Foxconned

Foxconned

Imaginary Jobs,
Bulldozed Homes &
the Sacking of
Local Government

LAWRENCE TABAK

THE UNIVERSITY OF CHICAGO PRESS · CHICAGO AND LONDON

The University of Chicago Press, Chicago 60637
The University of Chicago Press, Ltd., London
© 2021 by Lawrence Tabak
Published 2021
Printed in the United States of America

30 29 28 27 26 25 24 23 22 21   1 2 3 4 5

ISBN-13: 978-0-226-74065-2 (cloth)
ISBN-13: 978-0-226-74079-9 (e-book)
DOI: https://doi.org/10.7208/chicago/9780226740799.001.0001

Library of Congress Cataloging-in-Publication Data

Names: Tabak, Lawrence, author.
Title: Foxconned : imaginary jobs, bulldozed homes, and the sacking of local
      government / Lawrence Tabak.
Description: Chicago ; London : The University of Chicago Press, 2021. |
      Includes bibliographical references and index.
Identifiers: LCCN 2021016959 | ISBN 9780226740652 (cloth) |
      ISBN 9780226740799 (ebook)
Subjects: LCSH: Foxconn International Holdings Ltd. | Industrial development
      projects—Wisconsin—Racine County. | Economic development projects—
      Wisconsin. | Industrial promotion—Wisconsin. | Economic development
      projects—Political aspects—Wisconsin. | Economic development
      projects—Social aspects—Wisconsin. | Tax increment financing—Wisconsin.
Classification: LCC HC107.W62 R338 2021 | DDC 338.7/62138109775—dc23
LC record available at https://lccn.loc.gov/2021016959

♾ This paper meets the requirements of ANSI/NISO Z39.48-1992
(Permanence of Paper).

For my beloved econ-major son, Zach

Contents

Introduction

When I was growing up in Dubuque, Iowa, my best friend's father had an appliance store on Main Street. Its windows were crammed with wonders: blurry color TVs, clock radios with glow-in-the-dark radium dials, hi-fi consoles. Before leaving for college, I purchased a little stereo there from an up-and-coming Japanese company called Panasonic.

Back then, blue-collar workers were firmly part of the middle class, and a hardworking high school graduate could support a family by working the line at the John Deere Dubuque Works or at the Dubuque Packing Plant, home to the famous Fleur De Lis hams. Diversity was pretty much limited to religion—Protestants and Catholics—although a handful of African American families lived on a little triangle of land on Hill Street. The rest of the city was restricted either by covenants or by common practice. We had one public high school, and the wrestling star Jordan Smith was the only Black student in the class ahead of mine; there were no Black students in my class. The Hispanic population, as I recall, was the foreign exchange student from Venezuela.

But even during my childhood this world was already in transition. First Plaza 20, with Iowa's first Kmart, opened on the west side of town, followed by an indoor shopping mall. Downtown's largest department store, Roshek's, moved to the mall, and the mom-and-pop stores began to close. The city elders (they were all men back then) despaired at the ruination of their downtown and snatched up $7 million in available federal urban renewal funds. They razed empty buildings, moved the clock tower onto a pedestal, and turned Main Street into a pedestrian mall. All it lacked was pedestrians.

Then came the industrial calamities. In the late 1970s, a line worker at the Dubuque Pack made $25,000, the equivalent of $87,000 in 2020 dollars. Employment at the factory peaked at 3,500. But these high wages and associated benefits, along with an outmoded factory floor, made the plant noncompetitive against newer facilities elsewhere that were hiring lower-paid, often immigrant labor. There were layoffs and salary cuts, and in 1982 the plant shut down, pushing the town's unemployment rate over 17 percent. I wouldn't be the only Dubuquer moving away for good—the city's population peaked in 1980.

But like cities across the country, Dubuque's urban renewal efforts had given the city its first experience in taking commercial development into its own hands. Up until the late 1960s and into the 1970s it would never have occurred to most city officials to get into the business of managing retail or industrial development. Today, long after federal urban development funds have dried up, it is rare to find a town or city that isn't actively involved in promoting development and using tax advantages, infrastructure investments, land grants, and municipal debt to attract businesses.

In the 1990s, I landed an assignment to do a story for *Ingram's*, Kansas City's business-friendly city magazine, on a proposed $90 million ($160 million in 2020 dollars) expansion of the convention center, Bartle Hall. Not only was the expansion promised to reinvigorate flagging convention traffic; it also was promoted as a major cog in revitalizing a moribund downtown.

After a deep dive into the topic, I submitted a story that detailed how the investment was destined to disappoint—both in terms of ancillary downtown development and in the balance sheet for the facility itself. Something of a countrywide civic arms race to expand convention space was under way; overbuilding and the unlikelihood of sufficient expansion in convention business would lead to financial jeopardy for most of these facilities. I also found plenty of support for the notion that the economic impact studies that endorsed the building craze were deeply flawed and perhaps even cynical. One of my sad discoveries was that cities were encouraged to throw good money after bad: consultants would explain shortfalls by pointing to lack of exhibit hall space or hotel rooms and claim that for a city to make good on its current investment, it would have to spring for bigger halls and subsidized hotels—often at considerable civic expense.

The editor of *Ingram's* read my submission with horror and immediately canceled the assignment. But I continued to work on the story and eventually found a home for it in the *Atlantic Monthly*. The story was then republished in a number of venues, including the *Sacramento Bee* and the *Charlotte Observer*, papers in two cities contemplating convention center expansion.

In July 2017 I was thinking back on that story while watching President Trump and Wisconsin's governor Scott Walker on the news. They were at the White House, announcing a major industrial development for Wisconsin, where I live. A Taiwan-based company, Foxconn, had committed to building one of the largest factory complexes in the United States, promising to spend some $10 billion and to hire 13,000 workers. As I read about the frantic interstate bidding that had gone on for that factory and the grand projections of economic benefits, I couldn't help but think of the convention center arms race. Wisconsin offered Foxconn up to $3 billion in incentives to build the factory there, a figure that would expand to $4.5 billion when combined with infrastructure expenses incurred by utilities and the local municipalities. This amounted to $346,000 per job, an absurd figure. And it wasn't only the size of the subsidies—the announcement at the White House signaled a new level of politicization for economic development.

In early August 2017, I pitched *Belt Magazine* (an allusion to the Rust Belt), an online journal focused on issues of the Upper Midwest, where Trump's electoral victory had been sealed. I suggested looking into the economic impact justification for the billions in state incentives for Foxconn. The editor, Jordan Heller, encouraged me to go ahead.

It was soon apparent that Foxconn's proposed factory had driven interstate bidding wars to new highs. The cost per job was as much as ten times more than the usual public incentive levels. Over the following year, as hundreds of municipalities piled into the bidding for a new Amazon headquarters, America seemed like it was in the midst of out-of-control auction hysteria. Achieving the highest bid might be cause for short-term celebration, but it would likely lead to "the winner's curse," a well-studied auction phenomenon in which the prize goes to the bidder who has most overestimated the coveted object's value.

But Foxconn and Amazon were just the high-visibility cases. There is a broad and steadily growing trend of state and local spending on economic development. Every large city, region, and state in the country has a fully staffed, well-compensated economic development authority that fights to outbid or outmaneuver all the others in courting corporate investment. These are the real buyers. The shoppers are not just corporations but also their hired hands—site-selection and incentive specialists who are wooed by economic development professionals much the way that wedding planners are by country clubs. Keeping the engines of this process roaring is a cadre of consultants who pump out reports that make every dollar devoted to development look as smart as buying Microsoft stock at its initial public offering.

Where does all this money come from? The story of Foxconn might be exceptional in scale, but otherwise it is a window onto a deeply established, institutionalized process of city-versus-city and state-versus-state competition that beggars public coffers while enriching corporations. The love of economic development spending crosses party lines, but it has proved particularly popular in states like Wisconsin under the control of Republican governors and legislatures. As Governor Walker's campaign slogan had promised, Wisconsin was "open for business." Cutting business taxes and spending freely on economic development held out the promise of prosperity but contained the reality of slashed education budgets, cuts to social services, and deferred spending on deteriorating infrastructure. Even so, the political halo for governors and mayors granted by landing deals was incontestable. Everyone seemed to love a winner, even if they grossly overpaid.

Trump's promise in 2016 to bring back manufacturing jobs—like those in the Dubuque of my childhood—was a major part of his appeal in the Upper Midwest. It was welcome news to Racine County, in southeastern Wisconsin, the eventual site for the Foxconn complex. Even more so than Dubuque, the city of Racine had once been a bustling manufacturing center with abundant well-paid jobs. During and after World War II, factories short on labor recruited workers from the Deep South, making Racine a destination in that wave of the Great Migration. But like Dubuque, beginning in the mid-1970s Racine entered a period of steady economic decline. So Foxconn's promise of 13,000 "family-supporting" jobs was irresistible to local representatives of both parties. When it came down to designating which land to grant to Foxconn, not everyone was so accommodating. Lucky for the boosters, the village of Mount Pleasant—just outside of Racine, population 26,000—had not only plenty of wide-open farmland but also a Tea Party–led village board who jumped at the opportunity. Mount Pleasant's boosters believed—or said they believed—that by falling in line behind the Foxconn project, they would be helping make America great again.

Digging into the Foxconn project unveils the cozy relationships among corporations, contractors, consultants, and municipal and state governments. It illuminates a deeply ingrained economic development complex that rewards corporations with generous taxpayer-funded grants, politicians with political capital, and connected contractors and vendors with lucrative business. Public incentive spending engineers public support through promised job creation but ends up enriching the few. Our current means of economic development satisfies the definition of "plutocratic populism," developed by the political scientists Jacob Hacker and Paul Pierson. Plutocratic populism is a system in which the majority of voters end up supporting a process that helps concentrate wealth. Modern economic development is a below-the-radar machine that steadily moves money from public coffers to enrich the already affluent, helping to power the accelerating income disparity in the United States that is not only a national disgrace but also a looming danger to the republic.

We are all being Foxconned, every day.

Foxconn Timeline

2017

January 22 Bloomberg reports that Foxconn is looking to make a joint $7 billion investment with Apple for a US LCD display production facility. This joint venture never gained traction.

March 1 Foxconn breaks ground on a state-of-the-art, Gen 10.5 flat-screen LCD fabrication plant in China, with an estimated cost of $8.5 billion.

March 28 Ernst & Young contacts the Wisconsin Economic Development Corporation (WEDC) regarding an anonymous prospect (Foxconn) looking for 40 acres for an industrial development with an additional 750 acres for expansion, and an estimated 2,000 jobs.

April 28 Wisconsin governor Scott Walker and associates are invited to Washington to discuss with Foxconn executives "a significant foreign direct investment in the US," described as a "Liquid Crystal Display application plant." A WEDC official projects the employment numbers to eventually reach "30,000 to 50,000."

June 2 Scott Walker and associates tour Foxconn's Osaka plant. Foxconn predicts groundbreaking in the fall of 2017, a ridiculously aggressive schedule. Walker offers the company a $2.25 billion incentive package.

June 14 Trump leaks that a major company may be coming to Wisconsin.

June 17 The WEDC describes the deal as "two projects . . . which in total represent an investment of approximately $10.3 billion and employment of approximately 14,000 individuals."

July 7 Tim Sheehy, the head of the Milwaukee Chamber of Commerce, describes the project as "a next generation 10.5 liquid crystal module and final TV Assembly operations. The facility would have an enormous foot print requiring +1,000 acres, 15–20M sq. feet."

July 12 Foxconn chairman Terry Gou and Governor Walker sign a handwritten letter of agreement that Foxconn's investment will be $10 billion and 13,000 jobs, while Wisconsin will provide $3 billion in incentives, including a 17 percent payroll rebate and a 10 percent capital investment rebate. It is understood that three-fourths of the jobs will be hourly, blue-collar wage workers making around $54,000 a year.

July 26 The agreement is announced at a White House event at which President Trump, Gou, and Walker are the featured speakers and Paul Ryan, Speaker of the House (R-WI), is a prominent presence.

July 27 Walker has badges printed for a celebratory event with business leaders in Milwaukee. The cards read "Welcome to Wisconn Valley," a play on Silicon Valley, underscoring the belief that Foxconn will be the beginning of a high-tech cluster.

October 7 Foxconn announces Mount Pleasant as its US site, promising 20 million square feet of office and manufacturing space over 1.56 square miles, eventually employing as many as 13,000 people in "Wisconn Valley Science and Technology Park."

2018

April 26 The chief executive officer of Corning confirms that a new glassworks in Wisconsin is off the table—unless the state comes up with $700 million in subsidies and indefinite tax relief. A state-of-the-art Gen 10.5 fabrication facility producing large-screen TV displays cannot be operational without such a glassworks on site.

May 24 In response to reports that it plans to downsize its Wisconsin investment, Foxconn says, "Our commitment to create 13,000 jobs and to invest US$10 billion to build our state-of-the-art Wisconn Valley Science and Technology Park in Wisconsin remains unchanged."

June 20 Foxconn announces that it will build a smaller Gen 6.0 panel fabrication facility instead of a Gen 10.5 factory.

June 28 President Trump leads groundbreaking in Mount Pleasant as Foxconn unveils a large tabletop display of its sprawling future campus—some 22 million square feet of industrial development.

Fall Moody's downgrades Mount Pleasant's credit rating.

November 6 Governor Scott Walker is defeated by Tony Evers, the state's superintendent of public instruction, who wins 52 percent of the vote.

2019

January 27 Terry Gou's special assistant Louis Woo reveals that Foxconn's manufacturing plans in Wisconsin have been scaled back and will shift to a research and development focus, hiring mostly engineers and researchers, not manufacturing labor. He added, "In Wisconsin we are not building a factory."

January 31 *Nikkei Asia* reports that Foxconn is suspending its US investment in display production because of "weakening macroeconomic conditions" and the trade war. Foxconn reaffirms its commitment to hire 13,000 workers but does not disagree.

February 3 After direct intervention from President Trump, Foxconn contradicts Woo's January 27 interview, stating that it will move forward with its Gen 6.0 flat-panel factory.

February 5 Foxconn announces its first product to be built in Mount Pleasant—automated coffee kiosks for Texas-based Briggo.

June 2 Joy Mueller's house in Mount Pleasant, which was purchased by the Village of Mount Pleasant along with seventy-four others under threat of eminent domain, is bulldozed.

July 10 Foxconn announces that it will begin manufacturing in Mount Pleasant in May 2020 with 1,500 employees. Staffing at this level requires production far beyond coffee kiosks, but additional products are not specified.

April 29 Racine County and the Village of Mount Pleasant have borrowed $350 million to pay for Foxconn infrastructure based on the needs of a Gen 10.5 fabrication facility. Work includes expanding country roads and building a water main capable of pumping up to 25 million gallons from Lake Michigan each day.

August 27 Foxconn pledges $100 million to the University of Wisconsin for a new research center. A year later the university had received less than 1 percent of promised support and reported "no significant progress" on the remaining sum.

September 11 Foxconn puts a hold on opening an $8.5 billion Gen 10.5 facility in China after prices on flat panels collapse and tariffs make Chinese TVs less competitive in the United States. Reports indicate that Foxconn is looking for capital infusion from investors, possibly a complete sale.

December 31 Foxconn claims to have surpassed the 2019 minimum of 520 full-time employees in Wisconsin needed to trigger the first payroll and capital subsidies; the count includes an unspecified number of paid interns. The Evers administration appears skeptical of the numbers and reluctant to pay since Foxconn decided not to build the contracted Gen 10.5 fabrication plant; audits eventually reduce the count to 216 eligible employees, far below the threshold to trigger incentive payments.

2020

January 21 Terry Gou pledges to begin Wisconsin production of something in 2020, to drive Foxconn's "vision of manufacturing components for fifth-generation wireless and AI [artificial intelligence] applications." At the company's New Year's party in Taipei, Gou pitched stints working in the United States to employees.

Spring Foxconn completes its second building, a 990,000-square-foot structure it calls its "fab" building, but it doesn't meet specifications of a Gen 6.0 fabrication structure. A domed building designated as a data center is also under construction, which Wisconsin officials claim is not part of the incentive contract.

August 21 Foxconn begins making face masks in Mount Pleasant, employing seventy temp workers paid $13 an hour.

October 12 WEDC rejects Foxconn's claims for incentive payments as high as $50 million for 2019, stating that the company neither met its minimum employment target of 520 nor fulfilled the specific contract requirement to construct a state-of-the-art Gen 10.5 flat-panel display factory.

2021

April 20 The state of Wisconsin and Foxconn inked a new contract that formalized the diminution of the company's industrial plans, now projected to amount to 2.7 percent of the originally promised $10 billion. Wisconsin's hope: new, obtainable incentives amounting to $55,000 per job would keep Foxconn in the game, paying Mount Pleasant and Racine County property taxes on at least $1.4 billion of assessed property for decades, money needed to keep up with interest payments on hundreds of millions of dollars of municipal debt spent recklessly on infrastructure to support Foxconn's original chimeral plans.

CHAPTER 1

Your Dream House
Is Blighted

In 2008 Kim and James Mahoney finally found the perfect lot for their dream home. It was in rural Mount Pleasant, surrounded by farms growing cash crops and vegetables, a few miles west of Racine, Wisconsin. They liked that it had a country feel but was just ten minutes down low-traffic roads from the thirteen-screen Marcus Cinema and the Pick 'n Save supermarket, and just twenty minutes to their jobs in Racine. This was the very southeastern corner of the state, about ten miles west of Lake Michigan, ten miles north of Illinois, an hour's drive from Chicago. Even though they were a long way from having saved the money needed to build, and with saving getting harder with a three-year-old daughter, they couldn't let the land get away. For years they visited the property as one house after another went up in the little development. They mowed the grass and let their daughter have the run of the acre lot, knowing this would someday be her home.

The years of anticipation and planning made the groundbreaking of their home in the fall of 2016 particularly emotional. This was not a tract home: they had reviewed and considered and modified every detail. The microwave was not above the stove but at waist level because Kim is just five feet tall. Kim and James learned to do stonework and put in the full fireplace wall themselves. They did the same with the oak flooring—preferring to spend their money on premium wood and make up the difference with sweat equity.

"This was a house we planned to live in the rest of lives," Kim explains. "We wanted everything just right." They even decided to go with a one-floor plan so they wouldn't have to contend with stairs in their retirement years, decades away. They were delighted to move into the new house in February 2017. Their daughter had already made friends with the neighbors, and she fit right in.

There were rumors in the village of Mount Pleasant (population 26,000) that spring and early summer. Maybe a large industrial project was coming. But nothing official had been announced, and their little neighborhood, well off the major thoroughfares, seemed safely insulated.

The nature of the project was first revealed in July, at a White House event headlined by Donald Trump, Wisconsin's governor Scott Walker, and Terry Gou, who was chairman of a company called Foxconn, a huge Taiwan-headquartered manufacturing company with the bulk of its assets in China. The company was best known for its megafactories at which hundreds of thousands of workers assembled iPhones and other electronics.

Scott Walker was a Tea Party Republican who was first elected governor in 2010. In his Twitter biography he describes himself as "Christian, American, Husband," and "45th Governor-WI, Harley-Davidson rider." As a state legislator he had been a loyal and productive member of the American Legislative Exchange Council (ALEC), which promoted a hard-right agenda, including cutting environmental regulations, privatizing prisons and other government functions, establishing school vouchers to support private schools, making it harder to vote, and pushing action against undocumented immigrants. One of Walker's primary campaign slogans was "Getting government off the backs of people." Thanks to work that was likely concocted by ALEC and its prime backers, the Koch brothers, Walker took office as governor with a comprehensive plan to gut public unions through legislation that the historian Nancy MacLean characterizes as "devilishly lethal." Walker himself described the legislation as "dropping the bomb."

After his surprise attack on public unions and teachers, Walker soon found himself the subject of the state's first gubernatorial recall election. But he survived recall and was reelected for a second term in 2014. Throughout his time as governor, colleagues described him as having an unbending focus on his next election. From the start of his first term he had a run for the White House in mind, an ambition he continued to harbor even after his presidential campaign flamed out in 2015. One of his characteristic fumbles was his response to a question about his foreign policy experience. His practiced response was that defeating the Islamic State would be a breeze after his experience handling thousands of protesting grade school teachers.

Standing alongside Walker at the White House, Gou offered few details on the proposed industrial complex, but he did promise the return of TV manufacturing to the United States. A few years earlier Foxconn had acquired controlling interest in the ailing Japanese electronics firm Sharp, which had invested billions of dollars in a massive flat-screen liquid-crystal-display (LCD) panel fabrication facility, capable of producing the screens for the large TVs consumers were demanding. Foxconn envisioned a similar factory with colocated suppliers at its complex in Wisconsin. Standing behind the podium was Speaker of the House Paul Ryan, whose Wisconsin district was a prime prospect for Foxconn. Rumors had placed the factory in either Kenosha County or Racine County in the southeastern corner of the state. Real estate brokers had been gathering up options to buy farmland in both areas. Only on October 2, 2017, was the official announcement made: the largest factory complex ever built in Wisconsin would be sited in little Mount Pleasant. There had been no public hearings, no input from residents, and not a hint of a referendum.

The Mahoneys were already planning their first Christmas decorations for their new home when certified letters began circulating in early October. But they had not gotten theirs yet. They first heard the news from neighbors and friends. Kim was at her job at SC Johnson, maker of Johnson Wax, when her husband called: their neighborhood of nine homes was being condemned. "It was a shock, panic," she recalls.

She later showed me the letter. At the top it read "Village of Mount Pleasant." The letter used the ominous term "eminent domain" in declaring "you are the owner of a parcel of land affected" by planned road improvements associated with the Foxconn development. The Mahoneys would, the letter promised, in bold type, "soon be contacted by a relocation specialist." The houses would be bulldozed, the basements filled, and the acquired land deeded to Foxconn, a company few, if any, residents of Mount Pleasant, had ever heard of before.

On October 11, 2017, I drove the two hours from my home in Madison to Mount Pleasant to participate in Foxconn's first public presentation to its future neighbors. I anticipated a packed public meeting hall with a panel of Foxconn executives and local leaders briefing citizens and taking questions. The event was held at the village's new municipal headquarters, which like the Mahoneys' house, was surrounded by active agricultural acreage.

Instead, I walked into a public relations event hosted by Milwaukee-based Mueller Communications. The firm's owner and chief executive officer is Carl Mueller, whose client list includes the deeply conservative, pro-Walker, Milwaukee-based Bradley Foundation. The president and CEO of the Bradley Foundation had served as chairman of Walker's first gubernatorial campaign in 2010 and during his recall in 2012. The Mueller people had set up tabletop displays around the main hall with graphics showing the future Foxconn complex, projected jobs, and anticipated products. Mueller Communications had been hired by the Village of Mount Pleasant, and its invoices through early 2020 would total $651,786. That money would actually come to Mueller via a TIF district tax-increment financing but that's getting ahead of the story.

I soon discovered that the real action was in a crowded side room. Seventy-five area homeowners had received letters from the Village of Mount Pleasant notifying them that the municipality would acquire their homes under Wisconsin's eminent domain statute. Eminent domain, the power of a government to take private property, has a long history, going back to the Roman Empire. It was written into the US Constitution via the Fifth Amendment, which specifies that the government's power in exercising eminent domain must be limited to the "public good" and only with "just compensation."

For years US courts held that this power could apply only for public works, most commonly road development and expansion. But in a 5-4 decision in 2005, *Kelo v. City of New London*, the US Supreme Court ruled that taking land for private development was justified in specified circumstances, if that development would serve the public good through increased property tax levies and job creation in the service of revitalizing an economically distressed city. This decision, which was widely understood as an expansion of eminent domain authority, appalled citizens and politicians across the spectrum. Conservatives felt the affront on private property rights; liberals added their fears of the empowerment of corporations. Within a few years almost every state passed legislation intended to limit the powers of confiscation. Wisconsin's law went to some lengths to ensure that in a case like *Kelo*, the property would have to be truly blighted. The criteria for taking a single-family home was quite specific: "abandonment, dilapidation, deterioration, age, or obsolescence." Another: "The crime rate in, on, or adjacent to the property is at least three times the crime rate in the remainder of the municipality in which the property is located."

In one of many ironies of the Foxconn project, the state representative for the designated area was Republican Speaker of the Wisconsin State Assembly Robin Vos, who emerged as one of the biggest boosters for the project. A decade earlier, he had championed the personal property protections of the eminent domain bill, promising in 2006 that the bill would restrict government overreach. "This is what eminent domain is all about," he wrote. "Government taking private property in rare circumstances (after paying the fair market value for it) only when the property would benefit public use. Not when some members of the public might have an interest in seeing another private entity develop it."

Curiously, the area being taken for the Foxconn project was much larger than any industrial complex's footprint—3,893 acres, or 6.2 square miles. That is New York's Central Park four-and-a-half times over. Foxconn's sprawling, state-of-the-art LCD flat-panel manufacturing facility in Sakai, Japan, sat on 340 acres outside of Osaka and had room for further industrial development. The Wisconsin site was ten times larger for reasons that the company and public officials never addressed. If instead the development had been restricted to 340 acres and road expansions had been curtailed as soon as the project dwindled, almost no one in Mount Pleasant would have had to receive an eminent domain letter.

Some one hundred affected homeowners and their relatives had gathered in the side room. Many of them were senior citizens accompanied by their adult children. The session was conducted by Peter Miesbauer, heir to G. J. Miesbauer & Associates, Madison-based "right of way acquisition specialists." (Through early 2020 Miesbauer & Associates would receive $403,950 from Mount Pleasant.) The heavy-set Miesbauer paced the center of the room, patiently listening to the often quite specific questions from homeowners. He answered in repeated generalities, restating the statutory definitions of property acquisition and the statutory requirement that the buyouts would represent "fair market value." With no indication of how much that might be, the sense of frustration in the room was palpable.

An older woman explained that she was in the midst of a major remodeling project. "Should I have them finish the kitchen? Will my buyout reflect the improvements?" Miesbauer wouldn't comment directly on any valuation issues. That would be the job of the assessors Mount Pleasant would hire.

Others asked about being compensated for the turmoil this was clearly going to cause. Miesbauer was specific on this—there was no law requiring compensation for "pain and suffering." Everyone wanted to know the timetable, how long they had before eviction. Kim Mahoney's emotional comment was more plea than question. She explained that her family had yet to celebrate a Christmas in their new dream home. All Miesbauer could do is assure her, once again, that she would receive a "fair market buyout." With the final contract between the state and Foxconn still unsigned, Miesbauer had precious little to satisfy these questions, other than to note that construction was expected to begin in the spring of 2018.

Before the eminent domain meeting had begun, inside the main room, in front of the booth with a map of the future Foxconn complex, was a man with gray, combed-back hair whom Kim Mahoney recognized because his picture had been in the paper over the past few months. He'd been hired by Mount Pleasant through a third-party contractor to direct the Foxconn project. His $20,000-a-month fees had raised eyebrows, as had the contractor, Kapur and Associates, whose founder, Ramesh Kapur, had chipped in more than $100,000 to Scott Walker's campaigns over the years. Kim introduced herself, and he smiled.

"I'm the new project director," he said. "Claude Lois" (pronounced "loice," like "choice").

Mahoney pointed to her property on the map. "You can't take my property," she said, having already taken a dive into the Code of Wisconsin. "You can buy it, but you can't take it. We're nowhere near the roads and it's certainly not blighted."

Lois's smile dropped, and his face hardened. "Don't worry," he said, in the dismissive tone that would become familiar to locals. "We'll find a way."

CHAPTER 2

Foxconn Comes
to America

The July 26, 2017, event in the White House's East Room was an uncomfortable one. Scott Walker seemed particularly discomforted, perhaps given his proximity to Trump, who had been merciless in his blunt assessment of Walker and Wisconsin's economy during the 2016 presidential campaign. Walker repeatedly called Foxconn "Fox com." In an Austin Powers moment he proudly announced that the project would be valued at an amazing "$10 million dollars!" Paul Ryan tapped him on the shoulder and whispered to him, and Walker immediately corrected himself. "I mean $10 *billion*!" He went on to misname Foxconn's Sharp subsidiary as rival Sony.

Gou's speech had different challenges, primary his thick accent. But his repeated references to the new "AI 5G AK ecosystem" were also puzzling. I eventually figured out that AI was "artificial intelligence," 5G meant more data per second (in other words faster broadband), and that he wasn't saying "AK" but "8K," which meant more pixels per square inch on a TV screen—in other words, higher definition. But how was this an "ecosystem"?

The ensuing press reports were gushing. Foxconn was going to invest $10 billion and create 13,000 "family-supporting" jobs building one of the most popular consumer products around: a TV bigger than your neighbors'. The *Milwaukee Journal Sentinel*, the paper with the largest circulation in the state, headlined "The Foxconn Era Begins in Wisconsin." Walker held a victory celebration in Milwaukee and crowed, "This is something that will say to the world, 'We have arrived!'" His ebullience spilled over to the badges he handed out, which read, "Welcome to Wisconn Valley," heralding the belief that the Foxconn project would spark a tech cluster that would rival Silicon Valley. Wisconsin's side of the deal was to put up $3 billion in state incentives along with substantial investments from the local municipalities. The leading trade publication *Site Selection Magazine* rushed out a ten-page feature titled "Bagging the Big One." In the site-selection industry, having an economic development project announced at the White House was so exceptional that the event, rather than the project, was the subject of a rather gushing podcast the next day. The top Democrat in the Wisconsin State Assembly, the minority leader Gordon Hintz, felt his heart sink as his hopes of beating Walker in the 2018 gubernatorial election faded. "I thought we were screwed," he told me in 2019.

Foxconn's new interest in developing US manufacturing didn't occur in a vacuum. It fit neatly with Trump's campaign promises to revive US manufacturing while he also brandished tariffs to punish those that produced overseas. Trump particularly fixated on the balance of trade, and no matter how many tons of soybeans the United States sold in China, it would never match the enormous flow of Chinese-produced consumer products into the US, including big-ticket items like large TVs. Having those TV screens manufactured and assembled in Wisconsin seemed like a big step in the right direction for the MAGA crowd.

Back on April 20, 2016, Donald Trump had held a campaign rally in front of 4,000 supporters at the Indiana State Fairgrounds in Indianapolis. He referred to a viral video taken on a cell phone by a local worker at Carrier, the HVAC manufacturer. In it, a manager tells a large group of workers that "the best way to stay competitive and protect the business for the long term is to move production from our facility in Indianapolis to Monterrey, Mexico." The manager's comments were met with a chorus of shouts, moans, and curses.

Trump told his audience that he was focused on Carrier, which the highly profitable United Technologies had acquired in the late 1970s, "because it's such an excellent example. Now I could talk about Ford, they're moving, as you know, massive operations to Mexico; Nabisco, massive factory to Mexico." In a preview of his daily presidential routine he continued, "I'm sitting home, watching the news, and I see 1,400 people fired from Carrier."

Trump pledged to save those jobs and invigorate blue-collar employment generally—and that promise helped him capture a critical segment of Rust Belt voters, leading to his victory. And about those Carrier jobs? United Technology, unabashed, moved the manufacturing jobs to Mexico, despite a $7 million tax incentive granted by the state. As a newly laid-off Carrier employee Renee Elliott was quoted in a Reuters story in January 2018: "'Yes, he [Trump] saved jobs, yes he did. But he didn't save mine, he didn't save manufacturing jobs. He saved office personnel, okay?'" Elliott had supported Trump in the election.

In a later interview, Trump, undeterred by reality, recounted calling in his chief of staff, Reince Priebus, and saying, "I want to get a list of companies that have announced they're leaving. I can call them myself. Five minutes apiece. They won't be leaving. OK?"

Early in Trump's term the White House announced the new Office of Innovation, led by Jared Kushner, that would encourage Asian firms to establish manufacturing in the US. The response was quick and revealing. Even before the inauguration, Masayoshi Son, chairman of Japan-based SoftBank, stood in the lobby of Trump Tower and pledged a $50 billion investment in the US. At the time SoftBank was maneuvering to merge its subsidiary Sprint with T-Mobile. Son, no doubt with that merger in mind, stated that he was looking forward to "a period of deregulation." He held a piece of paper that showed the logo of SoftBank's manufacturing partner,

Foxconn. When questioned about its role, Foxconn issued a non-specific statement that it was also exploring opportunities in the US. Over the following few years, SoftBank did, through its venture capital fund, invest heavily in the US, including an $18.5 billion stake in the troubled WeWork commercial real estate company. But such investments would have had little or no impact on manufacturing jobs. Two days after the inauguration, Foxconn's chairman Terry Gou publicly pledged $10 billion for a nonspecific operation that, rather grandly, would employ between 30,000 and 50,000 workers.

A period of frenetic, behind-the-scenes activity preceded and followed the White House announcement of July 2017. Earlier that year, Foxconn had hired the global accounting firm Ernst & Young (E&Y) as its site-selection vendor. Brian Smith, a site-selection and incentive specialist at E&Y, put together a request for proposal (RFP) and circulated it to economic development agencies in areas that appeared to meet its stipulations. In March, Smith contacted Coleman Peiffer, a senior staffer at the Wisconsin Economic Development Corporation (WEDC, which insiders pronounced "Wee-Dick") with a proposal for 40 acres of land, and potential expansion to 750 acres, for a project that would employ 2,000 people. For an agency like WEDC this would have been big news—projects employing thousands of workers are rarities. Initially WEDC used the code name "Project Grande," indicating either a sense of self-importance, the sizable plot of land requested, or someone's preferred Starbucks order. Of course, other state agencies received the same RFP. Nearly every area of the country is covered by some sort of economic development agency, most commonly funded by taxpayers of the state or region. The auction was on.

As the auction heated up, the scope of the industrial development seemed to steadily grow. A month after the initial RFP, WEDC officials were informed by the Office of Innovation that the deal was much larger than initially stated: $10 billion in capital investment with 10,000 jobs. If the project hadn't been on Governor Walker's front burner, it was now. When Walker first ran for office in 2010, he had immense confidence in his ability to grow employment. To him, the formula appeared straightforward: cut taxes on businesses to as close to zero as manageable, eliminate "red tape" such as environmental oversight, and separate the state's economic development authority from its Department of Commerce (which Walker would soon eliminate) while taking over the WEDC's chairmanship himself. He envisioned earning glory leading the WEDC as it achieved his campaign promises of an exceedingly ambitious 250,000 new jobs within four years. But in the end, Walker's job boom didn't turn out to be easy at all. After seven years (2010–2017) in a steadily expanding national economy, he was still far short of that 250,000 goal. Ten thousand jobs in one fell swoop would help.

Before long the bidding for Foxconn was reaching new highs for Wisconsin, which was up against as many as seven other states. On May 5, 2017, Walker met with Foxconn executives at the White House. This led to additional bidding and a trip to Wisconsin by Foxconn executives to review sites. By the end of the month, Wisconsin had put a $1.25 billion incentive package on the table. The resulting per job cost of $125,000 was well above national standards, but the bidding still wasn't over. Soon, though, some states, including Ohio, assessed the deal as too rich and dropped out.

In early June Governor Walker and key associates rented a private jet from Northwestern Mutual Insurance in Milwaukee to fly to Japan (taxpayer expense: $37,500) to tour the large LCD flat-panel fabrication complex in Osaka that Foxconn had bought from Sharp. Suitably impressed, Walker upped the state's bid to $2.25 billion, but the auction was still open, with Michigan proving the most aggressive competitor. With a tight gubernatorial election coming up in 2018, Walker wasn't going to let this deal get away. Following an economic impact report that projected a huge ancillary windfall from Foxconn's factory, Walker and his team upped Wisconsin's offer again. Walker and Terry Gou met in Racine on July 12, and on Walker's personal letterhead the two inked a handwritten deal. Wisconsin would provide up to $3 billion in incentives based on a 17 percent rebate of Foxconn's Wisconsin payroll and a 10 percent rebate of its capital investment. Foxconn in turn would invest $10 billion in construction and equipment and hire 13,000 workers. But the company hadn't yet settled on a specific site.

Soon, Wisconsin's regional economic development agencies picked up the ball. Although Foxconn's specs were guarded, all evidence suggests that they were in flux throughout site exploration. One aspect that seemed consistent was the requirement that the location be near a population center sufficient to meet employment needs. For Wisconsin, this meant the southeastern corner of the state—Milwaukee, Racine, and Kenosha—just to the north of exurban Chicago.

What started with a request for 40 acres of land expanded to 200 acres by May. By mid-June, the agencies had been told major suppliers would trail in after Foxconn and that they should be looking for more than 1,000 acres to accommodate all of them. By mid-July Foxconn had informed site-selection officials that they were also looking to develop a "Smart City," too, and they needed 2,300 acres for that. The Smart City would include not only factories but also residential development and man-made lakes with elegant fountains. In their inscrutable words, it would "transform building data analytics through artificial intelligence and machine learning to advance smart building and smart city technologies and achieve comfort, security and sustainability goals."

One stipulation had been agreed upon early: Foxconn was not going to pay for the land. The host municipality would be responsible for buying up the thousands of acres and then pitching in to expand roads, build out sewers, and make millions of gallons of high-quality Lake Michigan water available each day. It was a big ask for the regional economic development authorities, but they eventually zeroed in on two sites that met these criteria: one in Racine County and one immediately to the south in Kenosha County. The local liabilities, once estimated at $100 million, had quickly escalated to closer to $500 million. Kenosha crunched the numbers and said no thanks.

But just outside of Racine was the village of Mount Pleasant, which had recently overthrown its moderate leadership and replaced it with a Tea Party–identifying village president and a loyal majority of trustees. The village president Dave DeGroot, a Tea Party supporter of Scott Walker, was all in.

DeGroot had grown up in Racine, had attended nearby University of Wisconsin–Parkside, and had lived in Mount Pleasant since 1998. He was first elected as a trustee in 2013. He'd been trained by the Koch brothers–sponsored American Majority organization, which is dedicated to electing local officials to fulfill the mandate to "reject the self-destructive policies associated with government expansion." The *Racine Journal Times* reported that "DeGroot campaigned on ensuring transparency, holding the line on taxes and responsible budgeting." Mount Pleasant paid him some $13,000 a year for his service as village president.

DeGroot was a small-time real estate player in town, managing some low-end rentals he inherited and rehabbing and flipping homes through his company, Action Homebuyers. At times DeGroot demonstrated confidence that crossed the line of arrogance, but he knew that a project as big as Foxconn would need more expertise and support than he could provide.

Lucky for DeGroot, the village already had a relationship with one of the state's leading eminent domain lawyers, Alan Marcuvitz, an octogenarian from the Milwaukee law firm of von Briesen & Roper. The law firm began charging the village some $100,000 a month to manage the upcoming land acquisition. The village also found just the person to handle the administrative aspects of the effort, a retired Republican mayor of the nearby town of Burlington. His services would cost $20,000 a month. These might have been seen as rich hires for a village whose operating annual budget was just $20 million, but as everyone involved, from Trump to Walker to DeGroot would explain, the old rules no longer applied.

When Scott Walker and Terry Gou inked their deal, it seemed clear what Foxconn would be building: a factory similar to the one Walker had toured in Japan. This would be a massive industrial development, projected to have a total footprint of 20 million square feet. In comparison, Toyota's largest assembly plant in the world, in Georgetown, Kentucky, covers 8.1 million square feet.

But even before the official groundbreaking in June 2018, plans had shifted. Foxconn announced a week beforehand that it wouldn't be building the massive plant to produce display panels large enough for the biggest TVs after all, but instead a more modest, still-substantial fabrication facility for smaller displays, suitable for consumer handheld devices and the automotive industry. This revelation didn't seem to reach Trump or his speechwriters as he stood in the farm fields of Wisconsin, holding his golden shovel. He called the coming Foxconn factory "the eighth wonder of the world," ominous considering that he had once declared the same of his disastrous Taj Mahal casino in Atlantic City. The casino had been built for $1.2 billion in 1990; it sold for four cents on the dollar in 2017.

Foxconn insisted the company would still be spending $10 billion and hiring 13,000 workers. But over the ensuing months, Foxconn officials repeatedly revealed major shifts in their plans and unveiled new projects, only to contradict previous plans while failing to execute the additional enterprises. This lack of clarity proved one of Foxconn's defining characteristics. At a February 2019 conference in Milwaukee, a Foxconn vice president, Bill Mitchell, described the process as "building the airplane while we're flying it." In a November 2020 editorial, Jay Lee, a vice chairman of the Foxconn Technology Group subsidiary, brought the still-enigmatic Mount Pleasant operation into sharp relief by describing it as "a World Economic Forum Lighthouse Factory and shining example of Industry 4.0 manufacturing." Wisconsin's cadre of Foxconn boosters stuck with their hopes and commitments even as the projected massive construction project clearly shifted and dwindled.

As Wisconsin officials were soon to learn, getting a handle on exactly what Foxconn was planning and what it was actually building was like trying to fish with your hands. The slippery object was rarely in focus, and despite some exciting moments when it seemed within grasp, it inevitably slipped away.

CHAPTER 3

What Does
the Foxconn Say?

As a Wisconsin taxpayer I was immediately curious about our new business partner. After all, if you were approached to put your hard-earned money into an investment, say, a new restaurant or a tech start-up, you'd want to know not only what was on the menu or what was being made but also your prospective partner's history and character.

I read what I could about Foxconn. The company employed more than a million people, and its core business was figuring out how to most efficiently assemble some of the most popular electronics in the world. Its most notably product was the iPhone, but it also assembled Blackberries, Kindles, Xboxes, Nintendo Wiis, iPads, and PlayStations. In other words, this was a company that had its hands on almost every electronic device covered with our fingerprints. Despite its massive workforce, Foxconn was also clearly intent on automation: it has an autonomous vehicle division and as early as 2016 manufactured its own assembly-line robots, "Foxbots," at a pace of 40,000 a year.

Perhaps because bad news makes for good headlines, one of the first things I found was suicide nets. Foxconn had received a wave of negative publicity because young, low-paid, despairing Chinese workers at the company's megafactories were ending it all with a dive off the dormitory roofs. Foxconn responded by installing safety tarps around their high-rises. Keeping employees on site was an important aspect of Foxconn's "just in time" efficiency. Housing in the China operation was barebones, with up to twelve workers bunking together in a single room. Similarly, Foxconn's Czech Republic assembly operation prefers young, single workers who are more likely to be flexible. Workers there are required to be available on short notice via text message to report for twelve-hour shifts. A 2018 study by two University of California sociologists showed how such unstable work schedules cause as much worker distress as low wages do. Despite this, everywhere Foxconn went it favored flexible employment and hours—preferring employment agencies and temp labor to direct hires.

Once I moved beyond the suicide nets and worrisome employment practices there was plenty of broad information about the Taiwan-headquartered company, whose main industrial assets were in China. First there was the founder Terry Gou, born in 1950 and estimated to have accumulated a fortune of $5 billion, putting him among the richest three hundred people on the planet. He had started the company in his garage with $7,500, making knobs for television dials. He didn't seem to give many interviews and seems on first investigation to have a personality that might make that a wise decision. For instance, he once brought in a zookeeper to help train managers to handle hordes of young employees. This seemed of a piece with a 2013 news story that showed "four young women wearing short skirts and sunglasses," standing outside a Shenzhen China Foxconn factory "to hand out masturbation gifts to help reduce stress and prompt harmony of the single male employees." Gou is also known to make subordinates stand for endless meetings and once professed that his greatest hero was Genghis Khan.

Foxconn had been sanctioned in China, despite Gou's reported access to the highest levels of the Chinese leadership, for abusing interns. It seemed he swung a deal with universities near some of his massive assembly operations. In order to get their diploma, students needed to spend a three- to six-month "internship" with Foxconn. The learning environment was twelve-hour shifts on the assembly line. This wasn't a one-off; the number of interns on the job at any given time was as high as 68,000. The company was also cited for using workers as young as fourteen years old, in violation of Chinese labor laws and Foxconn's stated policy.

Foxconn has a history of demanding relationships with governments. In December 2016, the *New York Times* unveiled the subsidies behind one of Foxconn's largest assembly operations in China: "The local government has proved instrumental, doling out more than $1.5 billion to Foxconn to build large sections of the factory and nearby employee housing. It paved roads and built power plants. It helps cover continuing energy and transportation costs for the operation. The city created a special economic zone for the project and provided a $250 million loan to Foxconn. The local government also pledged to spend more than $10 billion to vastly expand the airport, just a few miles from the factory."

Foxconn also had a history of broken deals. Take Harrisburg, Pennsylvania. In 2013 locals were ecstatic when Gou announced he'd be investing $30 million and hiring five hundred workers for a high-tech factory. The deal just dissipated over the years. The company had also reneged on major promises in India, Vietnam, Indonesia, and Brazil. These were not secrets. But Mark Hogan, head of Wisconsin's economic development authority, told a reporter that the state team didn't think background research on Foxconn was necessary because "we got to know these people so well."

Alberto Moel covered the LCD panel industry from Hong Kong during his seven-year stint at Sandford C. Bernstein, a major Wall Street research and brokerage firm. He noted Foxconn's propensity to promise more than it delivered. Even by the less transparent standards of East Asia, Foxconn was so opaque that he once characterized it as a "black box." He told Wisconsin Public Radio that the Foxconn project in Wisconsin was "a snow job," an assessment that proved literal, too. During its first year of lackluster activity, a Foxconn spokesperson explained that the company had been surprised by all the snow in Wisconsin. But there were deals that did go through. Outside of mainland China, Foxconn had assembly operations in Brazil, India, the Czech Republic, Mexico, Houston, and Plainfield, Indiana.

Hold on. Plainfield, Indiana? A current Midwest operation was something I could investigate. It was also enticing because when confronted with some of Foxconn's egregious employment practices overseas, Foxconn's Wisconsin boosters replied that US labor laws would make Foxconn an entirely different sort of employer here. Proof, I felt, wouldn't be in the pudding but in Plainfield.

Plainfield is a southwestern suburb of Indianapolis with a 2017 population of about 32,000. Although Foxconn promised in 2008 to expand its extant computer assembly operation by 1,400 workers, it appeared that the facility had been operational for some time with a workforce averaging about 900. From job postings and review sites it appeared the company was paying close to minimum wage. The job forums at sites such as Indeed and Glassdoor were intriguing. Among the bland positives and generic complaints were more suggestive notes. For instance, from someone on the professional staff: "Despite knowing full well that not everyone on the team speaks Chinese, business was conducted mostly in Chinese. If you don't speak it, then you missed out on a lot of information. . . . There is almost no chance for upward movement. The team I was on had workers who had been at their same exact positions for 8+ years and still far away from any kind of promotion." From assemblers: "Weird culture, horrible working environment, low pay," "long hours and low salary," and "high percentage of people are temps so turnover is high." Other terms that might have concerned a prospective business partner were "slave labor" and "sweatshop." The latter was apparently literal, as management seemed averse to air conditioning. An assessment of Foxconn culture published by Comparably, a group-sourced website that rates corporate culture on eighteen different characteristics, gave Foxconn a D–. What particularly caught my attention were three posts that mentioned the non-English-speaking workforce and the routine frustration of immigration-raid rumors leading to so many absences that the whole operation would be shuttered for the day. These posts have since been scrubbed from the websites. But I was intrigued.

No one at the local biweekly newspaper, the *Hendricks County Flyer*, could tell me more, nor could anyone at the radio stations. But I did finally locate a former employee named Carl Williams, who had spent a year and a half between 2008 and 2010 at the Plainfield facility as a quality technician and later a data analyst. He felt that the company treated him, as a manager, fairly and with respect. At the same time, he'd never seen Caucasians or African Americans in upper management. And he estimated that a majority of the 900 workers at the factory were undocumented. He cited one woman who had worked consecutive six-month stints under three different names and social security numbers. I wondered whether the Wisconsin legislators who had not yet approved the package of economic incentives and regulatory waivers for Foxconn would hesitate to support a company that relied on "illegals," as the Tea Party/MAGA set tends to call them. After all, Trump and the Tea Party Republicans who controlled Wisconsin said they considered illegal immigrants one of the gravest threats to our nation.

Williams referred to management's attitude toward undocumented workers as a "wink and nod." He explained that Foxconn executives declined to be certified as an E-Verify workplace (a system of checking worker identification). According to Williams, management acted on the pretense that it simply wasn't aware of, and certainly not responsible for, the documentation status of the bulk of the workforce, deferring to the temp agencies that brought them most of the workers. Foxconn also imported labor, relying on midcareer engineers from Asia who would work for less than a fresh engineering graduate from, say, Purdue University. Between 2014 and 2016 Foxconn filed for fifty-five H-1B visas, all associated with engineering positions that paid annual salaries between $46,000 and $82,000. H-1B visas allow higher-skilled foreigners to work for up to six years in the US.

After his stint at Foxconn in Plainfield, plus some time at one of the Mexican facilities, Williams became a labor unionist, joining Local 481 of the International Brotherhood of Electrical Workers. He had seen Foxconn's advocacy of disposable, replaceable labor, and it had made him into a strong supporter of workers' rights. "All employees," he told me, "who are working and contributing to the American economy deserve to be treated with dignity and have their wages, benefits and rights protected."

Williams referred me to a couple of his former Foxconn colleagues, including Andre Morris in Chicago. Morris, who had worked at Plainfield from 2005 to 2013, also cited his observance of a large number of undocumented workers there and recalled the lost days because of the rumors of raids. Although he did work his way up to manager from the assembly line, Morris felt that his opportunity for advancement was limited because he is African American; he reported seeing only white and Asian people above him. When asked if he would recommend working at Foxconn his response was an emphatic no. "There's just not enough opportunity," he said, adding that his most vivid memory of Foxconn was the endless, repetitive work in stifling summer heat in an airless warehouse with management too cheap to run the air conditioning.

Using these interviews, I published a story about Foxconn in *Belt Magazine* on September 11, 2017, while the Wisconsin Senate was debating the subsidy legislation. Two state senators read parts of it into the official record. My hope that these revelations might slow the process was a pipe dream. The objections were ignored and the legislation was quickly approved on partisan grounds, with nineteen of twenty Republicans voting for it. A grinning Governor Walker promptly signed it into law. He, along with his supporters, believed that in just two short years, big screen TVs would be rolling off the line in Mount Pleasant, stamped "Made in the USA."

CHAPTER 4

Who Made That TV?

"TV was invented in America," said Foxconn's chairman Terry Gou. It was even mass manufactured not too far from Mount Pleasant.

Melrose Park, Illinois, sits about fifteen miles due west of Chicago. The *Encyclopedia of Chicago* comes right out and admits that it's one of the "pre–World War II suburbs that do not fit the mythology of suburban affluence." It was industrial from early on, and the growth of one firm fueled the growth of others, as well as the need for housing for workers. By 1940 two-thirds of the jobs there were at manufacturers including National Malleable and Steel Castings and the American Brake Shoe and Foundry Company. During the war Buick made airplane engines in a sprawling new complex by the Proviso freight yard. Once the country shifted from war production to consumer goods, Zenith picked Melrose Park as the place to produce picture tubes for the emerging television market. All of this development was organic—this was before the modern age of economic development incentives.

John Cummins first visited the Zenith factory in the mid-1970s when he was fourteen years old. His father worked there. So did his uncle and a few of his cousins. As he recalled in 2008, "It was cavernous—easily a city block long." The factory was constant action and unending noise, running twenty-four hours a day, making up to 3.5 million cathode-ray tubes a year. The assembly line was a maze, "thirteen to fifteen miles of conveyers."

And then there were the explosions. "Implosions," Cummins self-clarifies. "Since there's a vacuum inside, it explodes in." On rainy days the roof would sometimes beginning dripping. "One drop of water hit that tube . . . sometimes one would explode and it'd set the one off next to it, and the one down from it . . . you'd see people get cut." The arrival of ambulances was a nearly daily occurrence.

Cummins followed his father to Zenith, working there nearly twenty years, until 1998. This was a company that had been founded in 1918, famous for its quality electronics and innovations. It was Zenith that invented the first remote control and pioneered high-definition TV. But by 1998 the final assembly of Zenith TVs was no longer being done in the US. The Melrose Park tubes were shipped to Mexico for that. Zenith, though, had held on longer than most. The same tubes were being made cheaper overseas; it was less expensive for Zenith to buy tubes than to make them. Zenith tried to automate in its last years, bringing in robotics, but they weren't sensitive enough to work with the fragile tubes.

Zenith might have been too loyal to its employees in Illinois—the company had been losing money for a decade and filed Chapter 11 bankruptcy a few months before announcing that the Melrose Park plant was closing, at the cost of 2,000 good union jobs. The corporation became a subsidiary of the Korean electronics giant LG, which still found equity in the Zenith brand name and in its research and development arm. For Cummins and countless others, though, it was the end of an era.

Today, approximately 3.5 million television sets are sold in the US each year. None is manufactured in the US, although a company called Element was doing some assembly in South Carolina before it went out of business in 2018, blaming the Trump tariffs. I bought one of Element's remaining red-white-and-blue packaged TVs on sale at Target. It's a nineteen-inch flat-screen television that, along with larger Element products, reliably brought up the rear in *Consumer Reports* ratings. Despite the patriotic packaging, I discovered a sticker on the back that said "Made in China."

Foxconn's Chairman Gou had promised a new era—but one that required a new technology. If you want to make modern TVs, you need to make flat-panel displays, which had never been made in the Western Hemisphere. But now they would. Never mind that automated LCD panel manufacturing had little in common with the work of places like the old Zenith plant, or little use for workers with only a high school education. The promise, or more accurately, illusion of blue-collar workers like John Cummins making modern TVs for good money and benefits was too powerful to resist. Boosters desperately wanted to believe that Foxconn was going to help America return to its era of manufacturing glory. Details be damned.

Made in America

The history of TV manufacturing in America is very much the history of twentieth-century American manufacturing. The first picture tube was patented by a Westinghouse researcher in 1923. In 1927 Philo Farnsworth made significant improvements and received patents for them, eventually producing the first all-electronic television system, giving him rights to the title "father of television." One of his first broadcasts was a fuzzy picture of his wife, which set the stage for endless hours of domestic dramas and family sitcoms. Production of TV sets began in the US in 1946, with broadcast stations covering all major cities by 1949. By 1962, 90 percent of American households had a TV.

The standard technology for televisions until the end of the twentieth century was the cathode-ray tube (CRT), like the one manufactured by Zenith. The core component was a vacuum tube in which cathode rays were projected onto a fluorescent screen to produce a luminous image. These CRT sets were bulky and heavy. (In 2019 I finally disposed of my sixty-pound thirty-two-inch RCA set from 1991, almost ruining my back.) Early models were not particularly reliable—a growth job in the 1950s was the house-calling "TV repairman." Families kept the service number handy because tubes went out regularly.

Color television sets became widespread in the early 1960s along with much more reliable transistor-based ("solid state") circuitry, although my household remained loyal to its somewhat fuzzy but reliable black-and-white Zenith until close to 1970. I never realized the full effect of *The Wizard of Oz* (which played annually on CBS to great ratings) until I saw it in a theater in the early 1970s. Oz was in color!

That there was a possible alternative technology for TV screens was known to the scientific community for many years. But the loss of TV manufacturing in the US wasn't a result of the abandonment of the CRT model for today's ubiquitous flat-screen TVs. The migration of manufacturing began decades earlier. Pat Choate, author of *Agents of Influence: How Japan's Lobbyists in the United States Manipulate America's Political and Economic System*, blames the migration on a "direct assault" by Japan. He details how "the Japanese government first created an anti-competitive cartel and then reinforced it with diplomacy, fraud and the influence of Washington insiders." By this account, a cabal of Japanese manufacturers illegally conspired first to monopolize Japan's domestic market and then to use the same strategy to conquer the US market. American companies licensed first black-and-white and then color technology to Japanese firms, a leak of tech know-how that Choate considered a major gaff. Using high margins from its protected domestic market, the cartel then began to sell its products in the US at a loss, using secret rebates to preferred American retailers.

The US television manufacturing workforce was cut in half between 1966 and 1970 and then reduced by an additional 30 percent

between 1971 and 1975. Another quarter of the remaining manufacturing jobs were eliminated over the ensuing few years. By 1971,
US government officials had concluded that Japanese companies
were indeed "dumping" their production in the US market at arti-
ficially low prices. Faced with possible retaliatory tariffs and other
diplomatic challenges, the Treasury Department opted for inaction
rather than taking on the complex calculation and assessment of
damages. Over the same period Japanese firms were aggressively
acquiring their US rivals, with the number of US-owned TV manufacturers dropping from twenty-eight in 1968 to six by the end of
1976. By the late 1990s you could still buy a TV with an American-
sounding name like RCA, but it was no longer made in America. But
the world of TVs was about to go through another disruption, and
this time the Japanese companies would be the losers.

The Age of LCD

An Austrian botanist, Friedrich Reinitzer, is thought to have been
the first observer of a strange material that seemed like an interme-
diary state of matter, in effect with two melting points. He shared
his observations with a German physicist who noted that the material (cholesteryl benzoate, for the record) showed characteristics
of a crystal. He named it "liquid crystal." For the following eighty
years the material remained a curiosity, widely known but its uses
unrecognized and untapped.

In the 1960s researchers began to conduct more focused studies
on liquid crystals. G. H. Heilmeier completed his PhD at Princeton
in 1961 and was recruited by RCA Laboratories at a time when much of
the fundamental scientific research in the US was under corporate
sponsorship. Previous work had shown that when heated liquid crystals were sandwiched between conductive-coated glass, electric cur-
rents produced interesting patterns in the crystals. Heilmeier added
specialized dye to the experiment and found that small amounts of
electricity could shift the color of the sandwiched material. By 1964
Heilmeier believed that large, flat-panel color TVs (liquid crystal
displays, or LCDs) would soon be hanging on household walls.

RCA pursued the work, discovering a room-temperature liquid crystal, and produced some sample displays that it demonstrated publicly in 1968. This sparked additional applied research in the US, Europe, and Japan and led to the first digital-display watches and pocket calculator displays. RCA, however, was not particularly interested in the new display technology because at the time it was a dominant player in the CRT market. While this might sound like one of those technological "Oops!" moments, it would be another twenty-five years before incremental discoveries caught up with Heilmeier's optimism and vision for LCD color TV screens.

The quantum leap took place at the Japanese electronics firm Sharp. In the late 1980s the company was producing small LCD displays through an expensive and laborious process. When the head of the effort, Isamu Washizuka, asked about the minimum screen size for a consumer TV, the response was fourteen inches. He tasked his engineers with making a massive leap to a fourteen-inch screen. As the industry insider Hiroshisa Kawamoto wrote in 2002, when the president of Sharp was shown the result in 1988, "his first reaction was that Washizuka was fooling him with a phony set up." The resolution and brightness were so superior to CRT screens that "the panel was too good to be true." When the results were publicly announced later that year, the writing was on the wall—where RCA's Heilmeier had envisioned future TVs. Other major electronics players, including Toshiba, IBM, and NEC, pursued liquid crystal applications. Sharp was the first with a commercial product in 1991. As Kawamoto summarized, the US may have been the innovation leader during much of the twentieth century, but "Japan's strength was in perfecting the implementation and moving it to mass production." By 2000, LCD TVs had caught up to CRT sales. Within a decade, CRT TVs were no longer being sold.

Modern LCD Production

Here's a revealing oddity: the factory required to make the nine-inch display screen in many cars today cost more than the factory that actually built the car. It's all about the precise and exacting technology. Even though car manufacturing retains much of the same hardware and assembly needs as those of a Ford Model T, you can't tinker with a LCD screen in your garage. When Honda constructed its plant in Greensburg, Indiana, to manufacture its popular compact Civic in 2009, it required a capital expenditure of some $550 million. Subsequent investments brought that figure up to around $1 billion. Of the two options that Foxconn has floated for LCD manufacturing in Wisconsin, the more modest is called a Gen 6.0 fabrication facility, or "fab" in the industry jargon, whose displays would not be large enough for modern TVs but could serve the automotive market. In 2016 Japan Display Inc. (JDI) opened a Gen 6.0 plant in Hakusan City, Japan, with an initial investment of $1.67 billion. The most expensive LCD plant making panels for the largest TVs is currently a Gen 10.5 factory, which would cost in the neighborhood of $8 billion to construct in China, and even more in the US.

The "Gen" designation stands for "generation" and reflects the growth of LCD screens, which now can be as large as 110 inches. The higher the generation number, the larger the glass substrate coming into the factory, and the larger the potential screens coming out. As the glass substrate increases in size, the cost per square inch of panel drops. In 1990 the largest LCD panels were being produced in a Gen 1 fab using twelve-by-sixteen-inch glass, somewhat larger than a sheet of legal paper. A Gen 6.0 factory works with glass substrate that is fifty-nine by seventy-nine inches, the size of a double bed. A Gen 10.5 fab is fed glass 115 inches (9.6 feet) by 132 inches (11 feet), larger than a one-car garage door. The glass itself is highly specialized and fragile. At larger sizes the panels are too large and delicate to be shipped: the glass sheets are made at an on-site glassworks and fed right into the LCD fab. In all cases, an extremely clean atmosphere is required, as the glass is coated and liquid crystals and film are added. A speck of dust can ruin an entire panel. Alignment of materials is painstakingly exact—within a few microns, and a strand of hair is forty microns thick. Human contact is minimal; all processes are automated and robotic.

The scale of these factories is hard to fathom. The Gen 6.0 fab built by JDI in 2016 for $1.67 billion has a footprint of 1.5 million square feet with three levels of operation—and yet just 250 workers, almost all technicians and engineers. The latest Gen 10.5 plant opened by China-based BOE is 1.3 kilometers long with a factory footprint of 15 million square feet. For comparison, the billion-dollar Honda factory in Greensburg, Indiana, takes up 1.3 million square feet but employs 2,900 mostly blue-collar workers. Auto manufacturing seems like a better deal for job-starved communities. But the automotive industry is a mature business, and the migration of foreign car companies to US manufacturing (at the considerable expense of mostly Southern states) is an old story. The idea of introducing a completely new manufacturing technology to North America had an entirely different wow factor.

During its courting of Wisconsin, Foxconn's Chairman Terry Gou took Governor Walker and some key aides on a tour of Foxconn's Gen 10.0 fab in Osaka, Japan, to what was clearly good effect. Among those given a second royal tour was Claude Lois, Mount Pleasant's Foxconn project director. He said: "I think the trip over there was instrumental in providing a number of us confidence and said to us, 'You know, this is real. These guys are for real.' And it's a very class operation."

The Fall of Japan's Giants

In a process ironically similar to the one that led to the fall of US television manufacturing, Japan's electronics giants began with a huge head start in the consumer electronics and LCD business only to find themselves boxed out of the game almost entirely. That advanced Gen 6.0 plant that JDI opened in 2016? It shut down before the end of 2019. The massive Gen 10.0 fab that so impressed the Wisconsinites on tour? It had lost money every year since 2009. Foxconn bought it for a dime on the dollar in 2016 when it acquired two-thirds of Sharp for $3.5 billion, billions less than just the factory alone had cost to build.

One factor in all of this was the rapidly changing nature of technology. In the years after World War II, Japan's electronic industry had benefited from lower wages than those prevailing in the US, newly constructed efficient manufacturing plants, and a dearth of the legacy costs that were accumulating for US corporations. In the twenty-first century, China and Korea were able to take similar advantage, sometimes in the form of lower labor and building costs and new factories, and sometimes massive government subsidies. For instance, in 2018 the Korean government committed a half billion dollars to set up a research facility to advance flat-screen technology. In China, the government has declared selected high-tech manufacturing as a strategic asset and poured support into it, all while regional governments commit billions of dollars to land and support large electronics factories. Although this regional support has some similarities to US economic development, the extent of the support is often well beyond what is normative here, where projected payback is a requisite.

Japan's losses were particularly hard in consumer electronics, where it faltered in the conversion from mechanical devices like the Sony Walkman to digital devices like Apple's iPod. Sharp was sold to Foxconn. Toshiba sold off its consumer electronics division to China's Midea Group. Today Sony makes most of its profits from insurance. Hitachi sold off its consumer electronics to concentrate on industrial manufacturing such as commuter trains.

Japan has also struggled to hold onto its LCD manufacturing business, without much success. In 2011 the LCD manufacturing capabilities of Sony, Hitachi, and Toshiba were combined with Japanese government support to form Japan Display Inc. In early 2020, with years of losses behind it, JDI agreed to an investment deal with a Chinese company that would eventually result in a transfer of ownership.

What happened was two-pronged. China made a huge commitment to LCD production, with massive local and national support. Not only did this allow China to undercut prices; it also produced a market glut that kept prices depressed. The second prong was new technology OLED displays. OLED-info, an industry website, defines OLED as "a flat light emitting technology, made by placing a series of organic thin films between two conductors. OLEDs are emissive displays that do not require a backlight and so are thinner and more efficient than LCD displays (which do require a white backlight)." Notably, OLED is a technology that competes with LCD. By 2020 it was used in most of the top-rated large-screen televisions sets, albeit at price points above those for comparably sized LCD screens. OLED images had better contrast, greater brightness, deeper blacks, wider color range, and faster refresh rates.

One of the advantages of OLED screens is that they can be manufactured to be flexible, even curved or foldable, which gives them additional capabilities and endurance. A bonus: they can be manufactured without the production of deadly and long-lasting heavy metal pollutants. But they are also more difficult to manufacture than LCD screens, which themselves are not technologically simple.

By 2020, OLED TV manufacturing was largely Korean, with LG taking charge after fellow Korean corporation Samsung abandoned the large-screen business in 2015, balking at high costs and technological challenges. Like other tech manufacturers, LG invested in China to take advantage of cheaper labor, existing supply chains, and government eagerness to subsidize or coinvest in such ventures. It opened a massive OLED flat-screen factory there in 2019. The projected cost for LG's Gen 8.5 plant was $4.5 billion, with the local government (Guangzhou Economic and Technological Development District) putting up 30 percent of the equity in the factory. However, three major Chinese display companies—BOE, China Star Optoelectronics Technology, and HKC—were also ramping up OLED capacity. In May 2019, Ross Young, the founder and CEO of Display Supply Chain Consultants, summarized his findings on display trends: "LCDs are losing to OLEDs in two key display markets: smartphones and TVs." By then, the latest and most expensive iPhones had switched to OLED screens. In 2020, Sharp, owned by Foxconn, announced it would begin selling OLED televisions with LG screens. Sony already had large-screen OLED TVs on the market, also using LG screens.

Foxconn had built its business by being the best assembler in the world. Other companies invented things: Foxconn figured out how to optimally build them. With its Sharp acquisition, Foxconn had made a bold decision in late 2016. It would stay at the forefront of LCD manufacturing, building a massive plant in China that would produce the sixty-five- and seventy-five-inch TV screens that consumers were demanding. The Gen 10.5 plant would cost $8.5 billion and would begin production in late 2019. Unfortunately for Foxconn, the price of large display screens dropped by 50 percent between the time the plant broke ground and its scheduled opening. Trump's tariffs added 10 percent to the cost of China-made products in the US, putting Chinese companies at a further disadvantage to Korean manufacturers in a vital market. The production of LCD screens was exceeding demand even before the COVID-19 recession. In early 2019 it appeared that Foxconn was delaying opening the plant and reducing production projections for 2020. Reliable sources reported in 2019 that the plant was actually on the auction block as Foxconn was contemplating taking an immediate hit on the project rather than face years of potential losses, similar to the ones at the Gen 10 fab that had helped bankrupt Sharp.

Meanwhile, stateside, Foxconn was still promising 13,000 jobs and LCD manufacturing in Wisconsin. It christened its million-square-foot warehouse structure due for completion in Mount Pleasant in 2020 its US "Gen 6.0 Fab." The consistently boosterish *Racine Journal Times* reported on October 10, 2019: "The building is to become North America's first and only thin-film-transistor, liquid-crystal-display fabrication plant or 'fab.'" However, the building seemed ill suited for LCD manufacturing of any scale, which requires specialized foundations to stabilize the massive machinery and three tiered levels of operation. It takes years to obtain fabrication equipment from limited suppliers—no such orders were in the pipeline according to industry observers. LCD plants have loading docks on their upper levels for crane-fed delivery of equipment. The single-story Mount Pleasant building is built on a concrete slab, with no visible upper-story loading docks.

Yet infrastructure work geared to the larger Gen 10.5 factory continued unabated. Hundreds of millions in municipal debt had been issued to pay contractors for grading, house demolition, six-lane roads, pipelines, and land acquisition. Foxconn boosters insisted that the company would come through—and if it didn't, boosters still had the contractual guarantee that Foxconn would begin paying property taxes on at least $1.4 billion worth of assessed valuation beginning in 2023 and continuing for decades, even if Foxconn was no longer in Wisconsin. This was the deal they had agreed to with Mount Pleasant and Racine County.

It was in writing. Terry Gou's associates had signed the contract.

CHAPTER 5

The Land Grab

On the evening of March 20, 2018, Mount Pleasant residents filled a room at their village hall to make and hear public statements before the board of the Community Development Authority, basically a working committee under the village board. One item was on the agenda: the authority's first step in taking eminent domain possession of the properties whose owners had not accepted purchase offers from Mount Pleasant. This required the designation of some 3,900 acres of agricultural land, farmhouses, and scattered and neatly maintained single-family homes as "blighted." It would be an essential step for the local authorities—vital cogs in the Foxconn-booster leadership chain that ran from local Tea Party officials through Governor Scott Walker and all the way up to President Donald Trump—to fulfill the promise to turn over to Foxconn the initial 1,100 acres for phase 1 by August 1.

Joe Janacek, in his late fifties, sporting a graying mustache and a crew-neck sweater, looked uncomfortable as he walked to the podium carrying a single sheet of paper. "I've lived in my home for twenty-eight years," he read to the board. "I'm a tax-paying citizen and I deserve better than this, to just be kicked to the curb and thrown out of my residence."

Connie Richards stood with her taller husband, as expressionless as the farming couple in Grant Wood's *American Gothic*. She said, "It will be a sad day when the wrecking ball demolishes the house and buildings we have put our hearts and soul into." Rodney Jensen, his voice breaking with emotion, pointed at the board as he said, "The village is telling us our land is worthless, while at the same time you're telling Foxconn it's the best property in the world. I don't know how any of you guys can sit here and do this."

The acquisition strategy mapped out by eminent domain lawyer Alan Marcuvitz (earning his $100,000 per month retainer) and project director Claude Lois, with some assistance from acquisition consultants, struck me as Machiavellian. The first step had been to send the designated real estate agents, Pitts Brothers, to the large landowners. The agents explained to the farmers they had two choices: sign an option to sell at $50,000 per acre or await eminent domain acquisition, which by law would involve compensation at predevelopment market prices, which could be as low as $5,000 per acre. A 250-acre plot could go for $12.5 million or for $1.25 million. Then they gave them a window of opportunity numbered in days. This proved both persuasive and expeditious. It also turned into a multimillion-dollar windfall for Pitts Brothers, which took a healthy share of the buyout as commission.

For many of the owners this was a sizable windfall, too. For instance, John Fork owned 152 acres, for which he could expect a settlement of about $7.6 million. For the larger landowners, the compensation was plenty enough to buy another farm or to retire with a nice new home in Wisconsin and another in Florida to snowbird. For those owners who had promised a deceased mother or father they'd never sell their multigenerational land, though, it was a bruising and heartbreaking decision.

The village told homeowners on smaller plots that their land was being acquired for road development. Some property did in

fact come under the well-established protocols for roadway ease-
ments, as rural roads would be expanded into highways of four
lanes or more. But many were well off those grids. Although someone as savvy as Kim Mahoney quickly challenged this ploy, it sent
a message to landowners that they had no case for refusal. Then
the village made them an offer: market value plus 40 percent. So
if a property was valued at $300,000, Mount Pleasant said, "Sign
here now for $420,000, or fight us and we'll pay you the $300,000
eminent domain settlement." This too proved persuasive, even
though property values were escalating fast given anticipation of
Foxconn's workforce and the influx into the market of all the displaced homeowners.

For a few recalcitrant owners, the village had a final gambit:
they showed the homeowners maps of the Foxconn plot with no
access roads to their property. If they held on, they wouldn't be
able to drive home. This moved some additional homeowners, although it turned out (after almost all the deals were sealed) that
the village had no authority to restrict access, a state Department
of Transportation matter, and that, moreover, state law prohibited
such manufactured isolation.

The one speaker at the public forum from outside the area was
Anthony Sanders, from the Minneapolis-based Institute for Jus-
tice, a pro bono law firm that employs some of the leading eminent
domain experts in the country. After reviewing the statutory backdrop, Sanders looked directly at the Community Development Authority board and told them: "Make no mistake. If there is a legal
challenge, you will lose. You will not be able to take these people's
homes."

Sanders's firm had argued—and lost—one of the most important
eminent domain cases in history, *Kelo v. New London*, before the
Supreme Court. That landmark 2005 case, decided 5–4, upheld a
Connecticut municipality's right, under specific circumstances, to
condemn property for commercial development. In its wake, forty-
two states passed eminent domain legislation to clarify the process
and fortify property owners' rights.

Sanders explained to me how he came to be at the March 20 meeting: "We've been involved in some eminent domain cases in Wisconsin so Foxconn was on our radar. One of the property owners reached out to us as did a couple of attorneys representing home-owners. Based on our experience with Wisconsin law we knew the village would have to do a blight designation."

The main complication in condemning the sprawling 6.2-square-mile area is how specific Wisconsin law is regarding blight. For in-stance, one of the qualifying criteria is a crime rate three times the rate of the surrounding community, which is nonsensical for the Foxconn property. There is also the clause that seems to directly subvert the goal of giving the land to Foxconn: "Property that is not blighted property may not be acquired by condemnation by an en-tity authorized to condemn . . . if the condemnor intends to convey or lease the acquired property to a private entity."

Sanders was blunt in his assessment: "This is a textbook case of eminent domain abuse." When he considered the authority's promise to Foxconn to have all the land in hand by August 1, 2018, Sanders said there were two possibilities: "Either they sold Foxconn a bill of goods or they've retained the financial resources to make some huge offers." Offers, one is tempted to say, that homeowners couldn't refuse.

One of Foxconn's earliest site criteria was that the land be pro-vided gratis. The Walker negotiating team quickly agreed. The key for Walker's team, though, would be for a municipality to agree to do two things: facilitate the establishment of an eminent domain authority and issue municipal bonds to raise the hundreds of mil-lions of dollars needed to buy the land and pay for the promised infrastructure. It was a long and winding road from the first Fox-conn RFP to the eventual acquisition of the 3,900 acres in Mount Pleasant.

As we've seen, the process began in March 2017, when Ernst & Young reached out to the Wisconsin Economic Development Cor-poration with the initial search for 40 acres that quickly ballooned to 750 acres. WEDC in turn reached out to the Racine County

Economic Development Corporation (RCEDC), one of the state's
eighteen such authorities. RCEDC has a full-time staff of sixteen
and an annual budget around $2 million, about three-fourths of
which is government sourced. The RCEDC's mission overlaps with
that of Milwaukee 7, a wing of the Milwaukee Metropolitan Chamber of Commerce, whose economic development mandate covers seven counties in southeastern Wisconsin. Milwaukee 7 has
a full-time staff of ten and is funded primarily from Chamber of
Commerce member dues. Other chambers around the country
have the same mandate but are taxpayer funded, including in some
places through a percentage of sales tax.

On May 6, 2017, state economic development officials took
Foxconn executives on a tour of three possible sites in Kenosha,
Racine, and Janesville. The memo circulated by WEDC before the
visit stated that the project required "350 to 380 acres of develop-
able land." But that same month Milwaukee 7 had prepared a report
summarizing the largest economic incentive deals across the country, sizing the Foxconn project at 750 acres. But at this point not only
were there other sites in Wisconsin under consideration; it was far
from clear that the state would even win the national bidding war.

Nevertheless, in mid-May, the RCEDC decided to share the most
recent Foxconn RFP with Mount Pleasant's leaders. Almost immediately locals began strategizing how they could meet Foxconn's
demands for land, environmental permitting, and huge amounts
of fresh water needed to wash the large sheets of glass used in LCD
production. The RCEDC official attached an aerial picture of the
Sharp Osaka Gen 10.0 plant to his introductory memo. It was a challenge to picture this sprawling industrial development in Mount
Pleasant's freshly plowed and seeded fields.

By late June a Milwaukee 7 executive discussed the potential
for rising costs for what had evolved into a 1,000-plus acre site as
landowners got wise to the value of their property and would no
longer accept $50,000 an acre, which was already about seven times
the average preproject price. He suggested budgeting $100,000 an
acre. At the same time, the development agencies were discussing

going after 2,000 acres in Kenosha or Racine counties. Not until late August did internal Mount Pleasant correspondence reveal that what they had in mind was 3,900 or so acres, with the prospect of declaring the entire area blighted.

Why would an industrial complex that could be built on 350 acres require the acquisition of 3,900? I asked one of the members of the Mount Pleasant Village Board who voted for the plan. "I'm not sure," Gary Feest told me. "We didn't make the maps. I know that Foxconn wasn't the only corporate tenant planned—there had to be room for all their suppliers."

Given the natural tendencies for politicians to seek greater power and bureaucracies to expand, I wondered whether officials in Mount Pleasant were taking advantage of the Foxconn project to obtain control of a much larger land footprint than Foxconn itself could ever use. When I asked Feest if the principal players might have been taking advantage of the project to expand their domains, he couldn't be sure. But for economic development professionals such as the chief executives at the regional economic agencies, RCEDC and Milwaukee 7, the "Foxconn plot" would be a huge asset. They could pitch projects for decades into a massive industrial park with virtually unlimited water, electricity, and terrific roads all paid for not by Foxconn or prospective corporate or industrial owners, but by taxpayers. After the site was established, they wouldn't have to negotiate any more purchases of acreage or go through any more eminent domain battles. Even better, the land had already been stripped of much of the environmental requirements that can slow projects and discourage new development. For ambitious politicians like the village board's president Dave DeGroot, it was a fast track up the food chain without having to go through a daunting electoral process. He would be catapulted from a small-time real estate player to being in charge of thousands of acres of land primed for development. As a *University of Chicago Law Review* article noted, one of the liabilities of municipality-based economic development is the temptation for elected officials "to act as entrepreneurs, formulating and implementing development plans." This is not to suggest that DeGroot or any other elected official involved in the Foxconn project benefited personally. No such evidence exists.

By June 26 the number of sites had been whittled down to two: the thousand-plus acre sites in Mount Pleasant and a similar plot in Kenosha. Unlike Mount Pleasant, Kenosha had a professional city administrator who put together a budget for the WEDC of the potential spin-off costs of the massive project. These included capital needs of $2 million for police, $9 million for fire, $138 million for facility and road expansion, $1 million for airport expansion, $2.5 million for an expanded bus fleet, and $125 million for the water utility: along with other miscellaneous costs it totaled more than $285 million. The anticipated annual operating load was $17 million. Kenosha would also require state backing for any related bond offerings and, intriguingly, a new mental health facility. Although such a facility had no direct link to the industrial development, it was a gesture that declared that the general community, and not just Foxconn, should benefit from the project from the start. When these requests were revealed to be beyond the state's capacity to give, Kenosha withdrew from consideration. Kenosha's mayor John Antaramian announced, "The job I have is to protect the city of Kenosha."

The reaction of Dave DeGroot and his followers in Mount Pleasant was just the opposite. Once Mount Pleasant was selected, activity became frantic. WEDC had promised Foxconn that it would have possession of the initial thousand-plus acres of land by August 1, 2018. Foxconn kept releasing unrealistic and fantastically aggressive start dates for its massive factory, even though it would take years to build and fulfill orders for the required fabrication equipment from Asia. Perhaps it just wanted to keep the heat on the land acquisition effort. Certainly there was a sense of urgency from state officials, regional economic development executives, and the village board of Mount Pleasant. But there were complications, including statutory wait times between the blighting of land and the legal transfer from citizen to government. Even though Mount

Pleasant residents received eminent domain letters in October 2017, the "blighting" process wasn't officially initiated until June 2018. According to eminent domain experts, it was the largest such blighting action in US history.

After attending the initial eminent domain meeting in October 2017, I stopped to talk with a distraught fifty-something woman with tightly bunned blonde hair and silver-framed glasses. Joy Day-Mueller and her husband owned a 5-acre homestead on Braun Road, a lightly trafficked, two-lane rural road that bisected the overall Foxconn site. A mile east stood a large produce stand her husband once ran, selling a wide range of vegetables cultivated on the adjacent land. More recently he'd passed the baton on the produce stand to concentrate on his snow-removal business. As the road continued west, toward Interstate 94, it formed the north side of Foxconn's 1,198-acre phase 1 area. The highway was slated for expansion to at first six and later four lanes—part of the local government commitment for land, roads, water, sewer, and broadband whose cost projections steadily expanded, reaching a high of $911 million. Six lanes would subsume Day-Mueller's home. When the road was later revised back to a two-lane highway, no longer endangering her home, the project director Claude Lois was quick to explain that such plans are always fluid, and besides, the Muellers sold their property voluntarily—it was never seized by eminent domain.

Day-Mueller's home sat outside the main proposed industrial area on the northern border of a 622-acre plot designated for construction staging adjacent to the main industrial site. She and her husband, Michael, had hoped that being on the edge would spare them from the eminent domain acquisition. She was shocked to receive the mailed notification that specifically noted road expansion. In reality, Claude Lois and Alan Marcuvitz weren't exacting about whether or not the homes in the greater Foxconn acreage were actually being taken because of road expansion plans. Eminent domain actions for road expansion are a well-established, accepted procedure with little legal recourse. Mount Pleasant's land grab would be less likely to be challenged if owners were led to believe their yards would soon be highways.

When Joy and I talked after the October meeting and the next day on her property she was clearly still in a state of disbelief. "They're taking my home, where I've lived for twenty-four years," she told me, repeating herself, as if doing so might somehow soften the blow. "We've got a pond, and a utility barn for my husband's business. It's all I've been able to think about for a week. I'm not sleeping well. This whole deal is such a bad idea. I don't see how anyone can support this."

As we walked from the driveway leading up to her ranch home across a carefully landscaped yard to the pond, a couple of hundred feet across and lined with rocks. A small pontoon boat was upended next to a sandy stretch with a sign that declared "Joy's Beach."

"We did all this work ourselves," she said, gesturing across the pond and to the yard behind us. "Everything but the original pond excavation. How are they going to pay us for all that?"

I asked if she'll stay in the area. "I want to get as far away from this as possible," she answered. I sensed she meant both from the Foxconn development and from local officials. "But my husband's snowplowing contracts are all in the area, in Racine." She shook her head. "I guess we'll be hiring our own assessor and begin the battle to get what we can."

In the end, their extra land plus her husband's on-site business structures produced a bonus, with the village paying them $991,000 plus $233,000 in relocation fees, mostly related to the business. Mount Pleasant proved more accommodating to the few small businesses within the Foxconn district than it was to homeowners. This was no doubt part and parcel of the overall pro-business disposition of the Republican leadership and may have been additionally influenced by sympathy: Lois had run his own family's small-town auto-parts store for years. All the same, what Joy and Michael got was years of stress, the loss of the only home they really wanted, and no windfall by the time they had found another place to live and work.

Among the cascade of impersonal business correspondence that streamed through the Mount Pleasant village offices during the period of land acquisition was a letter of a different ilk. Penned by a native of Mount Pleasant who was approaching seventy years of age, it was a carefully crafted paean to a tract of land destined to be ceded to Foxconn, something of a cross between nature rhapsody and memoir. It spoke to the now-towering white pines her mother had planted, to her childhood splashing along the farmstead stream. The bulk of her family farm, it turned out, had been sold some years earlier to pay for her mother's health care. But the family had kept the house and 37 acres, which included a few wooded acres designated for long-term preservation.

"I hope it can serve as a greenspace for the Flying Eagle project," the author, who asked to remain unnamed, wrote her village. "Flying Eagle" had been Foxconn's self-selected code name early in the project.

Claude Lois responded promptly: "Thank you for your email and the history of the parcel. I will do what I can but as I stated I can't make you any promises."

She received a second note from the village the next week: "The purpose of this email is to confirm the closing arrangement we discussed this morning for the closing of your property. . . . The closing will take place at the Waukesha office of von Briesen & Roper." Although no commercial development had been booked for this section of the Foxconn plot, Mount Pleasant closed on the property and promptly had the house and outbuildings bulldozed.

This woman's property was in what the project calls Area 2— north of the 1,000 or so acres that had already been transferred to Foxconn. "I haven't been back," she told me. "I prefer to remember it as it was." As of the summer of 2020, her land was still owned by the village of Mount Pleasant. Her family's house had been razed, but the white pines stood tall. In fact, in April 2019, the village had leased the tillable portion of this area back to two farmers who had been pressured to sell at $50,000 an acre. With no prospect of immediate commercial development, the village decided to earn a little money by growing corn and soybeans. The village's rental income per acre: $180.

By 2020 all the residents but three in the 3,900-acre blighted district had come to terms with the village. Ronald Jensen had a deep attachment to the home where he'd raised his children. They liked coming back with their children and wandering his 3 acres like they did growing up. Even so, he was willing to consider selling, but only if the village offered him the same kind of deal it offered to his neighboring farmers—around eight times market value. The village had taken title to Jensen's property via eminent domain, but in mid-2020 Jensen was still living in his house while petitions in both state and federal courts challenged the village's right to claim his property. Sitting in a kind of escrow account was the village's final offer: $569,300. That money wasn't going to buy 3 acres with an expansive house unless it was twenty miles or so out of town, a change in lifestyle Jensen didn't relish.

The second surviving homestead was Kim and James Mahoney's. Although Claude Lois had promised to find a way to take their dream house, he hadn't in the end. Instead, his apparent revenge for Kim's fortitude was to ignore all the Mahoneys' counteroffers after the village made an initial bid that Kim said fell at least $125,000 short of replacement value largely because of all the customized work they had done. Marcuvitz and Lois arranged to bulldoze all her neighbors' homes and leave her on an island, with her views reduced from bucolic farm fields to bulldozed dirt and Foxconn's industrial buildings. This is where Kim and James and their daughter continue to live—a lovely house on their personal dead-end road in the midst of a bleak stretch of stripped farmland. She occasionally posts updates on the activity and traffic involving Foxconn's new buildings, which she can see clearly from her kitchen window. Visitors to the Mahoneys take a turn just short of one of Foxconn's new guardhouses, driving past the remainders of their neighbors' homes, evident in rough piles of unearthed clay like bare humps of the area's Indian mounds, some with driveways to nowhere.

The third plot to survive the blitz was a farm owned by the Cruezingers, whose popular pumpkin farm is known as "Land of the Giants." They have not been willing to speak publicly. Some of the locals I spoke with admired their fortitude. Others thought they were just being savvy, knowing that their land would someday be even more valuable if it became the only available plots for future private development.

· · ·

Back in Madison as I looked through my pictures of the Foxconn property—mostly rich farmland, including fields of cabbages—my goldendoodle nudged me into a walk. I thought about how in the summer of 2014 the city began putting up fencing around an un-used area of our neighborhood park. More than a year prior, all the homeowners in the adjacent neighborhoods had been polled by the parks department. This was followed by a series of public meetings and open hearings with solicitations for comment. Although there was some dissent from adjacent homeowners, the consensus was positive and the 1-acre Walnut Grove Dog Park was opened in the fall of 2014. "Dog park" has become one of those phrases my wife and I have to spell out in front of our doodle. We walk the dog over there three or four times a week.

In contrast, the homeowners in Mount Pleasant had heard only rumors before that certified eminent domain letter arrived. Many recipients must have read it several times before realizing what it meant. It was more than many of them could grasp.

There had been no public hearings to determine whether resi-dents of Mount Pleasant were in favor of turning their largely rural community into the home of what Foxconn promised would be one of the largest factories in the country. There was no referendum on what would be the most momentous change in the village's his-tory. In fact, all the decisions had been made behind closed doors, with the help of economic development staffers in Madison and

Milwaukee, lawyers and contractors, including Ernst & Young's people in Chicago. The village's part-time elected officials had been working with consultants and a high-priced eminent domain lawyer, but they were mostly bystanders who'd hardly breathed a comment during the process, either in the closed-session meetings or to their neighbors, overwhelmed by the scale of the project and gagged as they seemingly were by nondisclosure agreements that, based on the reluctance to discuss, must have included provisions precluding speaking of them.

What had kicked into action was a massive economic development machine, one that had been honed over hundreds of smaller deals. Foxconn was the big one, the one that comes along once in an economic development career, if ever. No wonder people in Mount Pleasant used the metaphor "getting run over by a train." Once the engine was cranked up, nothing could stop it.

Throughout this hectic process, it was easy to forget about the purported motive for this massive civic investment. From Trump's announcement to the legislative pitch for the $3 billion in state incentives, it was all about the jobs. Over and over again WEDC and other boosters had repeated "13,000 family-supporting jobs." Not jobs for engineers and computer programmers, but hourly, blue-collar jobs, like the ones that had once made Racine County a great American manufacturing hub, before deindustrialization transformed it from a city of well-paid factory workers to a pocket of multigenerational unemployment and urban decay.

CHAPTER 6

Racine, Poster Child of the Rust Belt

When I spoke to seventy-two-year-old Gerald Karwowski in the spring of 2020, he looked back at his life in Racine, searched for the best way to characterize it, and settled on "charmed." His grandparents would have agreed. All four of them immigrated to Wisconsin from Poland as adults in the early years of the twentieth century. In Poland they would have been described as peasants—uneducated tenant farmers, barely avoiding starvation on what landowners left them. His favorite grandfather, his mother's father, told Gerald in broken English stories of their depredation; how he'd race with his sisters to hide them in the fields when the marauding Cossacks came through, protecting them from rape or abduction. Their grandson had completed the family's transition from Old World tenant to New World landowner. For years he has pursued his hobby of collecting artifacts that reflect the history of Racine. He lives outside of Racine on a farm with outbuildings crammed with his findings.

"The best thing we ever did," his grandfather often told him, describing the gamble of leaving the Old Country for Milwaukee and then Racine, thirty miles south. Both were hotbeds of Polish immigration. His grandfathers found jobs in Racine, a vibrant center of manufacturing and innovation. The grandparents otherwise lived an insular life in the Polish community, hanging out at the Polish club and attending mass at the Polish church.

The work they found wasn't easy. One of his grandfathers spent forty-one years in the oppressive heat of a foundry while his wife brought home extra money as a domestic, scrubbing floors and working in a more affluent family's kitchen. His other grandfather got a job at household appliance maker Hamilton Beach, one of Racine's famous-name manufacturers. His other grandmother worked in a laundry. Holidays were raucous affairs, with the extended family crammed into one of their small homes. They were all there in Racine back then, the four grandparents, every uncle and aunt, every one of their children. Now just a smattering remain.

Karwowski's father went into the grocery business, working a corner store that served mostly Polish clientele, undergoing a gradual shift to African American and Hispanic customers. In 1953 when Karwowski started at Garfield, the neighborhood elementary school, there were only a handful of Black students. By the time he moved on to junior high, there were only a handful of whites. The Black population in Racine County was just 484 in 1940; by 1949 it was 2,330 and by 1960 it was 4,700, population growth fueled by the tail end of the Great Migration. That diversity remains today even if the jobs don't—while most of Wisconsin lacks racial and cultural diversity, in 2010 Racine was 23 percent Hispanic and 23 percent Black.

When Karwowski was in high school his father asked him to think about joining him in the grocery business. Gerald had spent many hours stocking shelves, minding the register for a dollar an hour. He'd watched his father working from five in the morning to eleven at night, five or six days a week.

"I said, 'No way,'" Karwowski recalls.

Besides, it was the mid-1960s and American manufacturing was still in its heyday. As soon as he started high school, Karwowski had gotten a summer job at Rajo Motors, a machine shop that specialized in adding customized cylinder heads to soup up the performance of Model Ts, which were still popular with the hot-rod crowd. He liked it. He liked the pay even more. Suddenly he was the rich one among his peers, the one who'd put up the beer money on weekends. His parents begged him to finish high school, but his patience was waning.

"I was never interested in being a lawyer or something professional," he remembers. So after a few lackadaisical months in his sophomore year, he stopped by the J. I. Case office one morning and put in an application. They saw his machine shop experience and by the end of the day he had a job. J. I. Case was the biggest employer in Racine. At the time the company was making farm equipment at a million-square-foot factory in the heart of Racine.

Gerald's timing was one of what he sees as the serendipities in his life. Starting so young gave him a seniority edge that would come to serve him well. His classmates who joined the company a few years later never achieved the same job security. He wasn't laid off once, even though Case was in a highly cyclical and seasonal business. He earned enough from the start to pay for a decent apartment and keep up with bills. Over the years, his union, the United Auto Workers, worked not only at improving his pay and his benefits but also at making the work environment safer. By 1996 the workplace had been transformed and he was making $24 an hour ($40 an hour in 2020 dollars), had accrued seven weeks of paid vacation, and also had dental and vision insurance—the works. He was forty-eight-years-old and eligible for a lifelong pension and benefits. He took it.

• • •

The city of Racine is about a third of the way up the western side of Lake Michigan, the fifth-largest lake in the world. Modern Racine has a somewhat ambiguous relationship with its lakefront,

indicative of its complicated demographics and culture. A good part
of the lakefront is shielded by a sprawling marina of small pleasure
craft owned largely by boaters from outside the area, many willing
to commute a half hour to two hours from Chicago and its suburbs,
attracted by the relative discount over city marinas.

The city's downtown sits well away from the lake and is domi-
nated by civic buildings and a sense of decay. With the exception
of a few high-rise housing developments that look like transplants
from Chicagoland's North Shore, Racine has not yet experienced
gentrification. A few lunch spots remain open; the shutters come
down after five. Walking to the lakefront from downtown is a lonely
exercise, even on pleasant days, across parking lots and nondescript
strips of empty, grassy parkland. For much of the year it's positively
depressing—the bleakness matched by gray waters and the chilled
breeze off the lake. For a good stretch south of the marina a gray
concrete walkway is bordered by a jumble of ragged, gray break-
water boulders. There is no beach in this area—on its north side
Racine maintains an attractive beach that is family-friendly during
the days, not so much in the evenings.

Racine has been named one of the most affordable cities in
America, with the average house valued at a little over $100,000.
Of course, this statistic tries to mask the reality of Racine and many
other Rust Belt manufacturing towns across the Upper Midwest:
dwindling populations, deteriorating housing stock, long-standing
racial disparities. In 2019 the city was rated the second-worst place
in America—after Milwaukee—for African Americans based on racial gaps in education, employment, income, and opportunity. In
a January 2020 report conducted by Brandeis University's Heller
School for Social Policy and Management, the Milwaukee metro
area, which includes Racine, was rated as having the highest opportunity gap in the country between white and Black children.

For the area's first settlers, the appeal of what would become
Racine was the mouth of the Root River, said to be named for the
maze of roots that clogged its passage, particularly upstream. The
name Racine comes from the French for "root." The river enters

the lake through a relatively flat plain, providing a natural, protected docking spot for canoes and flat-bottomed boats, the fundamental means of conveyance for both natives and early European visitors, as well as easy access to the interior. Various Native American groups had populated the area for centuries. By the time the first French fur traders arrived, the Potawatomi were on hand. They cultivated the rich floodplain with corn while exploiting the bountiful fishery year round with hook, spear, and net. Among the species that were particularly abundant near the shore in the spring and fall were whitefish, lake trout, sturgeon, walleye, cisco, and Atlantic salmon.

The first nonnative settlers came in the 1830s, mainly from the northeastern states and England, and increasing numbers followed the 1833 Treaty of Chicago between the Potawatomi and the US. This deal, as bad for the Native Americans as any, ceded the Potawatomi's Great Lakes holdings and forced their removal within three years to Indian Territory west of the Mississippi. According to Carthage College historian Nelson Peter Ross, who wrote in the mid-1970s with some restraint, as might be expected with a coerced treaty, "it was difficult to convince many of these people to leave, and they did so only with great reluctance."

The years immediately following the Indian treaty were particularly tense. It should have been no surprise that Indian braves would occasionally show up at settlers' homes on what they considered their land and expect a meal, or browse through as if it were a cost-free store, taking whatever pleased them. On July 4, 1836, Captain Edwin Sumner met with the Potawatomi of the Racine-Kenosha area and wrote to his superior, "These men do not appear content; they complain of the encroachments of the Whites, in settling upon their lands before the treaty requires them to leave it, and I must confess, that is a complaint that I could not well answer, for the Whites are actually starving them, by rushing into the Country and destroying all the game." In June 1838 most of the Wisconsin Potawatomi were forcibly gathered in Milwaukee. Federal agents rounded up as many wagons and horses from the entire region as possible and moved them to western Iowa. Although a few bands remained in the area, the depletion of game forced most of them west well before the Civil War.

A few Potawatomi avoided the roundup and a few others made their way back. The wooded and less populated areas of northern Wisconsin proved their best sanctuary, where many began to work in the logging industry. In 1907, the tribe's numbers in Wisconsin were tallied at 471. In 1913 some reparations were approved by Congress, and many of the local Potawatomi bought land in northern and central Wisconsin. In 1990 the tribe bought 7 acres of one of its former tribal centers, now in the city of Milwaukee, and opened a bingo parlor, which evolved into the first off-reservation casino in America. In a sort of indirect reparation, by 2019 the residents of the Milwaukee area and tourists were contributing about $390 million a year in profits to the casino, producing a pre-COVID $70,000 annual payment to each adult member of the Potawatomi Tribe.

The white pioneers at first cultivated some of the open, sandy ground near the mouth of the Root River, planting corn, potatoes, and turnips, but their early yields were far from sustenance level. By 1836 the movement into the interior had begun, with areas of oak savanna being the first choice, having the dual attraction of the rich soil of open prairie and quality wood for cabin construction. These people were as isolated from society as the most remote Alaskan adventurers would be a hundred years later. It is hard for modern Americans to appreciate the harshness of their self-dependent lives, particularly during the long and dreary Wisconsin winters, which they often passed in rough cabins the size and quality of modern tool sheds. But by 1840, Nicholas Provost could write his aunt from the area, "There are only five years that this land is inhabited by the whites and it is astonishing the number of people already settled here." He also suggests the enormous financial risks involved when he notes that most of the plots had been purchased from the government "with borrowed money and there are some who pay as high as 50% for their borrowed money, the least they lend money for is 7%." And these exorbitant rates weren't a result of inflation, which was nonexistent at the time, but a demonstration of the eagerness of pioneering Americans to take on the risks of homesteading regardless of the costs and the willingness of an unregulated banking system to exploit them.

Farmers from the northeast were well-acquainted with wheat farming, having exhausted their previous lands with it. The virgin prairie expanses around the Root River proved highly productive for wheat, the most lucrative crop at the time. The settlers used oxen to pull inefficient iron plows, to which the thick dark soil adhered to in clumps that had to be constantly cleared. John Deere began experimenting with slippery steel plows in Grand Detour, Illinois, in 1836, but they weren't widely available until about 1849, the year after the first train service was established in Chicago. Wheat production in Racine County increased dramatically from about 40,000 bushels in 1840 to 225,000 in 1850, 300,000 in 1860, and 350,000 in 1870, a bounty that modern agricultural practices would come only close to matching in the late 1960s and 1970s.

The success of the wheat production and availability of quality land sparked a settlement rush, with Racine County's population quadrupling between 1840 and 1850 to 15,000. The 1839 construction of a government road between Racine and Janesville, some sixty-five miles to the interior, helped establish the port of Racine as a trading center, as farm produce was collected from the interior and imported goods came via the Great Lakes water routes.

The heaviest settled inland areas were on the lake plain, which includes the current village of Mount Pleasant, six miles of virtually flat expanse west of Lake Michigan. By 1855 the economic fortunes of the various small towns that had sprung up inland from Racine was largely sealed by the route of the first rail lines. For instance, the Racine-Beloit line bypassed the promising hamlet of Rochester and ran through Burlington, which soon overtook it as a commercial center. Burlington was later the hometown of Robin Vos, the state legislator and Speaker of the Wisconsin assembly who would become a key booster for the Foxconn project.

Through the Civil War years, agricultural trade, which gradually diversified away from wheat into dairy and other crops, was the lifeblood of the region. One specialty was cabbage, which benefited from the dual markets of export via refrigerated rail starting in 1880 as well as local sauerkraut factories. When I drove through the Foxconn zone in the late summer of 2017, thousands of rows of neatly planted mature cabbages flicked by like shuffling cards, many to be shipped into the Milwaukee and Chicago markets.

While the Racine area is today noted for its twentieth-century boom-and-bust manufacturing history, it suffered an earlier economic dislocation at the onset of the second wave of the Industrial Revolution. The mechanization of farming resulted in an exodus of the rural population between 1880 and 1910. At the same time, industrial development began to attract displaced rural workers, and the city of Racine's population grew nearly 150 percent over the same span. In a neatly balanced equation, a good part of the formerly agricultural workforce became involved in agricultural implement manufacturing, most notably by the J. I. Case company, which is the only Racine firm from the Civil War period still in operation there. From the early part of the twentieth century into the 1980s, Case was the largest employer in Racine, peaking at 5,600 in 1976.

Jerome Case came to Wisconsin from New York in 1842 at age twenty-three and brought with him one of the earliest mechanical threshers—machines that separate wheat kernels from the chaff. He immediately began working on improving the machine. By 1847 he had opened a factory in Racine to make his more efficient threshers, added steam-powered tractors in the late nineteenth century, and shifted to gasoline tractors as the twentieth century began. The modern Case Corporation, which has gone through numerous owners and iterations, is currently the world's second-largest farm equipment manufacturer (behind John Deere) and the third largest in construction equipment sales.

After a major dip during the Great Depression, manufacturing employment in Racine ratcheted up during World War II and its aftermath, eventually accounting for some 26,000 workers during its heyday in the late 1960s and early 1970s. S. C. Johnson & Son was largely responsible for Racine's growth as a manufacturing center for paper, chemicals, and rubber. By the mid-1970s, S. C. Johnson was the city's second-largest employer with 2,200 workers, making some of America's most popular household brands: Pledge, Raid, Off!, Glade, and Windex. Publishing was also well established, with Western Publishing, best known for Little Golden Books, employing 1,600 in the same period. In 1976 Racine County was home to forty-three manufacturing companies that employed 100 or more workers. This was a time that Gerard Karwowski described as having such a worker shortage that recruiters would stand in the street, pitching to the foot traffic. Another former manufacturing employee from this period told me how he had been let go from one job and recruited in the parking lot for another: "I didn't even have to fill out an application or anything."

Labor unions were a major force in Racine through the latter part of the twentieth century. L. R. Clausen, the long-serving president of Case from 1924 through 1948, was not a fan. He claimed toward the end of World War II that "the power of unions" was "inspired by Russia" and that their aim was "to invade the authority of management without responsibility. Their idea is a piecemeal capture of industry by making management their slave." A showdown was predictable and led to one of the longest strikes in US history at Case; it began in late 1945 and lasted 440 days. The robustness of the local economy was demonstrated by the fact that 75 percent of striking workers found alternative employment while waiting out the company.

Case's headquarters are still in Racine, but the company closed its 1.3-million-square-foot plant in 2002, relocating its remaining manufacturing operation to a 60,000-square-foot facility in Mount Pleasant, where it employs about 400 people. S. C. Johnson is still a major employer in Racine County, with a workforce of 1,400. Western Publishing, along with many other large employers, including Massey Ferguson, Hamilton Beach, and the once-expansive nearby Kenosha Engine works are long gone. Western Publishing closed its Racine operation in 2001. Massey Ferguson's last 250 employees were warehouse workers making $14.60 an hour. The facility closed in 1993; the company's farm equipment manufacturing had previously moved from Racine to Canada and Europe. Hamilton Beach now has all of its appliances made by contract manufacturers (à la Foxconn) in China.

● ● ●

The postwar influx of workers and residents had put pressures on both Racine labor unions and housing. Unions at first resisted accepting Black workers, but by the later part of the war the local industries actively recruited a large number of Blacks from the US South and Blacks from the Caribbean, especially from Barbados. William "Blue" Jenkins, whose father had moved to Racine from Hattiesburg, Mississippi, in 1917, when Jenkins was an infant, was one of these pioneering United Auto Workers (UAW) members and organizers. After he helped initiate a sit-down strike at his foundry in 1946, both Black and white workers recognized his leadership skills. He went on to become the first Black president of the Racine AFL-CIO Council and was also president of UAW Local 553 at Belle City Malleable Iron Company, where he worked for thirty-five years. He went on to take leadership positions with the local chapter of the NAACP. In 1974, the sixty-seven-year-old Jenkins recalled a critical union meeting after the war.

"When the war was over . . . the Whites wanted the Blacks out. . . . There were only three Blacks at the meeting that day. Some guy got up in the union meeting and said, 'Send them back in cattle cars if you have to' . . . I blew my top." Eventually Jenkins and other Black leaders negotiated to protect the jobs of the Southern Blacks, but the Barbadian workers were forced to leave the country. Racial tensions did not abate. In 1946 a white man was stabbed to death in a robbery perpetrated by two recent Black arrivals from Detroit. After the attackers were arrested, rumor spread that they would be lynched. The court handed out life sentences to both perpetrators in fewer than ten minutes, and the convicted were spirited to an out-of-area prison for their own safety.

One of the activist heirs of Blue Jenkins was Chester Todd, who arrived in Racine in 1951 as a nine-year-old, when his family moved there from Kentucky. At that time "industry was really swinging," he told me in 2020. For his family, he said, "this place was fantastic. It was heaven." The cost of living in Racine was relatively modest; pay for industrial workers was as high as anywhere in the Upper Midwest. Per capita income in 1959 was ranked 31 out of 380 American cites. A hardworking Black man could make enough to support even a large family. And yet "racism was always thick in Racine," Todd reflects. "But remember, companies sent recruiters down south to bring us here. We were wanted."

Todd dropped out of high school, had a short temper, and was prone to fights. Hoping to get away from the racism in Racine, he joined the navy when he was seventeen. "I didn't realize how bad it was in the navy. Back then I never saw one Black officer. They put me on a ship with six hundred sailors. Eleven of us were Black. I'd never been around Southern Whites before," he remembered. It was daily misery, and not only because the Black sailors always got the dirtiest, toughest assignments. He survived two years and a couple of courts-martial when finally a lieutenant commander on his ship realized he was at the breaking point and called him in. Todd remembers him saying, "I know what you're been through here and I'm sending you home." He was honorably discharged. The temper stayed with him for years, though; he says that in his thirties he "did a stint up north, if you know what I mean."

His stepfather was a beloved employee of Webster Electric, makers of hydraulic pumps—he'd never missed a day of work or challenged the racial hierarchy that kept Black workers in menial jobs. He worked nights, cleaning the company grinders. He got Todd his first steady job there. Although Blacks were an accepted part of the Racine workforce, there was a clear code. As Todd pointedly put it, "You never saw a white janitor." The better jobs were in the machine shops, where workers could get bonuses for beating their production targets. "They told us we were too dumb to work a drill press," Todd said, remembering the years working alongside his stepfather as a third-shift floor sweeper. "I mean, how hard is it?"

Todd found a white accomplice who trained him on one of the more specialized machines—eventually letting him take over for spells on evening stints so the worker could catch some sleep. When a listing was posted for the same job, Todd decided to fight for it. "At first, even the union worked to keep me out of that job," he remembered. But eventually he was able to demonstrate his proficiency, and his union bosses relented. He broke the color barrier for machine tooling work in that plant.

In many industrial Midwestern cities racism was considerably worse than it was in Racine. Janesville, Wisconsin, for instance, sixty-five miles west of Racine, was known as a "sundown" town. Blacks could theoretically work there or even own small businesses, but they had better be out of town when the sun set. The effect of this is still seen today, with only 2 percent of the town's population African American and 5 percent Hispanic. Some of these small business people of color lived twenty miles south in Beloit, on the Illinois border. But Beloit itself was hardly a paradigm of fair practice. Racine's Blue Jenkins recalled the first time he was ever refused restaurant service, at a drugstore counter in Beloit in the mid-1930s. In the 1960s he would return to the area on behalf of the NAACP to investigate why the large GM plant in Janesville refused to hire any Black workers, an investigation that was, according to Jenkins, never followed up. But as Blue Jenkins concluded, the boom in Racine's Black population wasn't because Black families from the South were assessing the relative racism of Wisconsin cities. They came to Racine primarily because Racine had jobs, which they often heard about from relatives already working there.

The most obvious and often oppressive area of discrimination was in housing. People in cities nationwide, including Milwaukee and Chicago, used codified federal redlining to justify restricted access for nonwhites to rental properties or home ownership. As a result, in the early and mid-twentieth century, most of Racine's Black population lived in the city's south side "Black belt," although there was a Black neighborhood on the north side and some Black families scattered around the city and in the countryside. In cities including Racine, Milwaukee, Chicago, and Detroit, housing was under particular pressure during and after World War II. One solution that emerged in Racine during and after the war was to house Blacks in trailer camps set up by the wartime federal Public Housing Administration. Conditions were spartan: they had no kitchens and shared communal bathrooms. When some employers gave out holiday turkeys, most of these families had nowhere to cook them and took them to Black-owned restaurants to be prepared for a fee. In 1944 the director of war housing in Racine found that some 2,000 trailers, apartments, or houses were hosting between two and five Black families each. The saving grace of living in such conditions was the work, which eventually lifted workers out of the endless poverty they'd faced in the Deep South, even if they had limited ways to use their income.

Todd recalled housing being a problem as well. There were plenty of restricted neighborhoods and landlords who wouldn't rent to people of color. Black families crammed into ill-maintained rental units. "We had one place," he recalled, "when the lights went out, you could hear the roaches popping off the ceilings onto the floor." Today Todd lives in one of two houses his stepfather and mother had bought, a testament to the kind of income once widely available to blue-collar, industrial workers, even in the face of racism. They were also the first Black family on the block. Todd remembers how the white neighbors would cross the street rather than use the sidewalk in front of their place.

Despite the harsh realities of racism, Racine did embrace many progressive policies. The county's schools, which Blue Jenkins and Chester Todd looked back on favorably, were consolidated into one district in 1960 and became a national model of voluntary desegregation. Between 1960 and 1970 the minority population in the schools virtually doubled to 20 percent, and busing was instituted to keep the newest high school, J. I. Case, which opened in 1966 in Mount Pleasant, at approximately the same racial mix as Racine's two older high schools. Thomas C. Reeves, a professor of history at University of Wisconsin–Parkside in Kenosha, wrote in 1977 about a recent school survey. It "showed that eight out of ten elementary school parents contacted believed that desegregation was working successfully. All of the elementary school principals agreed as did ninety percent of staff."

But this isn't to suggest some sort of egalitarian moment. Racial disparities in housing, income, and academic performance were deeply entrenched and only worsened as the blue-collar-job situation deteriorated. The sad historical irony is that the potential opportunities and freedoms that followed civil rights legislation in the mid- and late 1960s came just before the steady erosion of good jobs. And just as there was workplace prejudice during the good times, there was a pecking order when the manufacturing boom gradually began to go bust. The Black workers were often the first laid off and the last rehired if things picked up. It was a slow process and, as a result, hard for those like Todd who lived through it to pinpoint in terms of timing and cause. The erosion of work may have hit Black labor first, but it eventually hit everyone in Racine and across the industrial Midwest, punishing all blue-collar labor. Some of the jobs moved to suburban locations, some to Southern states, and even more left the country. Those most likely to leave the deteriorating cities tended to be the more affluent and mobile, which created a combination of white flight and an exodus of those Blacks achieving professional status. The result was a steady destruction of the tax base.

"An abundance of decent jobs," wrote University of Massachusetts economist Robert Pollin, is "fundamental to building a decent society." The loss of those decent jobs created a rent in the social fabric that got worse over time, not just in Racine but nationwide. By 2012, 24 million Americans who sought full-time work couldn't find it. Even as the US gross domestic product grew steadily for decades (with the exception of the 2008 global financial crisis and the onset of the COVID-19 pandemic in 2020), the standard of living for most Americans fell. Since 2000 the official unemployment rate in Racine has generally been higher than the Wisconsin average,

but it doesn't look disastrous at 8 percent or so. But the official unemployment rate for Blacks in Racine was double the city's average at 16 percent, and the real crisis in employment has been much
greater than even these numbers suggest, even before COVID-19.
At the start of 2020, 30 percent of the Black population of Racine
fell below the poverty line, four times that of the white population.
As Dartmouth economist David Blanchflower wrote in his book *Not
Working*, "The published unemployment rate, these days, is much
more unreliable than it used to be. . . . Low earnings and loss of
high-paying jobs have led to feelings of instability, insecurity, and
helplessness, especially for the less educated. Suicide rates in the
United States are up twenty-five percent since 1999. The United
States has a labor market crisis, one that has grown into a crisis of
desperation."

The employment crisis goes well beyond racial barriers: even a
high school degree (not a guarantee, with a 16 percent dropout rate
in Racine County) leaves young people with limited job prospects.
As jobs become scarce, college graduates take jobs that were once
filled by people with only high school diplomas, leaving the latter
in increasingly perilous states. In 1970 college graduates earned
40 percent more than high school graduates; by 2000 that number
had escalated to 80 percent. A Brookings Institution study showed
that accomplishing three things—high school graduation, full-time
employment, and marriage before having children—reduced poverty to only 2 percent. During the heyday of manufacturing, the job
was the easiest achievement of these three; now it's the hardest.

Research has shown that, once it is established, the cycle of
poverty creates a damaged and traumatized generation for whom
jobs alone are no longer enough to correct the downward spiral.
Local businessman Jeff Neubauer was hired in 2014 to head Higher
Expectations for Racine County, an agency charged with developing
comprehensive programs to break the cycle. Although the Foxconn
development was promoted to provide well-paying blue-collar
jobs for the unemployed and underemployed workers of Racine
County—a throwback to the 1970s—the reality on the ground was
more complicated. Not only was the Foxconn industrial location

logistically ill suited for an urban workforce, the urban workforce capable of stepping into industrial jobs, if they actually appeared, no longer existed—not after two generations of deprivation. When asked whether Foxconn in nearby Mount Pleasant could be an answer for Racine, Neubauer scoffed at the suggestion: "It might as well be a hundred miles away."

The overall stresses on the fabric of life in Racine can be seen in the social consequences. After decades of decline and its effects, Chester Todd talked with the weight of his years, of decades of distress and racism, about the inception of drug traffic and the rise of gangs. In midlife he'd gone back to school and received an undergraduate and master's degree, spending the latter part of his career as an advocate for Black youth. He cited the Republicans who didn't care about the fate of people like him, and the Democrats who only claimed they did.

Between 2011 and 2016, 16.5 percent of children born in Racine County were African American. These births accounted for 35.6 percent of the county's infant mortality. As the Central Racine County Health Department helpfully explains, "In other words, the percentage of deaths for blacks is disproportionate to the percentage of births." This infant mortality rate was more than three times the less-than-stellar national average.

At the other end of the life cycle, the number of drug-related overdose deaths in Racine County rose by more than 400 percent between 2000 and 2019; the heroin death rate spiked 1,122 percent between 2002 and 2017. Despite civil rights and equal housing legislation, Racine remains heavily segregated. The legacy of restrictive housing and discriminatory loan availability has made surrounding suburban areas expensive and largely white while depressing property values in Racine itself, particularly in minority areas. Within the city, neighborhoods show intense racial and ethnic concentration, with the Uptown neighborhood just south of the Root River 98 percent Black and Hispanic while other neighborhoods are 90 percent white.

Mass incarceration nationwide is a major part of the larger social problem, with the US putting seven times as many people in jail or prison in 2014 than in 1972, a rate five to ten times greater than other Western democracies. A 2013 study found that Wisconsin's incarceration rate for Black males was the highest in the country—twice the national average, at 12.8 percent, and twenty times above that for whites. In Milwaukee, four out of ten Black men had been jailed for minor offenses; one in eight had served hard time. As the University of Wisconsin–Madison sociologist Pamela Oliver explains, these rates "are not a legacy of Jim Crow, but are a result of policies implemented since the mid-1970s which created exponential growth in incarceration between 1975 and 2000. This growth was not due to growing crime rates, but to greater use of incarceration for lesser offenses and drug offenses." In just one generation, Racine went from a city where Blue Jenkins could look over two decades and tick off the names of the few Blacks sent to prison to a city where his activist mentee, Chester Todd, not only spent time "up north" himself but couldn't possibly name all of the ex-cons in his circle of acquaintances, let alone city limits.

Incarceration is socially destructive, especially to family cohesion, and it is a serious impediment to employment, even if jobs were to magically appear—say, at a massive Foxconn factory. The destruction of unions, which Scott Walker considered one of the hallmark achievements of his two terms in office (2010 through 2017), has eliminated another resource for Blacks as well as an institution that provided one of the few impetuses for interracial socialization. But this wasn't just a local phenomenon. Across the United States, the percentage of private-sector workers in trade unions declined from 24 percent in 1973 to 17 percent in 1983 to 6.5 percent in 2017.

One of Chester Todd's friends and activist colleagues is Al Gardner, eleven years his junior. When Gardner first heard about the billions being committed to the Foxconn plant, his reaction was one he would repeat many times—including in public meetings of the Mount Pleasant Village Board. "Will there be jobs for people who look like me?" he asked. He was skeptical from the first. He worried that "Chinese and Blacks don't get along so good." Gardner asked, repeatedly, to no avail, where the inclusion requirements were in the Foxconn contracts. He thought they should have guaranteed 20 percent of the workforce be African American. But that was probably never in the cards; as Gardner noted, "Just look where they placed the factory."

In the early stages of the Foxconn development, there were discussions about large mass-transit developments to enable thousands of workers, many of whom don't have cars, to commute from distressed areas of Racine to the plant. But as of early 2020, when Foxconn was claiming it had more than five hundred full-time Wisconsin workers on staff, mostly in Mount Pleasant, there was no bus transit from Racine to the Foxconn location. Oddly, in the fall of 2018, Foxconn executive Louis Woo told an audience in Chicago that he was looking forward to a commuter train from there to Mount Pleasant, part of the company's shift from its original projection of three-fourths of the workforce comprising blue-collar hourly labor to a model in which it would be at best 10 percent. That didn't seem to leave much opportunity for high school–educated workers in Racine who'd seen, and perhaps had their hopes raised by, promises of 13,000 jobs at $54,000 a year—one of the chief selling points for Wisconsin's multibillion-dollar commitment.

• • •

"I've been a lucky guy," Gerald Karwowski tells people when he describes his pensioned retirement at age forty-eight. The pension was solid even if he took another job, which he eventually did. He knows his children and their children will never have this kind of security, the kind that allowed him to spend the past twenty years pursing his hobby: collecting the history of Racine. His second job was at the local landfill. People would sometimes haul in interesting things. He now has a collection of more than 100,000 objects, most made in or related to Racine.

The popular History Channel TV show *American Pickers* paid him a visit in 2016. He sold the pickers a few items, including two old bicycles, but when Mike Wolfe, one of the costars, realized that virtually everything on Karwowski's property was Racine related, he told his producers they were done shopping. He thought the collection should stay together.

"Today, you have a family like my parents had, five boys, one a high school dropout like me, four no more than high school grads, and there's nothing for them. There's no jobs. No good ones, anyways. All they've been doing the past twenty years is tearing the old factories down," said Karwowski.

So what did Karwowski think when he heard Foxconn would be moving into the area, offering $54,000-a-year jobs? "It sounded good, but you know I was skeptical. Especially when they started spending millions on the roads and stuff. I thought about that air base they were going to build down in Kenosha. Everyone got all excited, they got the land all set, and they just never showed. Now it's a park. Maybe that's what the Foxconn deal will turn into. A giant park."

But none of original Foxconn boosters ever wavered as the project evolved and shifted, and the Mount Pleasant Village Board didn't blink when the project's director Claude Lois asked for a 20 percent compensation boost in 2019 to $24,000 a month, with an additional $150 per hour for overtime. Three years into the project he cited all the good things that Foxconn had brought to Mount Pleasant, praising the building of 5 percent of the promised industrial space and the busy manufacturing of face masks. The face mask operation employed about seventy people, a half a percent of the promised workforce, laboring for half the promised average wages. One of his listed positives was the steady stream of national media attention. What he didn't mention was that the visiting media went on to write and report relentlessly critical stories about the project. When asked to explain his work, he replied, "I look at what's best for the village, making sure that whatever agreements we come to not only make sense for the development but more importantly for the village."

It wasn't the first village he'd said this to.

CHAPTER 7

Sherrard, Illinois

Sherrard is a sleepy town of 640 people on the western edge of Illinois, about halfway between Chicago and Des Moines. If you've ever driven cross country on I-80, you've been just twenty minutes away as you crossed the broad Mississippi and Iowa border. Visitors take Exit 15 onto Knoxville Road south, driving through horizon-to-horizon farm fields with cash crops of corn and soybeans. Traffic is light, and if you lift a hand to the occasional pickup, you'll get a wave back. The main reason travelers detour to Sherrard is for a round of golf at Fyre Lake National, a surprisingly well-designed course miles from any amenities, including food or lodging. Getting a tee time there is no problem.

Since the downtown high school moved out into the country, the old, central part of the village has drifted into a sad and ramshackle state. It's never been a bustling hub; the village population peaked in 1910 at 906. The last restaurant, a pizza place, is shuttered, as is the old grocery store across the street, hardly larger than a convenience shop. The only businesses left are two bars. One un-inviting house had been subdivided into apartments years ago, but when the owner discovered that Illinois code required sprinklers, he abandoned the project, leaving it empty. If you need supplies, there's a new Dollar Store outside of town, across from a gas station 7-Eleven. But most residents make a weekly half-hour run into Moline or Davenport, where they can stock up at the Sam's Club or Costco. Sherrard seems like the most unlikely setting for a large commercial development that failed, costing investors millions, igniting a series of bankruptcies, putting the largest bank in the area into receivership, and sending a civic leader to federal prison.

Over the years, the population of the village has drifted east, into a development that began growing in the 1970s. The owner of this stretch of wooded, rugged land, agriculturally limited to grazing, had a vision. If he dammed up a stream, he could create a lake. People liked to live in the woods around a lake, he thought. He hired a farmer to create a 150-foot-wide earthen dam, and as the water backed up, he christened the place "Fyre Lake"—his wife had said the sunsets there made it look ablaze. They chose the Swedish spelling to make the development sound more exotic, and they built "an authentic replica" of a Viking vessel and used it as the sales office for the lots they had surveyed. It slowly caught on as a housing development. Today, a few hundred houses on narrow, weaving roads sit on the east side of the lake, a motley mix of styles: conventional ranch; two-story houses; a small, green log home across from a prefab. None could be called a McMansion. You can get into a three-bedroom home there for less than $200,000 or buy a lot for as little as $10,000. Most everyone in Sherrard commutes to the Quad Cities, with the exception of teachers, a village employee, and perhaps the bartenders.

The village offices are downtown. The village's annual income from all fees and taxes has averaged around $200,000 over the past decade. I dropped by on a Wednesday afternoon in 2019, but they were closed.

Given all this, it's a stretch to imagine Sherrard transformed into a community built around a top-notch multimillion-dollar golf course. But the idea was hatched in the early 2000s by a landowner on the largely undeveloped western side of Fyre Lake. This amateur developer had limited experience in the intricacies of a large public-private enterprise, but his vision was clear: a destination golf course designed by Jack Nicklaus's company Nicklaus Design, surrounded by expensive vacation homes and sponsored by a village tax-increment-financing (TIF) district.

TIF districts, first pioneered in California in 1952, are a popular tool for municipal economic development. An area that is in need of improvement is typically designated as "blighted," and the property tax revenue—which normally goes to various recipients such as schools—is frozen at the current level, most commonly for twenty-three years. Public funds are then used to make the area more attractive—razing slums, improving roads, adding infrastructure. In a successful TIF district, the subsequent improvements spark development that increases the tax base; the increase, or "increment," over the frozen amount is funneled to the TIF authority that oversees the district. The authority then pays back any debt or costs incurred by the TIF development, until the district either matures after twenty-three years or sooner if the debts are retired. In the Sherrard case, Illinois law precludes spending TIF dollars on golf courses, but they can be used to support housing infrastructure, such as housing around a golf course. As it turned out, creative accounting would allocate all kinds of expenses to the TIF fund—for instance, half of the $500,000 in course design costs, with the justification that those costs were really marketing dollars for home development. But before any of that could happen, the village had to annex the land that would become the Fyre Lake TIF district—a process that would require some municipal finesse.

An ambitious community banker in Aledo (population 3,600), about twenty miles southeast of Sherrard, took an interest in the golf course development. The banker's name was Dana Frye, of Country Bank. Frye arranged a short-term loan for the developer with the stipulation that the debt could be extended if he brought in some deeper-pocketed investors. The developer was optimistic he could get additional funding; Frye was confident he wouldn't. If the additional financing fell through, Frye knew the developer would have to default on the bridge loan, putting the project up for grabs. The banker had some friends who were ready for the grab.

By 2006 the new developers had squeezed out the original and started ramping up their efforts, retaining the name Fyre Lake Ventures while providing what the original promoter didn't have: experienced developers, a consulting municipal leader with TIF experience, a willing banker, and a network of potential investors who had the means to toss in a million bucks or two. In the spirit of the real estate euphoria that characterized the years before the Great Recession, the banker and his investor friends were convinced that this development would be a smashing success.

Three of the developers arrived for the village's fortnightly board meeting on February 20, 2006, to convince the village to create a TIF district for the development: Paul VanHenkelum, Kevin McKillip, and a figure who should be familiar: Claude Lois. Lois was at the time mayor of Burlington, Wisconsin (population 10,000), where he'd put together a TIF district for an industrial park—not without some controversy. McKillip was a real estate broker who'd played a major role in the Burlington TIF and was a longtime associate of Lois. VanHenkelum was president of RSV Engineering, a surveying firm in Big Bend, Wisconsin, who also had worked with Lois and the town of Burlington. He was the original link to the banker, Dana Frye. They'd been friends since college in the 1970s at Bradley University in Peoria, Illinois, and had subsequently done some real estate deals. McKillip and VanHenkelum's projects financed by Frye's Country Bank included one nearby. In 2004 they'd broken ground on a 250-acre housing development in Andalusia, Illinois, a Mississippi River town of 1,050 people located ten miles downriver from Rock Island and twenty-six miles northwest of Sherrard.

Lois, an affable forty-eight-year-old with an automatic smile and combed-back, graying hair, did most of the talking. He wasn't polished, but that worked in his favor. He seemed small town, down home. He was born and raised in Burlington in southeastern Wisconsin. He grew up in what he describes as the largest family in Burlington history—he had four half siblings and seventeen full brothers and sisters. He had run his family's auto-parts store for years before selling out to a brother. After serving eight years on the Burlington city council, he was in his sixth year of a similar stint as mayor.

Accounts from Burlington, including an interview with a former member of his city council, suggest that Lois was a competent mayor, although not a stickler for ethical nuance. According to this Burlington insider, he had no qualms about hiring his own floor-coating business for city contracts; likewise for contractors whose owners were personally close to him. But Burlington was a small town, and it would have been impossible to support local businesses without supporting some friends. Perhaps it would be stretching things in his final year of office when he arranged for his daughter to take over as city treasurer, but there were never any complaints about her dedication or competence. In the year after his last term he emerged along with a partner as the sole bidder on an abandoned city building, a deal eventually scuttled by the city council as too sweetheart. He was fond of using TIFs, as in the town's industrial park. Some select businesspeople were able to set up shop there after purchasing land for a single dollar while others were offered much higher rates. But bringing in those businesses was the primary goal of the industrial park and the TIF district, so the only complaints came from the businesses who didn't receive the preferred rate.

Several people told me that Lois was the kind of mayor who "got things done" and "knew how to work the system." So it made sense that he'd been recruited to serve as a consultant on the Fyre Lake development. Lois was effusive about the project: "It's such a beautiful piece of property," he gushed, "all along Fyre Lake with rolling hills and woods." He explained that the lots would cost $100,000 to $200,000, with individual house construction costing a minimum of $300,000. The developers would spend $1 million (one can imagine him pausing for effect) to promote the development as vacation homes for the wealthy, with Chicago, "only" 178 miles away, the primary market. With some two hundred lots and a classy golf course, the completed development would be worth at least $35 million.

Lois assured the mayor and village board that forming a TIF district was a no-lose proposition. He brought a similar message to the Sherrard School Board, whose sign-off on the TIF project was required because the part of its revenue stream connected to the TIF district was about to be frozen. At the board's April 19, 2006, meeting, Lois assured board members that the TIF project was a rebate program: "We [the developers] get rebated back. We're funding the TIF ourselves . . . really, it's no risk to the village at all."

All the village needed to do was complete annexation of the undeveloped land (a process that had begun with the earlier landowner), turn it into a TIF district, and issue $17 million in bond debt (eighty-five times more than the village's annual budget), which would be used to pay the developers to get the project rolling. The village and its operations would be walled off from the TIF and would retain no liability for the project. With the exception of a couple of skeptical citizens and a minority faction on the board, it was all systems go.

The developers followed their predecessor in retaining Nicklaus Design to lay out the course. They told the board that they expected to build about thirty houses a year, including duplexes and fourplexes, eventually totaling 274 living units. The new houses would substantially increase what Sherrard collected in property tax. At a projected value of $400,000 for each living unit, the completed development would have an initial real estate valuation of about $110 million. The golf course itself would not provide significant property taxes, since it was designated open space. At an effective mill rate of 2 percent of valuation (the level of property tax assessment), the completed development would generate about $2.2 million in property tax per year. The consultants went so far as to calculate a total of $60 million over the twenty-three-year life of the TIF district. However, the fine print made that windfall less enticing. During those twenty-three years, only 8 percent of the new taxes—about $176,000 per year—would go directly into the village's treasury. Twenty percent would go the Sherrard School District, and 72 percent—about $1.58 million—would go to the developers, who would in turn allocate a portion to other property tax recipients, such as the community college.

It took another year to tie up all the loose ends, with the groundbreaking ceremony in July 2007. In the publicity shot, the man at the center of the ceremony with shovel raised was Claude Lois, who had become the main face for the developers. He had been generous, too. In 2006 the village couldn't afford $14,000 worth of playground equipment it wanted to add to the city park. Lois said if the community could raise $3,000 the developers would foot the rest. Later, when engineers recommended a $16,000 backup generator for the city's water supply, Lois stepped up and bought it. The *Rock Island Argus* reported, "The generator won't cost the village anything." Lois would be "reimbursed for his cost through his tax-increment financing agreement with the village."

Lois was more circumspect about the cost of his numerous day trips from Burlington, which were piling up at $1,500 apiece—$1,300 for his time and at least $200 for his driving costs. These charges were later charged to the TIF pool, paid, and invoices filed, only later revealed when concerned citizen Bennie Garner insisted on reviewing the ledgers. Not counting mileage, Lois's pay rate was the equivalent of a $338,000-a-year salary.

The village's mayor, Terry Ayers, was the project's biggest booster. He worked as an insurance agent in the Quad Cities and lived in a small ranch house on a wooded lot in Sherrard. In the period following the developer's arrival, the mayor expanded his personal real estate holdings in the area and began to indulge his hobby, traveling around the Midwest to put his 1927 Super Comp Ford Roadster to the test in drag races. (His racing days ended in June 2018 with a serious crash that resulted according to reports from his neighbors, in broken bones and brain damage.)

As it happened, though, the village couldn't have had worse timing. Soon after the project was under way, the financial crisis of 2008–2009 hit, destroying the housing market and jacking up interest rates for high-yield bond issuers. It also became apparent that golf courses had overdeveloped in the years running up to crisis, which hurt both new and existing courses and country clubs.

And yet enthusiasm and optimism reigned in Sherrard for years. "We can't lose," Mayor Ayers and Claude Lois continued to assure the village board. A local builder put up a 2,600-square-foot house on spec and listed it with "Jack Nicholas [sic] designed golf course" as the teaser for an optimistic $1.2 million. As the golf course neared playability in 2009, the village board heard ideas from residents on how it should spend the projected windfall from the development. Like dreamers with a Powerball ticket, the wish lists rolled in, including rather modest and, in retrospect, heartbreaking proposals: a new library, a bike path, a grocery store.

While they dreamed of money coming in, actual money was going out. In 2008, the village's TIF spent millions for land acquisition (to the developers), engineering (largely to firms owned by the developers), site preparation (developer firms), and consultants and project managers (yes, largely the developers). In 2008, $1.2 million went to pay interest alone, although the original development agreement had projected total interest for the project at $200,000. The first set of bills the developers brought to the village, which would monitor the more than $16 million TIF fund, totaled some $12 million. Ongoing costs, such as Lois's travel and time, had mounted. It is perhaps worth noting that Mayor Ayers resigned in 2009, citing a "dysfunctional" board and stating that the village was headed for "financial disaster." They'd been there before; between 2003 and 2008 the longtime village clerk had embezzled at least $255,000 (rumored to be as much as $500,000)—more than 20 percent of the village's annual income— most of which ended up in the slots at Quad Cities casinos. She was convicted and sentenced to four years in prison in 2009.

Early on in the process there had been some strong resistance to the deal in Sherrard. At one of the village board meetings, Bennie

Garner brought in a printout from an internet forum that was critical of Claude Lois and his tenure as mayor of Burlington. The posts accused Lois and McKillip of cronyism and self-dealing. The printout was passed around the room until someone showed it to Lois, who became enraged. In July 2007 he and his friend McKillip filed a $100,000 lawsuit for defamation against Garner and Gene Mourisse, a township board member who was skeptical of the project. It was settled out of court, without admission of liability.

"It cost me $1,500" in legal fees, Garner recalled to me in a 2019 interview, still clearly bitter and with an enduring impression of the purpose. "It was pretty clearly a warning," Garner concluded, "to let people know what would happen if they tried to get in the way."

Gene Mourisse told me he was initially on good terms with Lois. "We were on a first name basis," he said. "Until he read a copy of those blog post comments. I didn't even know what a blog was at the time." Mourisse remains blissfully disconnected from cyberspace. He also coughed up $1,500 in legal fees to settle the matter.

Others had felt they were getting warned to back off any criticism as well. A couple of residents lobbied the village to hire an independent auditor to review the TIF spending. They hired one of the architects of the state's TIF statutes, a lawyer who made an initial presentation that was well received. But as a local officeholder at the time (who asked not to be identified) related to me: "After the meeting a few of the developers followed him out to his car. We never saw him again. He said it was a health issue. You judge for yourself." Another member of the Sherrard board was skeptical of the project. When the TIF district map was released, it had a little peninsula reaching into the city of Sherrard, surrounding the member's house. Illinois law precludes public officials from voting on TIF projects that involve their primary residence. The properties of board members in favor of the project were carefully excluded.

As the *Quad City Times* reported in June 2007: "Claude Lois is responsible for developing the relationship that exists between the Fyre Lake developers and investors and the Village of Sherrard and existing Fyre Lake Homeowners Association. Using his background as the mayor of Burlington, Wis., and as a small business owner, Lois played a primary role in getting a Tax Increment Financing district, or TIF, for this project." Some new housing development did occur at Fyre Lake, but somehow it didn't add up to the promised amounts. The TIF authority collected $499,000 from 2010 to 2013, an amount you'd typically expect from about fifteen new houses— far fewer than the thirty to thirty-five houses a year they'd projected. When the Sherrard board had voted on the TIF project, board members had in front of them projected increment prepared for them by the developer's TIF consultant. For 2010, the total real estate tax increment was estimated at an exacting $599,297; for 2011, $912,496; for 2012, $1,235,091; for 2013, $1,567,364. This makes for a projected total of $4,319,298, or 8.6 times what was actually collected.

The bond issuance itself was far from conventional. Sherrard had zero history issuing seven-figure bonds and no credit rating to speak of, so whatever bonds it put on the market would have to pay higher interest rates to attract investors. Before the financial crisis, the market rate for such bonds was close to 5 percent. Sherrard's were issued at 9 percent and 10 percent, costing the TIF project about $9 million over the life of the bonds. The annual debt service would amount to $1.6 million—a sum that a 100 percent successful golf development might support only barely through property tax revenue. And that was just debt service. In twenty years, when the bonds became due, the TIF would have to come up with a lump sum of $17 million to pay off bondholders. The TIF district didn't own any hard assets—its only source of income was property tax. The math just didn't work.

That is, the math didn't work for anyone except the bondholders. In a twist to the typical TIF project, the bonds were never brought to market. Instead, they were sold in a private placement, which is itself not terribly unusual. The oddity was the bond purchasers: a band of ten investors made up of the developers plus clients of Country Bank. The purchasers bought in for amounts ranging from $1 million to $2 million. $10.5 million of the $17 million bond offerings were picked up by members of Fyre Lake Ventures. Another

$1 million went to one member's father. A father-in-law took on $2 million. Another, who picked up $1 million worth of the TIF bonds, was a vice chairman of Country Bank.

Why would the Sherrard developers be interested in buying these bonds? Well, if the development succeeded, there would be a juicy yield. But there was another reason: Country Bank accepted the bonds as collateral on loans. The bank issued a $9 million loan to Fyre Lake Ventures, and $900,000 directly to McKillip and VanHenkelum. Two investors from around Kankakee, Illinois, Gregory Yates and Blair Minton, each bought $2 million in bonds and drew loans of $4.5 million and $7 million, respectively. In one of the many lawsuits to come, one bond buyer described how Dana Frye sold him on the bonds by promising a lower-rate loan in equal amount, allowing for tax-free arbitrage on the interest difference.

In the weeks before the bond issuance, there was a flurry of activity as the golf course and housing lots were transferred from Fyre Lake Ventures to individual members of Fyre Lake Ventures. All of this maneuvering made sense to the participants because Dana Frye kept informing them that he was about to close with a deep-pocketed buyer for the whole shebang. However, that never happened.

Still, the sweetest part of the loan deals was that the developers planned to charge the Country Bank interest payments to the TIF fund, allowing them to collect 9 percent or 10 percent on the tax-free bonds and keep it all. For a holder of $2 million in TIF bonds, this could amount to $200,000 a year tax-free, as long as the district could make its interest payments. Once it burned through the initial $16.3 million pool ($17 million less origination fees), the yield would be subject to how much property tax could be collected. In the end, it was Country Bank who was underwriting all the investors and the developers.

As Bennie Garner, a local carpenter and contractor, told me, "I would have had more confidence in the whole deal if any of them had put a dime of their own money in it." From the beginning he called the developers' faith "delusional," pointing out that no one was going to spend $500,000 on a golf course home in a distressed rural area where they couldn't go out afterward for dinner or even shop for groceries. No round of golf could be that good.

Even before the Fyre Lake development, bank regulators had looked askance at Country Bank's balance sheet. It wasn't normal for a small, rural bank to move from small business and agricultural loans to multimillion-dollar development deals. Dana Frye did receive some blowback from bank board members. But Frye was a formidable presence in Aledo. His father was a well-respected construction contractor, and Dana was a leader in the Aledo Catholic Church. He was a believer in divine providence and liked to exchange long e-mails with like-minded investors in Fyre Lake, proclaiming that they were being guided by the hand of God. He and the bank were major contributors to local philanthropy, often in ways that are especially visible in a small town. For instance, there was the Aledo High School Sports Hall of Fame. Dana Frye's son Todd, a three-sport graduate in 1994, was named to the very first class. He joined his father's bank after college and in 2010 was appointed its president. I was told Dana Frye was known as less than charitable at Country Bank, taking any dissent personally and famous for a fiery temper. People didn't cross him.

But what bank would want to issue loans to developers whose collateral required a virtually perfect execution of a golf development like Fyre Lake, a shaky proposition at best? It required self-confidence on a level that approached, if not surpassed, hubris. But it also involved ambition that rose to the level of greed. You see, Dana Frye was not only friendly with the Fyre Lake Ventures team—he had, in effect, drafted them for the task. He especially liked the way they surreptitiously cut him a piece of equity on the project, a fact he failed to mention to his supervisors at the bank, no doubt because it was blatantly illegal.

By mid-2011 the whole project had come undone. The TIF district had burned up almost all of its assets raised by the bond offering. The golf course was struggling to open and would have to depend on drawing customers from twenty and thirty miles away—customers who would drive by multiple, mature courses on the way. Few houses were being built. In July 2011 Kankakee's Blair Minton explained somewhat ingenuously that the investors, with Country Bank's approval, had agreed to default on their loans as "a step in the process to remove the existing ownership group and usher in new investors." Minton was holding $2 million in Sherrard TIF bonds and a $7 million Country Bank loan. The bonds no longer had any means of paying him more than pennies on the dollars of interest owned.

This foreclosure wasn't much help for County Bank's bottom line, since the collateral was a failed golf course development and the virtually worthless bonds. On October 11, 2011, federal authorities closed the bank, whose liability to the Fyre Lake development totaled more than $20 million. The Federal Deposit Insurance Corporation (FDIC) sued to recover losses, with some of the Fyre Lake investors settling and taking a hit while others fought. Blair Minton declared bankruptcy. Gregory Yates went to prison on unrelated fraud charges. McKillip and VanHenkelum took major hits—VanHenkelum eventually left RSV Engineering in 2012, ending a twenty-two-year career. His next stop was Kapur & Associates, a firm that would become a major contractor in the Foxconn development, including providing the Foxconn project director to Mount Pleasant. Dana Frye would later declare bankruptcy, and on February 28, 2020, Frye was sentenced to five years in prison and ordered to make $23 million in restitution for conspiring to make false banking statements in relation to the failed golf course development.

In 2015 a federal judge foreclosed again on the Fyre Lake golf course and associated property, and it was put up in a sheriff's auction. There were two bidders. The winners were two Quad Cities businessmen who took ownership for a mere $850,000. Around the country, golf course architects estimate high-end courses can be built for $2 million to $5 million. Where did all the money go?

Let us count the ways, starting with Claude Lois. Although Lois was never named in the FDIC lawsuits, he was one of the original equity investors in Fyre Lake Ventures, helping raise over $7 million and putting in a personal stake of $250,000. At the time, Lois, who was in office as mayor of Burlington from 2000 to 2008, received an annual salary of $7,200. In 2008 alone he pulled $300,570 from Fyre Lake, mostly from the TIF pool. By early 2010 his total compensation was $419,124, all but $25,837 from the TIF fund. In 2008, a Barbara Lois from Burlington, Wisconsin, made a $250 donation to Wisconsin Republican state representative Robin Vos. Claude Lois's wife is named Barbara. The employer she cited? Fyre Lake Ventures. There is no public record of her job responsibilities or salary.

In October 2006 Claude Lois had told a reporter from the Aledo weekly newspaper that he might keep a vacation home on Fyre Lake since "he will remain an owner in the Championship Golf Course." He never invested in such a home, and it's unclear how long he retained an ownership interest in Fyre Lake Ventures or the course itself, but he was completely out by the time the FDIC began to look to collect on Country Bank's debts.

By early 2010, Paul VanHenkclum's surveying firm, RSV Engineering, had collected $2,324,196 for site work on the housing lots, charges that were allowed to be paid out from the TIF district, and $129,538 for work on the golf course, which could not. That suggests that RSV did about 94 percent of its work on the residential lots, even though only a few were being developed, and about 6 percent of its work on the 140-acre golf course, which was completely surveyed, landscaped, and groomed for play. In 2013 a potential golf course buyer cited a mess of ninety-five liens on the property. Although the developers and their firms had been promptly paid, some of the contractors, particularly those working directly on the golf course whose bills could not be paid through the TIF, had been stiffed.

Lois's buddy Kevin McKillip had been pulling $20,000 a month for a total by February 2010 of $594,000, mostly from the TIF fund, for additional "project management." Another early member of the team, Chicago real estate developer Mike Assad, also pulled $540,000 for "project management." Glossy marketing expenses, which were a total waste, hit $1.4 million. Bennie Garner spent hours flipping through requisition bills, finding one for a $850 golf bag shipped to Aledo and another for $3,300 worth of Tiger Woods golf apparel. By early 2010, after all the bills were tallied, Fyre Lake Ventures had burned through $16,349,948 of the TIF account, effectively draining it.

Meanwhile at city hall, the new mayor and board were clearly worried about their recently annexed territory. In 2012 they found some remaining assets in the TIF fund and issued a zero-interest $375,000 loan to a Quad Cities real estate developer, Todd Raufeisen, who promised to manage and grow the project. He opened the course, but by 2015 the development was still stagnant and Raufeisen still owed Sherrard $375,000. In May 2017 Raufeisen entered a guilty plea for wire fraud and money laundering on activity unrelated to Fyre Lake. In September 2017 he was sentenced to six years in federal prison. Another $375,000 down the drain.

When I spoke to one of the early, lower-level investors who had taken a six-figure financial hit on the deal, he was clearly pained by the memories and his misjudgment of his fellow developers. Even as it was happening, his complaints about spiraling costs, particularly the way some of the principals were pulling big money for little work, went unheeded. When I summed up the costs of the project, he sighed and with some understatement said, "There was clearly some monkey business going on." If it seems as though everyone associated with Fyre Lake was cursed—or perhaps more accurately, tainted, if not convicted—that's not how Bennie Garner would sum it up. "I can't believe more people didn't go to prison for this," he says, shaking his head.

In 2020, the Fyre Lake golf course is more grandiosely named: Fyre Lake National Course. Golfers generally praise the layout, although there have been problems with upkeep, such as the quality of sand in the traps. One reviewer noted that you had a choice of removing your ball from the gravel-filled pit or risk "ruining your club." The clubhouse is in a triple-wide trailer, across the road from where the showplace building with expansive decks and a destination restaurant was supposed to be. They've had PGA golf pros from the beginning, but they haven't stayed long.

In terms of housing, the development is far from complete. At the projected thirty homes a year, the 240 housing lots would have been all filled by 2020. Instead, there are around twenty new houses total (an average of about two a year). That $1.2 million spec house is today valued at $335,000 by Zillow and Trulia. When I drove through in January 2019, one house was under construction. It's difficult to count the TIF homes, because the TIF boundaries jag in and out of properties like a gerrymandered congressional district.

In the end, the Fyre Lake development was a massive transfer of wealth. The citizens of Sherrard were put through the wringer more than once: embezzlement, unfulfilled promises of revenue, issuance of $17 million in bonds that would be virtually worthless within two years, a large loan to a swindler. While there has been some gradual development of the west side of Fyre Lake, most of the additional tax revenue will be sucked up to pay TIF debt (sold by the FDIC for pennies on the dollar to a specialist in distressed debt) until the district expires in 2030. In 2017 the Sherrard School District collected $130,742 less in tax revenue than it would have without a TIF district. That loss will only increase each year as houses are built in the TIF district and their corresponding property taxes are largely sent off to the bondholder.

The village now has responsibility for the annexed land, including the man-made lakes around the golf course, that one local resident pointed out contain some potential liability due to erosion and possible failure should, for example, a major rainstorm stress the dams. The bank collapse in Aledo was also a financial blow for residents who owned shares in the company, millions of dollars of which were sold under false pretense in 2010 when the bank was on its knees.

However, as is often the case in failed public-private enterprises, the major financial victims were American taxpayers. It was Country Bank that originated the assets behind the project. These loans ended up in default; the major recipients, in jail, bankrupt, or personally responsible for only a fraction of their loans. It is an open question as to whether any of the long list of contractors and consultants broke any laws when they cashed their checks. The developers' avarice appears incontestable. In the end, it was the taxpayer-funded FDIC that ended up holding the final $70 million debit.

But not everyone's reputation was permanently tarnished. Sherrard was just a warm-up for Claude Lois. When the really big deal appeared, he was ready and eager to take on the challenge and would do his work for the village in question for just $20,000 a month. It was a project that would also allow him to team up once again with one of his old Fyre Lake associates. When Claude Lois was determined to be the ideal project director, he wasn't hired directly. Instead, Mount Pleasant decided to go through a contractor, Kapur & Associates, whose founder was a major donor to the Republican Party and Wisconsin governor Scott Walker and where Lois's old Burlington colleague and Fyre Lakes partner, Kevin McKillip, was now on staff.

Mount Pleasant's village president Dave DeGroot announced Lois's appointment on August 22, 2017: "Claude is uniquely qualified to lead our economic development efforts. He has an extraordinary track record of success in fostering economic development, both as an elected official and in the private sector." Jonathan Delagrave, Racine County Executive and member of the Tea Party coterie, concurred, saying that Lois was the right person for the job. "I've been involved in a lot of development projects," Lois later explained. "but you just have to take that and times it by a hundred."

The Foxconn development directed by the experienced Lois rested on the foundational analyses of professional economic development consultants, the same kinds of firms that had written up the rosy TIF projections for Sherrard, Illinois. What could possibly go wrong?

CHAPTER 8

Monkey Business in the Middle

If Joy Day-Mueller had glanced out of her Mount Pleasant picture window on Friday, May 5, 2017, five months before she received her eminent domain letter, she probably wouldn't have noted the state-licensed SUV driving by, even if it had slowed in front of her property. The occupants weren't out there to admire her trim house, her husband's utility shed, or the neat landscaping or manicured pond. They were looking ahead to a future in which the entire area would be bulldozed as cleanly as Utah's Bonneville Salt Flats. In their most far-reaching projections, the little country road in front of Joy's house would become a bustling six-lane highway.

In the car that day was a Foxconn executive, Alan Yeung, and a Chicago consultant in his midforties who remained carefully in the shadows throughout the process, even though he was among the most important players. With a name perfectly matched to his low-visibility role, Brian Smith was Foxconn's site-selection and incentive negotiating expert. Smith had graduated from Penn State in 1995 and earned his law degree in 1998 from Capital University in

Bexley, Ohio. His entire twenty-year career had been with Ernst & Young. His title at the time of this drive-by was "US Location Investment Services and Central Region Credits & Incentives Leader." In early 2020 his LinkedIn interests included "Ted Cruz for President 2020" and "Jessica Alba."

Corporations connect with site selectors and incentive negotiators (functions that are almost always combined) in any of the many ways professionals are hired: internet searches, reputation, particular expertise, personal referral. It's not surprising that a global player like Foxconn hooked up with one of the world's largest global accounting and consulting firms, Ernst & Young. In terms of possible referral, Ernst & Young was serving as Apple's auditor at the time, and Apple had been Foxconn's largest client for years. In fact, Foxconn's designated leader of the company's first US venture was Louis Woo, a Stanford PhD who had spent twelve years of his career at Apple.

From the beginning Ernst & Young played a key role in Foxconn's plan to open a US manufacturing site. Foxconn began working with Ernst & Young's Chicago office in early 2017. As is typical of these kinds of economic development projects, Ernst & Young put together an initial requirements list and began to contact economic development agencies in areas it felt would be a match. The officials of these agencies usually work hard to develop personal relationships with site-selection professionals.

The site-selection business is virtually unregulated, and so a great example of how untrammeled capitalism unfolds when big business and government interests intersect. State economic agencies groom selectors the way lobbyists groom members of Congress, but free of any reporting or legislated restraints. Site selectors get entertained at the Masters Tournament in Augusta courtesy of the Georgia Development of Economic Development. Likewise, their Kentucky counterparts host site selectors at the Kentucky Derby. A lucky few get to go quail hunting with Mississippi's governor. There's even the Site Selectors Guild, whose major raison d'être seems to be an annual bash to match state officials with consultants. In 2018,

355 state officials and other attendees paid $2,000 each to attend the event in Cincinnati, which included a party at the Bengals' Paul Brown Stadium, where site selectors were given customized football jerseys and welcomed onto the playing field by cheerleaders.

In *Knowledge Is Power: Working Effectively with Site Selectors*, a publication by the nonprofit International Economic Development Council intended for economic development professionals, the process is laid bare. As site selection narrows, "The decision becomes a matter of who can structure the best opportunity for the company— not just in terms of incentives but including other key location factors for the project." The pamphlet bluntly continues, "Sometimes one community is a clear favorite, but the consultant will keep the remaining short-listed communities active to get the best possible incentive package for the client." What the report doesn't add is "caveat emptor."

In an industry podcast, prominent site selector Mark Williams of Strategic Development Group in Columbia, South Carolina, is more unguarded than the industry professionals I spoke with about the topic of compensation. In a discussion titled "Top Ten Mistakes in Site Selection," he highlights site selector bias. The client, he notes, "may retain a firm, and that firm, their advice may be driven by something other than pure fiduciary duty." For instance, the site selector "might receive a commission on one site and not another and may be driven to lean towards a site where their financial award is greater." Another site selector who doesn't do commission-based work recounted how he lost a large client who insisted on working on a commission, with the relocating company paying the site selector a slice of the publicly funded incentives. The company's thinking was that if no deal was reached, it would avoid any costs; if a good incentive deal was reached, it would be paying the site selector with someone else's money (tax dollars raised by the municipality or state).

Although a fee-for-service model is the compensation scheme that site selectors like to speak about, it's hardly universal. The existence of commission-based site location is not an entirely comfortable topic. The details of a deal like the one between Foxconn and Ernst & Young are confidential, but at least one site professional speculated to me that "it seems unlikely that Ernst & Young's compensation wasn't linked to the size of the deal." It's obviously a model with temptations on both sides. After all, half of 1 percent of $3 billion is still $15 million. In his first nineteen years at Ernst & Young, Smith had arranged for a total of $6 billion in incentives. In the year after the $3 billion Foxconn incentive package was approved by the Wisconsin legislature, Smith received a promotion—his new title: "Partner/principal: Americas indirect tax inbound and US location investment services leader."

State legislation to make economic incentive compensation more transparent or to prohibit commissions has been launched in various states, but it is the state's own economic development division that has lobbied hardest against such measures. Its staff lives in dread of being handicapped in competing for major business deals.

So it's really no surprise that Coleman Peiffer, an official at WEDC, introduced Smith to his colleagues and the governor's office as not only a personal friend but also "a great friend of the state of Wisconsin." It was April 2017 and WEDC was pushing Governor Walker to take a trip to Washington to meet with some of the Trump administration's economic development officials and a businessman who at the time was unknown to Wisconsin officials: Foxconn's chairman Terry Gou.

Getting Walker on board was a bit of a chore. His initial consent was for a phone-in, but as WEDC officials explained, if Gou was flying in from Taiwan, a phone-in would be considered a slight. Peiffer was upbeat from the first, assuring the governor that "we are on the top of a five state list for this project. Other state's [sic] being considered are Ohio, Indiana, Michigan, and Illinois." In the end, the promise of 10,000 jobs plus a White House meeting convinced Walker to rearrange his schedule. On April 28 he and his chief of staff flew to Washington.

Walker met later that day with Gou, Louis Woo, and four other Foxconn executives at the White House. The host was chief of staff

Reince Priebus (a Wisconsin native) and members of Trump's Intragovernmental and Technology Initiatives, working under Jared Kushner. Also at the table: Ernst & Young's Brian Smith.

One WEDC note that circulated among Wisconsin officials prior to this meeting was a harbinger of how difficult it would become to get Foxconn pinned down: "Foxconn has communicated very little details on the meeting agenda." But the stakes were clearly being ramped up. During the meeting Smith let it be known that Pennsylvania and North Carolina were also among the competing states. There was also a hint that key WEDC staffers had not been self-educating on the LCD flat-panel industry: Peiffer describes Foxconn's product in an e-mail that day as "AK" technology—exactly what 8K (a super high-definition screen spec that is the next step up from 4K) sounds like in Chinese-accented English.

The meeting was clearly a success. Within days WEDC was scrambling to set up a Wisconsin visit from Alan Yeung, Foxconn's director of US strategic initiatives and a University of Wisconsin graduate. Joining him was a figure whom WEDC chairman Mark Hogan described as also "representing Foxconn": Brian Smith. Ernst & Young let Wisconsin know that the same Foxconn team had toured sites in Michigan the previous day and had not one, but two meetings with Governor Rick Snyder. Prior to that, they had visited sites thirty to fifty miles from Cincinnati, Columbus, and Cleveland in Ohio—distances that Smith indicated were probably too far from the needed workforce. Hence one edge for southeastern Wisconsin, which could be as close as fifteen or twenty miles to the suburban Chicago workforce. This requirement, never publicized, undercut the repeated booster promises that the Foxconn jobs would go to Wisconsin residents.

On May 5 Governor Walker hosted a breakfast meeting for Smith and Yeung. Foxconn presented two possible factories: a smaller Gen 6.0 panel factory and a state-of-the-art Gen 10.5 factory that could make panels for the largest TVs It was left up in the air whether they would build one or both. In the many thousands of pages of WEDC e-mails that I obtained through Freedom of Information Act requests, WEDC carefully redacted details of the Gen 6.0 factory, likely because the job numbers were so modest as to call into question the entire incentive deal. The larger factory was similar to the footprint of the firm's Gen 10.0 plant in Osaka. The briefing paper for the May 5 meeting stated Foxconn's "high expectation that the land be offered as a local incentive." In this offhanded way, free land for Foxconn became a given, even though it could end up costing the chosen municipality tens of millions of dollars and hundreds of residents their homes.

Another notable topic was the highly aggressive time frame, with construction to start in 2018 and production to be under way by 2020. Perhaps this reflected not only the streamlined building culture of China but also mobilization capability, demonstrated in February 2020 when two hospitals with 1,000 and 1,500 beds respectively were built in China in one week in response to the COVID-19 outbreak. Gou would soon learn that the American process was considerably more cumbersome, even with a pressing governor and a compliant Republican-dominated legislature.

After breakfast, the visitors toured Janesville, Racine, and Kenosha. Afterward, Smith passed along questions from Foxconn chairman Terry Gou, which included his concerns over the available labor force and the potential involvement of unions. Chinese management's distaste of unions was sharply portrayed in the 2019 documentary *American Factory*, the story of the opening of a Chinese-owned automotive glass factory in a former General Motors plant in Dayton, Ohio. The film details how the Chinese firm, Fuyao, spent $1 million on an anti-union consultant to successfully suppress a unionization vote and afterward aggressively removed union organizers and supporters from the workforce. Gou's concern was music to the ears of Governor Walker, who had made his national reputation by effectively destroying the power of public unions in Wisconsin and crippling organized labor in the private sector via so-called right-to-work legislation. He would later brag about how this union bashing had set the stage for the state's landing of Foxconn.

Mark Hogan of WEDC sent Smith a fawning letter on May 28, revealing his awareness of Smith's crucial role. After detailing a first bid of up to $1.25 billion in state and local incentives, he concluded: "Thank you for this unique opportunity that will positively impact friendships and relationships for generations to come. It will be a distinct privilege to work with you."

By late June at least two states were still in the bidding, and Smith was playing Wisconsin against Michigan. On June 25, Michigan offered Smith a deal that included $3.8 billion in tax relief, but Wisconsin's offers had an advantage: Walker had waived almost all taxes on manufacturing firms. As a result, his offer of "refundable tax credits" would translate into cash payments to Foxconn.

On June 26 Mark Hogan distributed a worksheet that showed the payback schedule for a project that would provide Foxconn with 15 percent payroll and 10 percent capital expense incentives. In other words, for a specified period the state would pay for largely cash subsidies to Foxconn equal to 15 percent of Foxconn's Wisconsin wages and 10 percent of its construction and equipment expenses. This worksheet's calculations revealed how long it would take to earn back those costs through state income tax on the workforce. And it also revealed a major problem: payback would take thirty-eight to forty-four years, without accounting for inflation. It was as if they'd calculated the thirty-year payback of a mortgage without considering interest, and the house was still too expensive. Hogan wrote, "Clearly the payback period and ROI [return on investment] for the state has to improve in order for us to substantiate the elevated levels of incentives."

His next statement was as revealing as anything that would follow in the Foxconn saga. He wrote, "The economic impact analysis is critical." The economic impact study would show the cascading effects of the Foxconn factory and its workforce, including induced jobs in Foxconn's supply chain. For instance, by July 2017 boosters were speaking confidently of the billion-dollar glassworks that would employ four hundred technicians and engineers. Tim Sheehy, president of the Metropolitan Milwaukee Association of Commerce, made it seem like a done deal, explaining, "Corning Glass will *have* to put in a plant where they manufacture glass screens right next to the Foxconn plant."

On top of these indirect jobs, the study would calculate the induced impact of all these workers buying housing and cars and shopping for food and eating out and getting haircuts. Depending on the economic models, it could make the math work for a $1.25 billion incentive package, or even a larger one—perhaps $2 billion or $3 billion or even $4 billion. Incentive levels at the higher end of this range would make this one of the biggest economic development projects in American history, certainly the largest involving a foreign corporation. And as Brian Smith regularly communicated to the Walker team, other states were still in the game.

When the economic impact report arrived in early July, it was a game changer. Walker's team told Smith they were willing go higher, much higher. Gou liked what he heard and let the Walker team know he was willing to hammer out the final deal. He and Walker met in Wisconsin on July 12. In a handwritten agreement on a sheet of the governor's letterhead, Gou increased his promised workforce to 13,000, and Walker increased his payroll reimbursement to 17 percent. The state's incentives could go as high as $3 billion: $2.85 billion in cash payments and the remainder in sales tax abatements. The local municipality's commitment wasn't spelled out, but the previous figure of $100 million to $125 million was still on the table. This number would increase by a factor of seven or eight over the following year, pushing the total incentive package to close to $4.5 billion when considering state and federal highway expenditures and electrical infrastructure.

As the incentive structure rose, it wasn't only Foxconn that benefited. If there happened to be a commission involved for Ernst & Young, as industry insiders suspected, then increasing the incentives could be a major windfall for them as well.

And who had crunched the numbers, producing that critical economic impact report? Using a software modeling program called IMPLAN, it was none other than Ernst & Young itself.

CHAPTER 9

Wassily Leontief and Input-Output Economic Impact

In 1854 a member of England's House of Commons announced to the assembly that advances in science might soon allow London weather to be forecast a day in advance. He was greeted with derisive depredations and laughter. Weather, it was widely believed, was chaotic, and proposing to foretell the future was the province of mystics and charlatans.

Since then, weather forecasting has steadily advanced so that today we look with some confidence on ten-day forecasts. The six-day forecast of 2015 was as accurate as the three-day forecast of 1975; by 2025, events like hurricanes might be modeled twenty-five days in advance. Behind the scenes of such projections are whirring supercomputers and complicated mathematical formulas, but in essence, weather forecasting is the output of an enormous amount of data. The inputs are weather observations from around the globe and the history of past weather events used to build a model of the real world. Of course, the farther out the forecast, the less accurate it becomes. Truly long-range forecasts are limited to generalizations such as the likelihood of a heavy hurricane season or a harsher-than-normal winter.

Weather forecasting is perhaps our most familiar exposure to a kind of input-output analysis. Yet if it is possible to model something as complex as nature itself, shouldn't modeling man-made endeavors be even more accurate?

Something like this must have occurred to an exceptional young student of economics in St. Petersburg, Russia, in the early part of the twentieth century. Wassily Leontief was born in 1905 into what he later described as "a typical intellectual" Russian family. In reality, the young Leontief lived a life of great privilege under the auspices of his academic economist father, whose family owned textile mills, and his Jewish-born mother of some means, who held a graduate degree in art history. (After the Russian Revolution, she helped catalog and preserve the neglected czarist art collection in the Hermitage, at one time sledding over the parquet floors that were, like a hockey rink, coated in inches of ice from burst water pipes.) Like the young author-to-be Vladimir Nabokov (seven years his senior, and four hundred miles southeast in Moscow), Wassily had foreign-language-speaking governesses (German and French) and accomplished private tutors. The family maintained a dacha in nearby Finland, where his father introduced Wassily to his lifetime passion for fly-fishing.

At age sixteen Leontief began advanced studies at his hometown Petrograd University (St. Petersburg's name from 1914 to 1924), with false starts in sociology and philosophy before settling on economics. He went far beyond his formal studies, reading widely and absorbing original texts and articles in English, French, and German. He was attracted to the statistical side of economics and made his first mark while still in his teens by showing how the abstract work of a Swiss economist, Leon Walras, on price and supply equilibriums could be quantified. He was of the mind that academic economics was concerned too much with producing beautiful equations and not enough with looking at facts and statistics, what he later called "looking under the hood." He earned his degree, the equivalent of a master's, at the age of nineteen.

He imagined an academic career in Russia until an early paper was suppressed for political reasons. Times were precarious in Russia for outspoken intellectuals—which he was, having been incarcerated for months at the age of fifteen for speaking out against the communists. Somewhat luckily for him, after a growth on his jaw was incorrectly diagnosed as cancerous, he was granted rather rare permission to travel to Berlin for further treatment. He entered the University of Berlin in 1925.

Leontief later characterized these first years in Berlin as "a beautiful time," even though he was dirt poor and sustained himself on a diet of sour milk, potato pancakes, and the occasional frankfurter. By then his family's wealth had been almost entirely confiscated in the name of revolution. A few years later his parents joined him in Berlin. His father served in the Soviet embassy, a dangerous assignment not because of unrest in Germany, but because civil servants in Stalin's Russia had the life span of songbirds. By 1933 Stalin's attentions had turned to Leontief's father, who was called back to Moscow, where a kangaroo court awaited. He declined the invitation and the family became part of the vibrant émigré society in Berlin that included novelist Vladimir Nabokov and the painters Wassily Kandinsky and Leonid Pasternak (father of Boris Pasternak).

Leontief received his doctorate in 1928, having already landed a position at an economics institute in Kiel, in northeastern Germany on the Baltic Sea. There, he continued to work on demand quantification, hoping to expand the existing work, which had primarily focused on agricultural and consumer products. In 1929 he published a framework for applying mathematical formulations to the industrial economy that was widely cited and discussed, giving him international status at the age of twenty-four.

In 1930 an American agricultural economist, Mordecai Ezekiel, visited the Kiel Institute. He took a liking to Leontief and gave him four suggestions for positions in the United States, for which Leontief promptly applied. In the fall of 1931 Leontief was met on Ellis Island by Stanley Kuznets, an earlier Soviet émigré who would go on to win the Nobel Prize in Economics in 1971. He was soon ensconced at the National Bureau of Economic Research in New York. That provided a bridge to Harvard University, where he would remain for the following forty years.

Leontief believed that the ideal economist worked with real-life data under an umbrella of theoretical concepts. As he wrote in 1937, "The most elaborate statistical investigation furnishes nothing but shapeless heaps of raw material, utterly useless unless fitted into a firm theoretical framework." From his perspective, economics should not match the model of physics, where a theorist could produce elegant equations that might take decades to be resolved by experimental colleagues.

What Leontief had in mind was audacious. He envisioned a model of the entire American industrial machine. In practice, it would be a giant matrix in which every component of the machine would be itemized. This matrix would be constructed in such a way, mathematically, that changing one cell would shift the quantities of all related cells, which would in turn shift their related components. The lingua franca of these interrelations was dollars. In this manner the user of the matrix could, say, increase car production by 10 percent, and in a cascading reaction, amounts spent on inputs like steel and rubber would perforce increase in a predictable way. One of the beauties of this model was that relationships were linear: ten more cars would shift each of the supply fields exactly ten times more than one more car would. As the Massachusetts Institute of Technology professor Karen Polenske describes of Leontief, "He wanted to look under the hood of the machine [the economy], in fact, to take the motor apart and subject each of its components to many desired tests and measurements." Although Leontief insisted that his concept was a marriage of theory and data, in one way it was a bit like a theoretical physicist waiting for the invention of the particle accelerator. Grinding out all the necessary calculations by hand (think of a factory floor full of human calculators with slide rulers) was impractical. And the collection of data was painstaking and slow, so that Leontief and his associates might be working in the 1930s on a model for a decade earlier. But the computer age was just around the corner.

At Harvard, Leontief published his first major input-output paper in 1936, which led to an invitation from Washington to work on a 1939 input-output table. Before long, he built the first major operational input-output matrix for the US Air Force's war production planning. He had proposed solutions that would only later find the means of testing, but he was quick to see the value of emerging computer technologies to provide those solutions. His official wartime assignment was with the Office of Strategic Services, the precursor to the Central Intelligence Agency.

After the war Leontief's input-output models began to find broad application and grew in power and utility along with computing power. He was awarded the Nobel Prize in Economics in 1973 for his work in this area. Interestingly, one of his postwar interests was the impact of automation. His first impression was that automation would eventually lead to large-scale unemployment, but by 1985 he believed that new jobs would be created to balance displaced ones.

From an early stage, Leontief and colleagues were well aware of the limitations of input-output modeling. In 1955, for example, Leontief addressed the complications of quantifying inputs. When describing the reliability of something as carefully measured as retail prices, Leontief admitted that the measurement required "considerable explanation." He continued, "There is even good reason to doubt whether such an explanation could ever be unequivocal." These concerns didn't keep the Soviet Union and other planned economies from making wide use of Leontief-based input-output models. Although the models achieved some success in areas such as coal mining, they proved less than potent in predicting demand and sustaining production for staples and consumer products. During the peak of the Red Scare in the 1950s, the US government temporarily shelved input-output models for fear that they appeared too communistic.

But that would soon change. More recently, for example, conservative Republicans have been enthusiastic cutters of education, infrastructure, and social service budgets while beating the drum of the economic wonders of pro-business tax and regulatory cuts. They have been particularly keen on economic incentives to spark industrial development. Even though the enthusiasm for company-specific incentives crosses political lines, no one has been more enthusiastic about committing funds than Republican governors. One of the sad ironies of their propensity to pick industrial winners like Walker's Foxconn in Wisconsin or the petrochemical industry in the Louisiana of former governor Bobby Jindal is that the process relies on economic impact reports that in turn rely on Leontief input-output models that were once the backbone of failed planned economies in communist countries like the Soviet Union. It is hard to square how the kind of top-down industrial management that characterized the inefficient and eventually self-destructive planned economies of the Communist Bloc has become a mainstay and prized strategy for American politicians, even those (like Scott Walker) who trace their roots to the most ardent of free-market anti-communists, particularly Ronald Reagan. In an even stranger irony, Walker credited the fall of the Soviet Union not to bad economic policy but to Ronald Reagan's crushing of the air-traffic controllers' union—an argument that made little sense economically or historically but fit his self-narrative of being a heroic anti-unionist.

The problems demonstrated in planned economies suggest other limitations of input-output analysis. In an early critique, the 1976 Nobel laureate Milton Friedman focused on the mathematical relationships: "The central feature of input-output analysis as a predictive device is, as has been repeatedly emphasized, that it proceeds to make predictions *as if* all coefficients of production were fixed. . . . Now, it is obvious that coefficients of production are not rigorously fixed, that all sorts of variations are possible and do occur." The models, that is, are too static.

A real-world example of the difficulties of using current trends and data to project years ahead was a 1976 United Nations project to look at broad trends through the end of the century using a robust input-output model. Although the exercise correctly predicted important and realized issues, such as large trade deficits in certain nations of Latin America and Southeast Asia, the project suffered, in retrospect, from the same errors as other comparable projects of the time. They were unable to take into account sharp changes in commodity prices such as those wrought by the oil crisis of 1979 following the Iranian Revolution and technological change, which occurs in unanticipated ways in unpredictable areas of the economy. More recently, the COVID-19 global shock is a perfect example of the fragility of long-range economic forecasting.

Another pertinent critique was summarized by Emilio Fontela, a professor at the Universidad Autónoma de Madrid, in 2004: "Exploring the future [using input-output models] should never be identified with forecasting." When Leontief wrote his 1985 automation paper, he didn't produce a single result but ran four different simulations to see four possible futures. As Fontela explains, "It is useful to build long-term models—even if only to help us understand, a posteriori, the reasons for change."

In short, the creators of input-output models and the economists who best understand these models have been careful to explain their inherent limitations even as they exploit their strengths. A robust model can be quite accurate in showing the results of a specific change in, say, adding a third shift to an automobile factory. It can demonstrate the local economic impact of a new football bowl game, given the stadium capacity, the mix of local and visiting attendees and the average length of stay. Then again, you would have to run any number of results to account for the possibility that paid attendance could be far less than a full stadium. What if you built the stadium on the hopes of a bowl game or the possibility of landing a professional team? As the guesswork of inputs goes up, the utility of the output drops, in a classic "garbage in, garbage out" scenario. As Fontela stated, it would be a mistake to confuse possible futures with a forecast. And like weather predictions, the farther ahead you try to project, the fuzzier the outcomes.

The US Bureau of Economic Analysis warns that "regional I/O models can be useful tools for estimating the total effects that an initial change in economic activity will have on a local economy. However, these models are not appropriate for all applications and care should be given to their use. . . . Key assumptions of these models typically include fixed production patterns and no supply constraints. . . . Ignoring these assumptions can lead to inaccurate impact estimates." In other words, if you ask the input-output model, or I/O model, to calculate the impact of 13,000 new jobs, it assumes that all 13,000 workers are available (no constraints on labor supply).

Ray Cordato, senior economist at the John Locke Foundation, a conservative, free-market think tank, was even blunter when he spoke to me from his office in Raleigh, North Carolina: "The main flaw in economic impact studies is that they do not look at alternative uses of resources, do not provide a true cost/benefit analysis. In fact, the most common models, such as the IMPLAN one used by E&Y for their Foxconn study, are incapable of producing a negative number. So it's not a question of whether a project will have a positive impact, but how big an impact it will have. They are based on a series of false assumptions: that all resources are free, that every worker hired is unemployed, that every piece of steel and lumber would otherwise go unused. The premise is ridiculous."

A typical description of the process is provided by one of the larger players in the field, KPMG (a firm not involved in the Foxconn studies), on its website: "Economic impact analyses measure the direct and indirect effects of a business, organization or event on the local, regional, state or national economy. The presence and contribution of a particular project or business generates total economic impact that is substantially larger than the project's or business's activities on its own." The telling point is the assumption that the enterprise being studied will have not only a positive impact but also one "substantially larger" than its immediate business. This assumption is belied by experience. Imagine the projected impact of a nuclear power plant, taking into account its substantial construction and operational workforce plus the spin-off economic benefits of a new source of cheap, clean electrical power. Now suppose that plant is called Chernobyl.

The limit on qualified or specialized labor is especially problematic for the mechanical models that grind away without a care for this kind of practical consideration. As Cordato put it: "Where are these workers going to come from? They will have to bid them away from existing employers. So you are basically creating a wealth transfer from the employers who are not subsidized to the new employer who is."

Today's commercial practitioners of the black arts of the dismal science—Ernst & Young among them—are often less forthcoming, far less.

I/O Becomes a Business

In 1976 Congress mandated that the US Forest Service create a five-year management plan that would take into account various logging strategies and their associated impacts on local communities. One of the results was the development of a model called Impact Analysis for Planning (IMPLAN). The Forest Service began using IMPLAN routinely in 1978, but as the government agency demand grew, it found the collection of data from regions across the country imposing and in 1985 turned the project over to researchers at the University of Minnesota via a private corporation, Minnesota IMPLAN Group. IMPLAN was first used outside the government in 1988, and in 1991 the company took on its first commercial client. In 2013 IMPLAN relocated to North Carolina.

IMPLAN today describes its ideal use on its website as estimating "the impacts of 'shocks' to an economy and to analyze their resulting ripple effects." I was particularly interested to see how the company's software is used to justify megaprojects like the Foxconn development, in which the "ripple effects" were projected out over decades. This became more important especially after speaking with leading practitioners—like Dr. Julie Harrington, the director of Florida State University's Center for Economic Forecasting and Analysis—who explained in detail that IMPLAN needed to be understood as "a snapshot in time," not one that attempts to include even likely changes in the future.

I had a chance to get answers to these questions on the last day of April in 2020 in a phone interview with IMPLAN's chief economist Dr. Jenny Thorvaldson and Devin Swindall, the company's vice president of customer operations. The IMPLAN model, like its modern competitors, including RIMS II (the Bureau of Economic Analysis's Regional Input-Output Modeling System that competes with IMPLAN) is a powerful tool that retains the fundamental theoretical and functional underpinnings of Leontief's earliest conceptions. But this is like saying that a Boeing 767 retains the aeronautics of the Wright brothers' first planes. The amount and currency of the data are incomparable: IMPLAN is designed to provide county-by-county models for the entire US. And the engine behind it is written in software and spun by computer capabilities that couldn't have been imagined in the first half of the twentieth century.

On the day of our conversation, the US economy had been paralyzed by the COVID-19 shutdown, and it was particularly revelatory to hear how that "snapshot in time" works. While in the first days of I/O modeling data might have been a decade old, IMPLAN is constantly updating its model, allowing it to crunch data that is only a year or two old. As Thorvaldson explained to me: "In 2020 we're using 2018 data. You are assuming that when the impact occurs the underlying economic assumptions are still true. This is typically not a terrible assumption, and honestly it's that or make something up; it's based on real data, the most solid assumption you can make."

I wanted to know whether IMPLAN ever reviews the reports that companies like Ernst & Young produce using IMPLAN software and whether IMPLAN bears any responsibility for those projections. The answers were basically no and no. "Anyone can buy the software," Swindall noted. Thorvaldson added that sometimes clients come back and request a "stamp of approval" on a report. "It's not something we're comfortable doing," she explained. "We haven't spent the time collecting the data; we don't have enough knowledge to provide that stamp."

We then talked about the complications of employment impact. Thorvaldson and Swindall explained that in the absence of any adjustments, IMPLAN assumes that all jobs on a project are new jobs. This can be misleading if left to the software alone. Swindall gave the example of a new supermarket in his area of North Carolina that created sixty-five jobs. Within a few months, the new supermarket drove the old supermarket out of business, eliminating a similar number of jobs. The net economic impact of the new store was close to zero. However, an IMPLAN analysis on the new store alone would not automatically take that into account, thereby producing an overly optimistic impact.

So how did Ernst & Young consider the 13,000 jobs that its client Foxconn stated it would be scurrying over to the Mount Pleasant campus within a few years? It's unknown, because commercial impact studies don't reveal their inner workings. Given the incentives, it seems likely that Ernst & Young ran IMPLAN on the assumptions that these were all new jobs that would not cannibalize existing employment.

When I spoke by phone in December 2019 with Tom McComb, a statistician who works with the Bureau of Economic Analysis's RIMS II, he was upfront about the model's capabilities. He revealed that his most common conversation with potential clients involved him saying, "You can't really do that." This echoed my interview with IMPLAN's Swindall, who said staff have similar conversations "every day."

As we know from our reliable short-term weather forecasts, input-output models are one of the wonders of modern science. But their use requires extreme care about the assumptions—you can't project July weather with December inputs.

A deeper look at how the Foxconn project was rationalized is a window into justifications for thousands of projects across the country. It shows how business development professionals and their friendly consultants put together scientific-sounding reports that almost always show that a project is too good to forgo. And just as was true in Sherrard, Illinois, there are always plenty of boosters and contractors in the wings, eager to get their slice of the latest pie.

Wisconsin Map of Counties

From the beginning Foxconn showed a location bias for the far southeastern part of Wisconsin, with its denser population and proximity to exurban Chicago.

Foxconn in Mount Pleasant

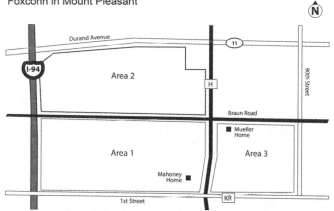

Foxconn Site in Mount Pleasant, Wisconsin

A. Although a massive factory complex similar to the one Foxconn touted had been built on some 350 acres in Japan, Foxconn's footprint in Wisconsin was much larger from the onset. Area 1, where Foxconn envisioned its initial massive factory, was more than 1,000 acres. The company has options to acquire Area 2 as well. By the fall of 2020 Foxconn had been deeded 1,015 acres of land in Mount Pleasant.

B. Before Foxconn's arrival, the area was largely agricultural, with scattered housing along rural roads. Photo credit: Erins-Imaging.

Handwritten Agreement

On July 12, 2017, on the governor's letterhead, Scott Walker and Terry Gou agreed on up to $3 billion in state incentives for 13,000 jobs and a $10 billion capital investment by Foxconn (file obtained via a Freedom of Information Act request by the *Wisconsin State Journal*).

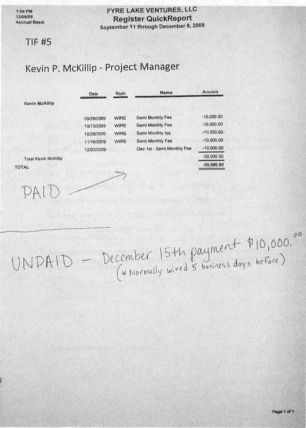

FYRE LAKE VENTURES, LLC
Register QuickReport
September 11 through December 8, 2009

TIF #5

Kevin P. McKillip - Project Manager

	Date	Num	Memo	Amount
Kevin McKillip				
	09/28/2009	WIRE	Semi Monthly Fee	-10,000.00
	10/13/2009	WIRE	Semi Monthly Fee	-10,000.00
	10/28/2009	WIRE	Semi Monthly fee	-10,000.00
	11/16/2009	WIRE	Semi Monthly Fee	-10,000.00
	12/03/2009		Dec 1st - Semi Monthly Fee	-10,000.00
Total Kevin McKillip				-50,000.00
TOTAL				-50,000.00

PAID ⟶

UNPAID — December 15th payment $10,000.⁰⁰
(* Normally wired 5 business days before)

Sherrard Page

A. ROAD TO SHERRARD—Despite the isolation of Sherrard, Illinois, and lack of amenities such as a grocery store or restaurant, a high-end golf course and lakeside homes captured the imagination of local bank official Dana Frye and a core of associated investors. Photo by the author.

B. MCKILLIP PROJECT DIRECTOR LEDGER—Multiple "Project Directors" contributed to the draining of the village's $16 million development fund. Ledger from the public records of the Village of Sherrard.

C. FYRE LAKE CLUBHOUSE—Originally conceived as a showplace clubhouse with a destination restaurant, the project ended up with a triple-wide trailer. A key player in the golf course disaster, which would end up with banker Frye in federal prison, was Mount Pleasant's anointed director of the Foxconn development. Photo by the author.

The DeJonge House

A. BEFORE **B.** DEMO **C.** AFTER

The DeJonge family moved into their expansive home in 2011. They received an eminent domain letter in October 2017. Their property was declared blighted by the village, and their home demolished on November 8, 2018. Figure 5a by Kim Mahoney. Figures 5b and c credit: Erins-Imaging.

The Richards House

A. BEFORE **B.** INTERIOR **C.** DEMO

Richard and Constance Richards owned one of the many carefully maintained, nineteenth-century farm homes in the 6.2-square-mile "blight" zone. The house and its outbuildings were destroyed on December 26–27, 2018. In addition to the owners' buyout, village taxpayers paid $71,404 for the demolition costs. Photo credit: Erins-Imaging.

Aerial View of Foxconn

Foxconn's initial building would have been more of a plus if it hadn't amounted to just 5 percent of the promised capital investment and if local municipalities hadn't gone all in on hundreds of millions of dollars in infrastructure costs to support the promised industrial development. Photo by Mark Hertzberg.

Foxconn Dome

The most impressive structure so far is the Foxconn dome, known locally as the Foxconn Disco Ball. Foxconn calls it a data center, although like the rest of its business plans, the details remain obscure. Photo by Kim Mahoney.

The Homeowners

A. THE MAHONEYS—Jim and Kim Mahoney were marked early by the development authorities for their in-depth knowledge of their eminent domain rights and insistence on a fair buyout price. Their reward was being left the sole house in the vicinity after having watched every neighboring home bulldozed to the ground. Photo by Kevin Miyasaki.

B. JOY MUELLER IN DRIVEWAY—Michael and Joy Mueller were shocked to receive an eminent domain letter in early October 2017. Their five acres on Braun Road included utility buildings for Michael's snow-removal business and a painstakingly constructed pond with a sign that announced "Joy's Beach." Photo by the author.

Groundbreaking

A. GOVERNOR SCOTT WALKER, DONALD TRUMP, AND FOXCONN CHAIRMAN
TERRY GOU—The Foxconn groundbreaking in July 2018 was celebrated by guest of honor President
Donald Trump as "the eighth wonder of the world." It was a Tea Party affair, including the area's
congressional representative, Speaker of the House Paul Ryan; Governor Scott Walker; and all the
way down to the Mount Pleasant village president Dave DeGroot. Photo by Reuters/Darren Hauck.

B. MODEL OF WISCONN VALLEY TECHNOLOGY PARK—Foxconn proved more ready to supply expensive models and videos than real factories. Photo by Mark Hertzberg.

CHAPTER 10

Flying Eagle Economic Impact

The report that would set the stage for the movement of billions of dollars from the taxpayers of Wisconsin to the coffers of a highly profitably Asian tech company arrived in early July 2017 from Ernst & Young (E&Y) in a tidy package of just thirteen pages. It was titled "Quantifying Project Flying Eagle's Potential Economic Impacts in Wisconsin" and was leaked publicly by the Wheeler Report, an independent legislative news service, later that month. These reports tend to be something of a boilerplate exercise for consultants—the numbers change, but about half the copy refers to methodology and terminology and reads the same from client to client.

The conviction that all economic development spending results in a whole greater than just the development itself is a foundational aspect of the Foxconn impact report, as is standard in economic impact reports of all ilks. This is known as the multiplier effect. The multiplier is the impact report's secret sauce. The always-positive multiplying number used, though based on seemingly hard evidence, such as regional qualities and industry-specific metrics, is in actuality subject to considerable judgmental oversight and wiggle room. A new enterprise like a realized Foxconn industrial complex does not exist in isolation. It will create ripple effects through the local and regional economy. This can be seen in any number of examples, such as the commercial districts that grow up around a military base or college campus, or the restaurants that pop up near a new amusement park. The quantifying of these ancillary developments into additional jobs is expressed as a multiplier. For instance, a 2.7 multiplier means that for every position a new enterprise creates, another 1.7 jobs are created by this ripple effect. The total multiplier effect comes from adding together the indirect and "induced" impact. Indirect impacts come from increased economic activity and new jobs to support, say, the Foxconn factory. Induced impacts involve the jobs created by all the money that those Foxconn employees, direct and indirect, will spend on food and housing and consumables. E&Y used established benchmarks to predict that for every ten jobs Foxconn creates, another seventeen jobs would be created in Wisconsin.

The E&Y report details impacts that, if realized, would be simply breathtaking. For boosters this report was a jolt of adrenaline; for anyone willing to dig into the numbers, it would be revealed as audacious. The project would absorb $10 billion in capital expenditure and employ an army of 10,100 construction workers per year for four years. Pictures of a similar plant going up in Osaka a decade earlier show so many construction cranes it looks like the uncountable sailboat masts lined up in a marina. According to the study, more than half of this $10 billion would be spent with Wisconsin suppliers—even though most of the capital expense would go to the massive fabrication equipment built exclusively by suppliers in Asia. The industry expert Bob O'Brien, of Supply Chain Consultants, told me in an interview in January 2020 that the cost of the fabrication equipment is as "at least two-thirds the total cost" for a flat-panel plant. Again, this simple fact, available from just a brief phone call to an expert, was never raised or used to challenge the economic impact studies or the payback calculations.

According to the E&Y report, those 10,100 construction jobs would lead to indirect and induced employment of another 6,000 Wisconsinites. And once the factory was operational, the promised 13,000 Foxconn workers would be earning an average of close to $54,000 a year. The active Foxconn complex would "support over 35,245 jobs in Wisconsin." Not "approximately 35,000 jobs" or "30,000 to 40,000" jobs. This exactitude is perfectly standard in economic impact reports, and it is also intentional, to add to the mystique of the behind-the-scenes formulas, to give the appearance of a machine so precise it can calculate results down to the individual worker, to the very dollar. All these new jobs would, the report concluded, produce $181 million a year in additional tax revenue for the state.

Yet despite the precision of its predictions, the report is full of caveats. The inputs, the fine print reveals, are dependent on the client and have not been audited. The software used was licensed from IMPLAN, and E&Y is not responsible for its accuracy. The Wisconsin supply-chain effects are extrapolated from existing relationships between industries in the area, even though the Foxconn factory would be the first of its kind in the Western Hemisphere, meaning that the relationships, then, were based on different industrial models. Another big problem was how the giant Foxconn complex was designed to be much more insular than a normal factory, both because of its location and its design. For instance, not many existing factory complexes include residential facilities. Many of Foxconn's employees (think engineers from Asia on H1-B visas and dormitory-dwelling immigrant labor) would not be seeking commercial housing in the neighboring communities, or spending as freely there as the technicians and engineers at the kind of electronics companies that were used as models. These regional companies also are typically owned and headquartered locally, keeping profits in the community rather than exporting them out of the region to distant executives and shareholders.

As the Iowa State University economist David Swenson, who has completed dozens of commissions using input-output models, explained to me in September 2018, "You can't get good output without precise knowledge of the inputs and I'm confident that Foxconn was not willing to reveal all the details of their business plan. You also have to have specifics about the supply chain—do these businesses exist in Wisconsin? I doubt they do. Without this information you're forced to rely on the default model which may not match the realities of the project." When I described the report's use of Wisconsin as the sole source of supply-chain effect to IMPLAN's chief economist Jenny Thorvaldson, there was a long silence. I asked if I was correct in sensing a cringe. After another moment's pause, she responded, "You felt that over the phone?"

The manner in which the report looked only at Wisconsin as the source of both material and employee supply to the new Foxconn factory had a direct impact on the number of Wisconsin jobs the report projected. An extra irony of this flaw was that it was E&Y's location team that was following Foxconn's directive to locate a site close to Chicago. As the Bureau of Economic Analysis's Tom McComb told me, if there are glass factories in the impact area (Wisconsin), then the software will assume they will be providing the glass to the new company. If they can't produce the kind of glass needed you'd have to feed this additional information into the model. Would E&Y analysts be informed on glass substrates? Would they take the time to customize the model to account for this even if it diminished the projected impact? We'll never know because of the proprietary nature of the data, but given the turnaround time, the amount of industry-specific expertise available, and the possible financial incentives for E&Y, it seems to me doubtful.

Although internal communications from Foxconn through this period consistently referred to two possible industrial scenarios, a smaller generation Gen 6.0 LCD flat-panel factory and a state-of-the-art Gen 10.5 LCD panel factory, the E&Y report was charged with calculating only the impact of the larger factory. This was not an insignificant decision. The smaller one would require around $6 billion less in capital investment and would need only one-fourth the employees. This Gen 6.0 plant also would not require colocated factories, including a glassworks capable of producing the giant, proprietary sheets of glass substrate; its smaller glass could be shipped in. But the E&Y impact study assumes that a $1 billion glassworks, employing four hundred people, would be part of the deal. The E&Y report casually folds it into the overall economic impact, even though Corning—the most likely partner for such a plant—had already indicated publicly that it thought LCD fabrication was a terrible business. It also had clearly demonstrated its hesitancy in preceding years by insisting that any of its colocated plants in Asia be subsidized by two-thirds of capital expenses—$700 million or more. But Corning's reluctance was conveniently ignored by boosters and E&Y. Rob Lang, director of Wisconsin's Legislative Fiscal Bureau (the state's equivalent of the Congressional Budget Office), later explained to me that they were not charged with doing industry-specific research. Rather, once they found E&Y's premises "reasonable" they focused entirely on extrapolating the provisions of the pending legislation. This is not to say they did no due diligence. Lang and his team did contact economic incentive expert Tim Bartik at the W. E. Upjohn Institute for Employment Research in Kalamazoo, Michigan, to assess the projected additional job creation that a large Foxconn fabrication facility might engender. Bartik found that if you accepted the premise of the $10 billion development, the ancillary effects as expressed in the multiplier were reasonably estimated. He was not asked to comment on the size of the state's subsidies, which he would later roundly criticize, nor was he in a position to analyze the feasibility of a LCD factory in Wisconsin, even if asked. The industry-specific issues were simply not in his wheelhouse.

The difference in scale between Foxconn's two industrial scenarios was never part of the ensuing legislative debate or general discussion, even though it was the equivalent difference between buying a minivan or a forty-foot custom motor home. In public, Foxconn spoke only of the larger plant, and that became the basis of its contractual obligation with the state and the municipalities: Mount Pleasant and Racine County.

As is the case with large projects of all kinds, this report was circulated to key decision makers, in this case, Wisconsin state legislators who would soon be asked to approve the $3 billion in state incentives. It was in turn passed on to the nonpartisan Legislature Fiscal Bureau (the state's equivalent of the Congressional Budget Office), which would look at the legislation and E&Y's projected benefits and calculate the payback period.

If the economic impact study had been done in a rush, it was consistent with the pace of the project. Governor Walker and his team could feel the competitive pressure from other states. The auction was still open at the time of the report in early June 2017, and although Foxconn was tilting strongly toward Wisconsin, the deal was far from done. In particular, Foxconn wanted a signed contract by September 30, 2017, or else it would consider walking away. At this stage of negotiations, Foxconn executives told Wisconsin officials that they planned to have the plant operational in 2018, a timetable so impractically aggressive it begged to be challenged. There is no evidence it was. This need for speed might have raised red flags for state officials if they hadn't been so absorbed in the scramble to land the deal. If this factory, whose output the state was counting on for decades to come, was so integral to Foxconn's long-term business plans, why would a few weeks or months make such a difference?

It is hard to overstate the importance of this E&Y report. It became the foundational document justifying the massive state incentives for Foxconn and was in turn used by all subsequent studies. It gave Mount Pleasant and Racine County the confidence to begin issuing debt and building up hundreds of millions of dollars in infrastructure. Sensing resistance from not just Democrats but also small-government Republicans, the WEDC and Walker's team sought additional economic impact justification. Baker Tilly, an accounting firm headquartered in Chicago, used the E&Y report for an August 2017 follow-up study commissioned by the Wisconsin Economic Development Commission, which would be in charge of managing the contract and details of the Foxconn agreement. A University of Wisconsin–Madison professor, Noah Williams, was also commissioned to produce a paper on short notice, also in August 2017, evaluating the proposal's economic impact; it, too, relied heavily on the E&Y report. It was the E&Y numbers that the Wisconsin's Department of Administration and the nonpartisan Wisconsin Legislative Fiscal Bureau would use to calculate the twenty-five-year payback schedule for a completed Foxconn industrial complex, a report essential to the passage of legislation authorizing the Foxconn subsidies and related matters.

All the reports have a common flaw: they were commissioned by interested parties. Even Noah Williams's report turns out to be tainted. His chair is funded by conservative sponsors (including the Koch brothers, who were big Walker supporters), and he personally sought an economics consulting position on the Walker presidential campaign. This might help explain why he generously expanded the E&Y multiplier of 2.7 to a potential 3.2, producing an even rosier prediction of economic bounty, with an additional 12,000 jobs.

You might imagine that the major assumptions in the E&Y report would be reviewed, if not challenged, in subsequent reports, considering the $3 billion stakes involved. You'd be wrong. As is the case in megaprojects across the country, the consultants received deference on the order of oncologist diagnoses or papal pronouncements. When members of Wisconsin's Foxconn negotiating team first looked at the incentive levels that were being tossed around, they balked. The direct income tax revenue of construction and Foxconn employment, even at their most optimistic projections, would never pay back the costs of the incentives offered. But they were brought around by the value of the indirect and induced benefits that were reflected in the multiplier.

It would be wrong to suggest that the studies went without any initial critique. One of the first objections to the E&Y report was its failure to consider commuters from Illinois. Their economic impact would largely shift to Illinois, where they would be spending their Foxconn wages on housing and retail goods. This inspired the Baker Tilly report. In the haste, signals must have crossed, because

Baker Tilly's initial report counted 40 percent to 50 percent of construction workers and full-time Foxconn staff as out-of-staters. This conclusion blew up the entire economic case for Wisconsin's investment. After what must have been a heated clarification meeting with WEDC, Baker Tilly came back with revised figures of 100 percent Wisconsin residents. When the first, "uncorrected" version of the Baker Tilly report leaked, WEDC officials scrambled in reaction, insisting that it was an early, flawed draft.

Noah Williams's report was also clearly inspired by the out-of-state worker concerns, as he spent considerable energy juggling numbers to show how Illinois workers wouldn't undermine Wisconsin's payback. His argument was that more Wisconsinites commute to Illinois than vice versa, so Foxconn would simply stem the flow. But neither of these reflexive and unconvincing studies got specific about how the drive time from the Foxconn site to the Illinois border is nine minutes, whereas it takes twenty-five minutes to drive from there to downtown Racine, the local area with the heaviest poverty and unemployment. Add to this convenience and demographics. The interstate running past the Foxconn site leads to Lake County, Illinois, which has a population of 704,000, compared to Racine County's 195,000. Residents of western Lake County currently put up with the highest commute times in the greater Chicago area. Next door, in McHenry County, Illinois, also bordering Wisconsin, 21 percent of the working population currently commutes an hour or more, mostly into Chicago metro traffic. Reverse commuting to the nearby Foxconn plant would be considerably less painful for them. As for the higher-paying Foxconn jobs requiring postsecondary education, Racine County and adjacent Kenosha County have college graduate populations of 24 percent compared to Lake County's 44 percent.

In the wake of all these studies, the nonpartisan Wisconsin Legislative Fiscal Bureau prepared an important report for legislators. The final version was released on August 8, 2017, using E&Y numbers to calculate the projected income and payback schedule. It was this report that produced the twenty-five-year payback figure, which quickly gained currency in the legislative debate and in a wide range of media reports.

The Legislative Fiscal Bureau did show some skepticism. It assumed that 10 percent of Foxconn workers would be out-of-staters, but at the time of calculation it was not cognizant of just how close to the Illinois border the development actually would be. The bureau took for granted the E&Y projection of an average salary of $53,875 and did not take into account the time value of money—the widely acknowledged understanding that a dollar spent today is not the same as a dollar earned ten or twenty years in the future. Most grievous of all was the failure to understand that the designers of the software used to produce the initial impact are regularly on the phone telling people why they can't use these numbers for long-term projections or forecasts.

Finally, the December 1, 2017, Tax Incentive Financing deal in which Racine County and the Village of Mount Pleasant committed to hundreds of millions in bond-raised revenue for infrastructure in support of the Foxconn project also used E&Y numbers to justify the expense and project payback, based on increased property values on site, which in turn relied on Foxconn's estimates of capital expenditure. As Mark Fralick, a Texas-based industry expert on automated production and a contributing editor to the most prominent US trade magazine in Foxconn's industry, *Supply Chain Digest*, told me in August 2017 as the project was getting under way: "Foxconn has a long history of overpromising and underdelivering. I just hope the government entities and municipalities involved don't get screwed." When I spoke with IMPLAN's executives, I explained how the Foxconn impact results were annualized and projected to calculate a twenty-five-year-or-more payback for the state's incentive costs. This result became a fixture of the resulting legislative debates and press reports. After a long pause, they explained that this kind of projection is one of the most common misuses of IMPLAN results. Even a five-year projection is stretching things. IMPLAN and its competitors are highly evolved and powerful tools, but results will vary, often to the point of disaster, when the tools are ineptly or inappropriately applied. IMPLAN is at its best when measuring the initial effects of a specific project in a constrained geographic area. The ideal example the IMPLAN staff gave me was a new hotel in a county that had no previous establishments. These temporal limitations are well established. In a declassified 1963 report on the centralized economy of the Soviet Union, analysts at RAND noted that, despite the Politburo's known reliance on I/O models, the time gap between ordering specific industrialization and production was too long for any effective use: "For long-range planning, presumably, the appropriate framework is some form of a programming rather than an input-output model." In short, even spies in the 1960s knew that I/O shouldn't be used for forecasts. Peter Fisher, an economist at the University of Iowa and research director at the Iowa Policy Project, has spent his career studying economic development efforts. He is particularly leery of the multiple-decade payback calculations used for projects like the Foxconn deal. "The average life expectancy of a new enterprise is under ten years," he told me.

Despite the expert consensus and all the peer-reviewed critiques from economists, politicians continue to enthusiastically commission reports and projects continue to be approved. As we will see, the potential political gains and opportunity to reward donors overwhelm the economic evidence. Partisan lines seemed well etched in some large corporate subsidy deals like Foxconn's, with Republicans forming the key booster coalition. But large cities like Chicago that are bastions of Democratic hegemony are equally attracted to large incentive spending. Some of the most vocal critics of the Foxconn-type megadeal actually come from the far right. One of the loudest such voices is that of Ray Cordato, senior economist at the John Locke Foundation, the conservative, free-market-oriented nonprofit think tank.

"The missing ingredient in economic impact studies is economics," Cordato told me. He lambasts the shallowness of the software used by consultants and their typical dearth of the academic economics background needed to understand and explicate the inherent flaws. "All of these studies ignore basic principles of economics and, as a result, do not meaningfully measure what they claim to be measuring—economic impact," he said.

The most comprehensive quantitative economic critique of the Foxconn project came in late 2019 from economists at the Mercatus Center of George Mason University, part of the Koch brothers–sponsored conservative think-tank complex. These free-market academic purists operate in isolation from the political considerations that powered the Republican establishment behind the Foxconn deal. They were also a world apart from the boosterism seen from a politically ambitious economist like Noah Williams, despite their commonality of Koch financial support. Their concluding view of targeted subsidies in general is that they "have little to no effect on local community welfare." They used Wisconsin's Foxconn project as their core case study and concluded through an analysis of likely scenarios and alternative uses of the funds expended that the net effect for Wisconsin would not be the economic windfall promised by the consultants but a long-term burden on the state and its taxpayers.

The philosophical underpinnings of Cordato's bile and the more measured critique from the Mercatus Center must have also struck a nerve in many ideological conservatives as they watched Wisconsin's Tea Party–aligned conservatives jump on the Foxconn bandwagon. How can you support smaller government, free markets, and an "America-first" agenda while handpicking a foreign corporation implementing a very particular technology as the best possible recipient of billions of taxpayer money? Even accepting all the shaky assumptions, for the state's investment to pay off, Foxconn would have to be a long-term winner in an intensely competitive and rapidly evolving flat-panel industry—a call that even top industry experts would be unwilling to make. For Cordato the answer is betrayal: "A lot of Republicans talk the talk about free enterprise but don't walk the walk. In our battle against corporate welfare we find ourselves aligned with advocates from the left with whom we might be normally in conflict."

CHAPTER 11

A Tea Party for Foxconn

When ebullient Republican leaders stood in the East Room of the White House on July 26, 2017, to announce Foxconn's $10 billion project in Wisconsin, it was something of a Tea Party celebration. Wisconsin's governor Scott Walker was a self-identified Tea Partier, as was Speaker of the House Paul Ryan, into whose congressional district the factory was headed. While pinning an ideology on Donald Trump is as quixotic as his inchoate verbal joists with "windmills" (wind turbines), the case is plenty strong that the Tea Party laid the foundation for Trump's election.

In Wisconsin, the search for a site for the massive industrial campus found compliant supporters among conservative Republicans in the statehouse and, most important, at the municipal level. In tiny Mount Pleasant, a usually reliably Republican rural village, longtime residents were in agreement that the person calling the shots was Dave DeGroot, the authoritarian president of the Mount Pleasant Village Board. Although candidates run for local office unaffiliated, it was understood by anyone who paid attention that

DeGroot had led a campaign of conservative Republicans to retake control of the village after a period in which the power had shifted to less-partisan centrists. Before running for office, DeGroot had been trained at the conservative boot camp run by the dark-money-supported organization American Majority. When first running for a seat on the village board, he proudly claimed his loyalty to the Tea Party. In 2017, after serving two two-year terms as trustee, he ran for both village president and a regular trustee seat with the plan of being able to name a like-minded trustee to fill his own vacancy if he was elected president. He won, but the two major factions ended up with a three-three split (the village president being a voting trustee), and to DeGroot's rising indignation, all of his nominees were blocked by three-to-three stalemates. He refused to compromise on a candidate and the seat remained open until finally an election filled the spot; the winner was a DeGroot supporter who would prove the tiebreaker. Although almost all the village business in that "stalemate" period was conducted with unanimous votes, DeGroot characterizes those times through a lens of his frustration.

"Our village is at a crossroads," he wrote for his campaign for a second term as village president. "There is a small segment that wants to take us back to the dysfunction and stalemate we had two years ago . . . we need to come together as a community and put politics aside. Let's stop the negativity and focus on positive ideas. My leadership is about results. . . . We need to make our government more efficient, keep cutting taxes and decreasing our debt."

In 2018 the village, with an annual operating budget of $20 million, put out a request for proposals for bonds in support of Foxconn infrastructure. The village was issuing $142.5 million in TIF bonds and $56.3 million in sewerage system revenue bonds, a debt load of about $20,000 per household. To service the debt, Mount Pleasant would send some $8 million a year to bondholders for decades—about 40 percent of the village's pre-Foxconn budget. In 2019 DeGroot won election for a second term, running unopposed.

Taking a broader look at the political movers and shakers in the Foxconn deal showed that something was amiss, and not just at the village level. A question which bears repeating: Weren't the primary tenets of the Tea Party smaller government, free enterprise, and America first? How could these align with a project that would devote up to $4.5 billion of Wisconsin taxpayer money and resources to a handpicked winner, one of the world's largest corporations, a Taiwan-based company with the majority of its assets in China?

The oddity of an alliance between a foreign corporation and Tea Partiers is exemplified in the brouhaha over the Export-Import Bank. The Export-Import Bank is a long-standing government program that had operated for seventy years well below the radar screens of even avid government critics and observers. The first act of the Export-Import Bank was loaning Cuba $3.8 million in 1934 (about $70 million in 2020 dollars) to purchase silver held by the US government. At first glance this might appear akin to loaning someone money to buy your house, leaving you poorer and homeless, but political economics can often defy common sense.

In short, the Export-Import Bank helps finance trade by providing loans that would not otherwise be available in the private market. According to one extreme analysis, without the bank, the US would lose $50 billion in export revenue and 250,000 jobs. A good percentage of the Export-Import Bank's energies go to supporting a few US businesses, with Boeing having been the largest, absorbing about a third of its resources. One of the Koch brothers-supported libertarian think tanks, the Mercatus Center at George Mason University, popularized renaming the Export-Import Bank as the "Bank of Boeing"—along with other like-minded institutions, it devoted considerable effort to promoting the idea of disbanding it. Specific reasoning excluded, this fits with the Koch brothers writ large and the libertarian ideal of less government means better government.

All this might be confined to the backwaters of government esoterics if the Export-Import Bank had not become a banner issue, even a bête noire, of the insurgent Republican Tea Party movement after its stunning upset in the 2010 midterms and subsequent depression over the inability in 2012 to unseat the Tea Party nemesis,

Barack Obama. On July 24, 2015, Texas senator and presidential hopeful Ted Cruz declared on the Senate floor that the Export-Import Bank was "an egregious example of corporate welfare," with the American taxpayer "on the dime for hundreds of millions of dollars in loan guarantees given out to a handful of giant corporations." He explained that the bank was "a classic example of cronyism and corporate welfare . . . it is career politicians in both parties who are kept in power by looting the taxpayer to benefit wealthy, powerful corporations." This tirade was baffling to many—the *Washington Post* reported on it the next day by referring to the bank as a "seemingly obscure government agency." Cruz ended his speech with a rare public display of intraparty rift, accusing Senate Majority Leader Mitch McConnell of lying about his support for the bank. Many Democratic senators seemed baffled by the Tea Party's stridency on this seemingly insignificant issue, akin to being held up at gunpoint with a demand to turn over your shoelaces. But the core conservatives in the Republican Party echoed Florida senator Marco Rubio, who explained his opposition to the bank in April 2015: "The government should not be picking winners . . . when it comes to the free market."

So it is not the Export-Import Bank that is the subject of interest but the Tea Party consensus revealed in opposition to it: a uproar over government spending to support business as a hallmark of corruption and cronyism, a underlying belief that markets must be left free, and a conviction that the government's worst transgression is "picking a winner." Given this kind of ideological backdrop, how did a group of Tea Party–aligned Republicans find the Foxconn deal so enticing? It represented the largest US incentive deal ever for a foreign corporation, and one of the largest of any such deals, domestic or foreign. Its cost for job development was up to ten times more expensive per job than the norm. It selected a winner not only in terms of corporate partners but also down to the granular detail of the manufactured product: LCD panels suitable for the largest TV sets.

The nominally "populist" Tea Party movement loved this deal from the get-go and immediately proceeded to act on it without the populace having any direct input on this giant commitment. The project was rushed through the Wisconsin statehouse, thanks to compliant Republican majorities, with minimal debate and then approved on largely partisan grounds. At the municipal level the site selection was accomplished behind closed doors and with all the principals muted in a way that pointed to broad nondisclosure agreements; none of the local residents whose lives were about to be upended were informed, let alone invited to voice an opinion.

To understand this conundrum, it is necessary to understand the deep contradictions of the Tea Party and Trumpian Republicanism, which is to say, contemporary Republicanism. The Foxconn project is a large and clear window—say, bigger and clearer than a sixty-five-inch 4K LCD TV—into what we can expect beyond the rhetoric when the modern Republican Party rules the roost from village to state legislature to the White House.

On February 19, 2009, with the market still reeling from the mortgage-backed-securities-induced financial crisis, the CNBC broadcast switched over to the Chicago Board of Trade. From there Rick Santelli, a former Chicago Mercantile Exchange and hedge-fund trader, gave regular reports, usually focused on the bond market. His fifty-two-year-old face was often locked in something between a grin and a grimace while he shouted above the trading-floor noise.

Santelli was in a particular dander over a bill President Obama had signed to provide relief for homeowners who were being squeezed out of their homes as a result of ballooning mortgage payments. In what has become known as "the rant heard 'round the world," Santelli sputtered: "This was America! How many of you people want to pay for your neighbor's mortgage that has an extra bathroom and can't pay their bills? Raise their hand. [Cheers can be heard from traders in the background.] President Obama, are you listening? . . . We're thinking of having a Chicago Tea Party in July. All you capitalists that want to show up at Lake Michigan, I'm going to start organizing."

The resulting groundswell culminated in the Republicans' stunning 2010 midterm victories. In Wisconsin, it was as momentous as anywhere. The Wisconsin statehouse went from a 50–45 Democratic majority to a 60–38 Republican one. The state senate rolled from an 18–15 Democratic control to a 19–14 Republican majority. The open governor's seat went to Scott Walker. Conservatives had held a 4–3 majority on the increasingly politicized and partisan Wisconsin Supreme Court since 2008, a majority that expanded to 5–2 in 2014. Working in secrecy even before Walker took office in January 2011, Wisconsin Republicans began engineering a sophisticated, big-data-driven gerrymandering plan that would virtually guarantee their dominance in the election cycles preceding the next round of redistricting in 2021 and, they hoped, far beyond.

This swing back to conservative, "government is the problem," nativist candidates after Obama's resounding win in 2008 was puzzling to many. The Tea Party movement has since been probed and dissected like a laboratory frog by social scientists and historians, even as it has dissipated as a political entity and morphed into Trumpism.

What the Trump years have proved is that the Tea Party was an alliance of factions joined not by any coherent ideology, but by a common hatred of Barack Obama and what he represented, including a "postracial" America. The Tea Party was also an early example of what came to be known as "astroturfing" (a takeoff from the term "grassroots"): the co-opting and uniting of disgruntled Americans by well-funded and well-organized conservative groups such as the Kochs' Americans for Prosperity.

But as well dissected as the Tea Party has been by academic and political writers, not much attention had been given to its elected leaders' positions on business or business incentives. An exception was an essay by San Francisco State University professor Charles Postel published in 2012. He wrote that "the Tea Party only oppose some types of government intervention in the labor market." When it comes to "right-to-work" and other anti-labor laws, "the conservative movement has consistently supported state interventions.... More broadly, although the Tea Partiers deify the free market, that does not mean that they want corporations to be free of governmental support. Except for some hesitation on the libertarian edge of their movement, conservatives embrace the system of federal and state contracts, subsidies and regulations that make corporations—from military suppliers to drug companies—so profitable."

He expanded on this when I reached him at his office. He compared the Foxconn development with his experience living in Michigan: "It was the same thing with Detroit. Try to do something to help with poverty or homelessness and there'd be a general outcry in Lansing. 'This is socialism, this is throwing money away, this is outrageous.' If it were a suburban high-tech development, it was great. As long as Black people couldn't get there."

While Scott Walker's Wisconsin was governed by the slogan "Open for Business," no state experiment on pro-business Tea Partyness is more illustrative than Sam Brownback's Koch-sponsored gubernatorial tenure in Kansas from 2011 to 2018, which Brownback called "the Kansas experiment." I lived in Kansas from 1991 to 1997, years before Brownback's election. Like the bulk of white-collar workers in Kansas City, Missouri, we lived over the state border in Kansas, where one of the attractions was the terrific public school system. In 1992 my son began attending Tomahawk Ridge Elementary School in the Blue Valley schools in Overland Park. He was enrolled there through third grade when we moved to Wisconsin. When I tracked down the school's now-retired principal, Michael Sportsman, he surprised me by remembering my son, recalling specific conversations about him that he'd had with his third-grade teacher, Elaine Nelson. Sportsman and Nelson, along with the school's talented-and-gifted specialist, were among the most dedicated and accomplished public school employees we ever met. It turned out that we had benefited from the heyday of Blue Valley schools.

Principal Sportsman was highly tuned to my interest in the Brownback years. Brownback had achieved wide support for his pro-business austerity measures, in part by demonstrating and raising ire over how tax dollars from affluent areas like Overland Park were being siphoned away to city schools in places like Wichita, to support the education of largely minority populations. These broad educational cuts became less popular as parents in suburban Kansas City and other cities began to see the steady degrading of their own schools.

Sportsman told me "the Brownback years were dreadful, and it's not over yet." He recalled his subsequent tenure during Brownback's terms as principal at another Blue Valley school with a more diverse, less affluent student population. As budget cuts ripped through the educational fabric, schools began to rely more on fundraising and parent-teacher associations. He told me about the dismal results of his attempt to match a successful rummage sale another school had held: "Our parents couldn't afford to buy each other's discards."

Nurses and guidance counselors were cut from high schools; where parental-organized fundraisers saved the positions at one of the wealthier schools, students at the lower-income school, who needed the support most, had to get by without. Eventually the Republican-controlled legislature rebelled against Brownback and passed tax increases to stem the deep erosion of public services and infrastructure. The economic boom that Brownback promised would materialize from eliminating state business taxes and reducing regulation simply never happened. In the middle of his term in 2018 he left for a position in the Trump administration, oddly decrying the state's underfunding of hospitals, prisons, and other facilities, institutions he had beggared.

The magic pixie dust that politicians chase is jobs. Brownback and other Tea Party governors like Scott Walker wrongly believed that cutting state budgets and programs would create a boom in jobs. Despite the demonstrated failure of this idea, it is Republicans and their wealthy donors who don the mantle of "job creators." It's an appellation so felicitous that the bearers of it, some of whom have spent the better part their lives outsourcing jobs to China and India while installing the latest robotics at home, actually believe it to be accurate. They can only agree that their heroic service in stoking the engines of commerce earns them their boundless compensation, tax cuts, and government subsidies.

A study conducted by the University of Texas's Nathan Jensen and Duke University's Edmund Malesky uncovered empirical evidence that supporting large government-incentivized projects wins votes. Politicians who join the bidding wars for factories or corporate headquarters wear a sort of halo that lingers whether or not they land the project or whether or not the project pans out in terms of employment. This was the driving assumption that convinced Scott Walker to commit to winning the Foxconn deal. He believed that if a politician was rewarded for landing industrial projects, the reward should be commensurate to the size of the project bagged. And Foxconn was "the big one." The arrival of the RFP from Foxconn must have seemed, to Walker, the born-again son of a preacher, absolutely providential.

For the onetime Wisconsin Republican insider Joe Britt, the Foxconn project exemplified one of the key qualities of modern conservatism that had turned him away from the party and particularly from Trumpism. He had spent almost twenty years working on Wisconsin Republican staffs, including stints in the US Senate and in the statehouse. He told me, "What the Foxconn deal exemplified was the primacy of party discipline in today's Republican Party, as well as the greatly diminished role of ideology." In the wake of the Tea Party movement, moderate Republicans were squeezed into obedience or retirement by the threat or actuality of being "primaried" and via selective access to campaign funds from the party and political action committees. By 2016 and the triumph of Trump, it was no longer surprising that projects like Foxconn could be supported without a word about the fundamental principles of free enterprise or fiscal conservatism. "You would think that some of the Republican legislators from northern or western Wisconsin would have had some pause about spending billions of dollars for a project in the far southeast corner of the state, but not a peep," said Britt.

Britt also identified two elements that made the Foxconn deal attractive to Republicans: serving donors and the upcoming election. His insight supports the notion that the line from the Tea Party to Trumpism is short and direct. As Britt explained in an observation that might fit the Trump White House as well, "For eight years the Walker administration devoted very little thought to issues that wouldn't make a difference in the next campaign."

This quality of modern Republicanism is an underlying theme for another former Wisconsin insider. Ed Wall had worked for thirty-two years in law enforcement when he was recruited to Scott Walker's cabinet as director of corrections. He served for four years before being summarily dismissed, which he says put him on the brink of suicide. He published *Unethical: Life in Scott Walker's Cabinet and the Dirty Side of Politics* just before the 2018 gubernatorial election. From his initial election to the governor's office, Wall writes, Walker was determined to make his national reputation by doing something "big and bold." As Wall served, he gradually became aware that his own "opinion and sense of what is right and wrong" didn't matter. In a description that is surely familiar to observers of the Trump cabinet, Wall described his and his fellows' roles as "nothing more than being a cheerleader for political catchphrases and pledges your boss made while pandering for votes. . . . In some cases, it was embarrassing to watch these fawning performances." From Wall's perspective, Walker emerged from his beatdown in the 2016 presidential race looking "like a man who was afraid he'd lose his job . . . my deepest fear was that he and his party, desperate to hold onto the governorship and legislature, would plan some other big, bold plan that would further cast the state into chaos."

When Scott Walker's promise to create 250,000 jobs in his first term was falling short, despite his having created the WEDC, he decided the political liability trumped any personal loyalties. In 2012 he called in WEDC chairman Paul Jadin and, according to Jadin, told him, "I hope you understand that I cannot be accountable for the job numbers." Jadin was out.

If all politics are local, as former Speaker of the US House of Representatives Tip O'Neill is credited with saying, then the focus of Republican politics from the White House through to Speaker of the House Paul Ryan and Governor Scott Walker, burned like a magnifying glass's refracted pinpoint of heat on the village of Mount Pleasant. The result on 3,900 acres of bucolic Wisconsin was a kind of politically driven scorched-earth policy.

CHAPTER 12

A Bright, Shining Object

When President Trump declared that the Foxconn development in Wisconsin wouldn't have happened without him, it was hard to prove him wrong. Foxconn's chairman Terry Gou clearly prized his access to the American president, and Jared Kushner's White House Office of Innovation was involved in the early stages of Foxconn's US initiative.

But for Trump the bragging rights clearly mattered: fulfilling his promise of "bringing back" manufacturing jobs to the US. One of the oddities I discovered in internal Wisconsin governmental correspondence was the repeated use of the word "re-shoring" to describe Foxconn jobs. Even though these jobs would, if achieved, represent a flat-panel industry that had never existed in the Western Hemisphere.

A good part of the nostalgia in Trump's banner slogan "Make America Great Again" is for the well-paying manufacturing jobs that, for a thirty-year stretch after World War II, raised a large number of high school–educated, blue-collar workers into at least the bottom tier of the middle class. In France this period of relative income equality from 1950 to 1980 is known as Les Trente Glorieuses. I was raised in this halcyon "Glorious Thirty" world, on the southern edge of Dubuque, Iowa, in a small housing development of modest ranch homes. All the early 1960s homes on our cul-de-sac had one-car garages for the family's one car, one television set, and most had more occupants, if not children, than bedrooms. The 1950s were the peak of America's relative global industrial output. With Europe and Asia shattered from the war, the US was responsible for 40 percent of global production. While my father was establishing an optometric practice, our neighbors were an executive chef, a supermarket manager, a carpet salesman, a deboner at the meatpacking pack, and the retired president of the University of Dubuque. This was a world apart from today's gated communities and economic ghettoization. One of the ironies of Trumpian nostalgia is the role of unions in raising blue-collar workers into this broad middle class, even as sworn enemies of unionization like Wisconsin's Scott Walker worked to crush them.

As has been documented in award-winning case studies like Amy Goldstein's *Janesville* and Matthew Desmond's *Evicted*, the alternatives to relatively high-paying, often unionized manufacturing jobs have often been grim. Laid-off workers lucky enough to find jobs are often forced to work longer hours for paltry wages that leave them short of earning a living income. Those who find work often struggle in multiple part-time jobs that pay well less than half of their previous salary, and typically without health-care benefits. The social consequences of lost jobs are deep and tragic: broken families, increasing substance use and opioid addiction, and spiraling suicide rates. This dissolution was first seen in urban areas with high minority populations. They were the first to suffer from deindustrialization and the least positioned to adapt. But the malaise is now widespread, particularly evident in largely white, rural communities where relative prosperity was once supported by a single industry or company. In several such afflicted US counties, life expectancies are now lower than in Cambodia or Bangladesh.

As the economist Anne Case and Nobel laureate Angus Deaton at Princeton have detailed, the damage has been particularly focused on people of color and white, middle-aged men and women without college degrees. The strongest regional correlation they found to the disturbing trend of dipping life spans in the US was percentage of employment. During the middle of the "Glorious Thirty," the unemployment rate for men between twenty-five and fifty-five across the US was 5 percent. In 2010, in the wake of the global financial crisis and subsequent recession, the number had ballooned to 20 percent, and the subsequent recovery largely passed by this demographic. Case and Deaton reveal that by 2018, only one in five of these unemployed men were still actively looking for work and as such included in the unemployment statistics.

Politicians who pointed to the official domestic jobless rate as a sign of general prosperity through most of the first decades of the twenty-first century either misunderstood the calculus involved or were being disingenuous. For one, they conveniently overlooked the degrading, destructive effects of working poor. Although some people may think that fast-food counter jobs are for teens, 40 percent of people in those jobs are older than twenty-five and close to one out of three has some college education. The methodology of unemployment statistics can be deceptive: people who work as little as an hour a week count as employed. The official numbers also ignore the millions who have dropped out of the workforce in despair, and they don't measure underemployment in terms of salaries or hours. As jobs have shifted from manufacturing to service, with particularly strong growth in retail and hospitality, the number of workers unhappy with their hours has steadily risen. Involuntary part-time employment is a particular scourge of the young and undereducated, as well as racial minorities. The loss of good manufacturing jobs is one of the important forces behind the well-documented escalation of the increasing American disparity in income and wealth. No single statistic better illustrates this reality than the calculation made in 2019 by the Berkeley economists Gabriel Zucman and Emmanuel Saez that the total net worth of the bottom half of American households was actually negative.

Another troubling employment problem is geographic. As manufacturing jobs moved to the suburbs, many workers were unable to follow, even if they had been welcomed. Reverse commuting required car ownership. Those with homes in the city could sell only at depressed prices while suburban home ownership escalated above their means. Hot spots for jobs, such as those in North Dakota during the fracking boom, require considerable mobility, and Americans have become increasingly less able to pick up and move. In 2005 there were only three Black people working in all of North Dakota's oil fields; by 2015 that number had risen to six hundred. While this is a huge percentage change, it is hardly a ripple in employment in the Upper Midwest.

Families who struggled for decades to own a home in a manufacturing city like Racine become bound to their property, since there is little market for their houses and prices are too low to sell and relocate even if they could find a buyer. Social factors have also become more complex as nuclear families have broken down: working mothers need extended families for childcare to maintain their incomes, however inadequate that might be.

Exactly what happened to create decades of relative prosperity for working-class Americans and then their subsequent, well-documented descent is the subject of considerable popular and academic literature. On the academic side, income-disparity expert Thomas Piketty acknowledges the leveling force of the Great Depression and World Wars I and II, but he places most of the credit for the good times after World War II on engineered political policies. He likewise blames policies for sparking the income inequality that today is approaching not only all-time highs for the US but also historical extremes. Piketty and others find the key characteristic of work in the US today the income disparity between minimum wage and executive jobs, which he describes as "probably higher than in any other society at any time in the past, anywhere in the world."

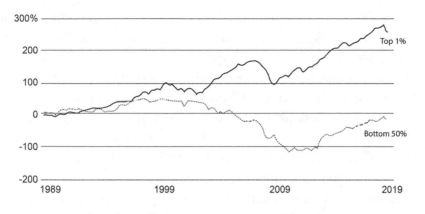

Example 1. Since 1989, the wealth of the top 1 percent has skyrocketed by nearly 300 percent
Cumulative wealth growth in the United States between 1986 and 2018, adjusted
to 2019 dollars using the GDP Price Index. *Source*: Federal Reserve

On the popular literature side are memoirs like J. D. Vance's
Hillbilly Elegy, in which a member of the underclass perseveres by
dint of grit and talent in support of the conservative notion that the
bottom side of income disparity is at least partially self-inflicted. In
contrast, Sarah Smarsh's memoir *Heartland*, a finalist for the 2018
National Book Award, uses her Kansas upbringing to detail the institutional barriers and social forces that promote the cycle of poverty.
Either way, among the most commonly cited factors that have led
to the loss of high-paying, high-benefit manufacturing jobs are immigration, globalization, and automation.

Immigration

In Donald Trump's 2019 State of the Union address he railed that
"working-class Americans are left to pay the price for mass illegal
immigration: reduced jobs, lower wages, overburdened schools,
hospitals that are so crowded you can't get in, increased crime, and
a depleted social safety net." This wasn't a new theme; in July 2015
at the beginning of his presidential campaign, he told an audience
in Phoenix, "They're taking our jobs, they're taking our manufacturing jobs, they're taking our money, they're killing us."

By any measure other than demagogic pronouncement and the public imagination, immigration has had an insignificant impact on US job loss or reduction of wages. Actually, immigrant labor on balance has been shown to have positive economic effects, including expanding the job market and boosting US innovation. Immigrant labor is much more likely to flow to low-wage, physically demanding jobs in agriculture and service, such as maids and restaurant workers. The industrial jobs immigrants find tend to be of the ilk of minimum-wage rural meatpacking, neither coveted nor logistically available to urban residents. A few high-profile cases of US businesses abusing H-1B visas may have contributed to this notion, but on balance, the immigration argument is a nativist political tool to rouse populations who are suffering for entirely different reasons.

Globalization

In 2017 the *New York Times* related how a quality manufacturing job had been a life saver for a female Indianapolis steelworker. In 1999, at age twenty-five, a job at the Rexnord steelworks had given her a path out of a troubled personal situation and what had seemed an inevitable descent into poverty. Although being a woman and a mother in this physically demanding world wasn't easy, the job would help support her daughter's college education and would be critical in providing services to her son, a preschooler with disabilities.

In October 2016, the steelworker and her coworkers who manufactured bearings at the Rexnord factory in Indianapolis received the word. Their jobs were moving to Monterrey, Mexico. Over the following twelve months, the factory slowly wound down. Workers were faced with taking a bonus for training their Mexican replacements or leaving the money on the table in protest. Most worked as long as they could, knowing that their chances of finding a similar paying job were slim.

Trump's stump speech in Indianapolis in April 2016 capitalized on just how bitter a pill it's been to swallow for American workers to experience jobs like these moving to lower-wage markets in foreign countries. The pressure to shift low-skill labor to low-paying markets has been inexorable. As the English-American historian Tony Judt bluntly put it: "Globalization of the labor market favors the most repressive and low-wage economies . . . over the advanced and more egalitarian societies of the West." Companies who fight this trend, like Zenith with its Illinois factory, have difficultly producing goods that can compete with the lower-cost competition. Producers of modern consumer products like the iPhone have just automatically outsourced production overseas. For years Foxconn's largest client has been Apple. In response, Foxconn has built megafactories in China—cities, really—where hundreds of thousands of young workers have produced as many as an astounding 500,000 iPhones a day.

As long as wages are a bigger factor than logistic costs such as shipping, the pressure for production to shift or remain overseas is overwhelming. We've already seen a substantial rise in Chinese salaries (five to nine times what they were just a few years ago), which has in turn led to some manufacturing shifting to even lower labor-cost markets, such as Mexico, Vietnam, and Indonesia.

One way to mitigate the difference in labor costs is to subsidize them, and this was the Wisconsin method. Early in the project Wisconsin's economic development team estimated the labor costs for the full-bore latest-generation Foxconn factory to be $230 million a year more in the US than in Asia. At the time the factory's workforce was estimated at 6,000–10,000 workers, meaning that Foxconn would be paying between $23,000 and $38,333 more per year per employee in Wisconsin than it would abroad—a daunting barrier and a reason Wisconsin agreed to subsidize 17 percent of Foxconn's payroll.

Yet these massive subsidies still paled in comparison to what China and Chinese provinces were willing to pay to support such facilities. The LCD panel expert Bob O'Brien, of Display Supply Chain Consultants, told me that China considered the capability a strategic asset and provided government subsidies up to 90 percent of capital costs for some of the most advanced flat-panel factories—approximately double Wisconsin's maximum support. No wonder flat-screen producers like Japan's Sharp and JDI couldn't compete.

Since the peak of US domestic manufacturing in 1979, some 7 million US manufacturing jobs have been eliminated. But this hasn't been a gradual process. The Great Recession of 2008 hit hard. Even with the ensuing economy recovery, job losses between 2000 and 2018 saw one out of four manufacturing workers out of a job—a drop from 17.5 million to 13 million. The Massachusetts Institute of Technology economists Daron Acemoglu and David Autor put the number of total US manufacturing jobs lost in the 2000s to globalization at 2 million–2.4 million. That's a lot of jobs and a lot of damage. But it's clearly just part of the story.

Automation

In July 2017 *Bloomberg Businessweek* profiled a new steel mill in Austria that told the harsher truth. Here was a mill that produced 500,000 tons of steel wire a year. In the 1960s such a factory would have employed about 1,000 workers. The new mill was run by a team of engineers and technicians ensconced behind a wall of monitors. Their number: fourteen. In the United States, the steel industry lost three out of four workers between 1962 and 2005, some 400,000 jobs. But steel shipments remained steady throughout the same period. Much of blue-collar work in America had been part and parcel of the mechanization of production. Working this industrial and power equipment on assembly lines and in machine shops and foundries created a large number of quality jobs. Automation, however, eliminates the human interface altogether. The economist James K. Galbraith direly describes the result: "Many of those displaced are not only unemployed but obsolete."

The sad fact is that, should the domestic manufacturing sector see a revival, it will be a return of production, not jobs. When labor-cost differentials are sufficiently suppressed or when labor cost as a percentage of production is sufficiently reduced, it will simply make economic sense to bring manufacturing closer to markets, and the US remains the world's largest consumer market. The use of industrial robots and automated systems is not just a manufacturing phenomenon. We're already seeing the creep of artificial intelligence and automation carve into jobs like phone representatives and checkout clerks. Before long, we'll see it in truck and Uber drivers.

In such a world, a new industrial complex that hires 13,000 workers or a new Amazon headquarters with 50,000 high-paid workers is like a desert mirage to a thirst-crazed traveler. Mayors and governors see these shiny reflections and are willing to up their bids into the stratosphere to win them.

But what about the millions of hardworking Americans who have lost their relatively high-paying manufacturing jobs over the past decade? Can they be trained to move from the assembly line to a desk at the new Amazon headquarters or transition into a white-coated technician behind a computer screen at an automated Foxconn factory?

In 2009 when GM shut down the longest continuously running auto plant in the country in Janesville, Wisconsin, a concerted, sometimes heroic, effort was made to retrain workers. For the instructors at the local community college, one of the surprising revelations was how many GM workers didn't even know how to turn on a computer. Retraining a midcareer autoworker to qualify for even entry-level office work was daunting: how could they ever compete with the young kids who had grown up in front of screens, pounding on keyboards? Both the instructors and students soon recognized they couldn't.

Misunderstanding Leads to Mismanagement

When the Foxconn project first emerged, it seemed that creating "family-supporting" blue-collar jobs for motivated high school graduates in the age of globalization and automation was an admirable mission. However, spending billions of taxpayer dollars to subsidize a highly automated, modern factory that has little room for blue-collar workers is an odd way to achieve that goal. While the Wisconsin state legislators were considering the $3 billion subsidy package, the gap between promises and reality was there for anyone to see—that is, anyone who took the time to look. Perhaps the frantic pace to pass the legislation and Foxconn's steady deadline pressure reflected just this.

A major piece of the problem in Wisconsin was the politicians and economic development professionals who were pushing the deal. These were not precise technocrats. They weren't even particularly curious folks who were willing to take the time to understand the basics of the industry they were promoting. Trump, Walker, Mount Pleasant's state senator Robin Vos, Dave DeGroot—these were Republicans who thumbed their nose at science and facts. Walker wouldn't allow agencies under his charges to employ terms like "global warming" or "climate change." He had even gone so far as to issue a gag order in 2015 that forbade Department of Natural Resources employees from even talking about climate change on the job. These were and are faith-based politicians who see what they want to see and believe things will just work out—for them, anyway.

Robin Vos, the leader of Wisconsin's house, has never wavered from his confidence that the Foxconn deal was "one of the biggest accomplishments we've probably had in our state's history." Vos achieved some national notoriety in April 2020 when he led the charge to require Wisconsinites to head to the primary polls despite COVID-19. His picture from a polling site in full protective gear from head to foot as he uttered "Perfectly safe to vote" became an internet meme. (His theory that forcing voters to appear in person would suppress turnout, to his party's benefit, proved incorrect.)

Vos has been very much the Mitch McConnell of Wisconsin, promoting his narrow agenda, reflexively opposing anything that comes out of the Democratic executive branch and disdaining compromise. When confronted about the gerrymandered Republican majorities that the state legislature maintained in 2018 (after 54 percent of the state's voters cast their legislative ballots for Democratic candidates, 64 percent of the seats went to Republicans), Vos explained that it was absolutely justified. "If you took Madison and Milwaukee [the state's two largest population centers] out of the state election formula, we would have a clear majority." In other words, the votes of the "educated elite" in Madison, home to the University of Wisconsin, and the people of color in Milwaukee were, to his mind, worth less than largely rural, heavily white votes. Scott Walker expressed this same dubious logic in a July 5, 2019, podcast, saying it's a "flawed argument" that "a vote in Madison counts the same as a vote in a very rural community or in a suburban community." When Walker was upset in the 2018 election, it was Vos who championed an "emergency" lame-duck legislative session in which the gerrymandered Republican legislature felt compelled to curtail as much of the newly elected governor's power as it could engineer. The bill was expeditiously signed into law as Walker's last act as governor.

Vos had been a major booster of Foxconn from the start, to no little extent because the factory ended up in his district. (Among other things, he championed $542 million in new state road spending there.) Vos spoke about his vision for Foxconn on August 26, 2019, by which time most of the original objectives of the deal were in disarray. Vos, a master of the superior, smug grin, looked into a camera and compared unproven Foxconn with the S. C. Johnson Company, a backbone of Racine's economy and civic development since 1886: "For anyone who thinks about Racine probably the best known employer are the Johnson family of companies. Johnson Insurance, Johnson Wax, Johnson Diversity, Johnson Bank. If you add up all of their employees together in our community it's about 4,500 people. So you think of the amazing impact Foxconn is going to have even if they would only have 5,000 people (we know it's going to be more)." He continued to explain how all of Foxconn's well-paid workers would have an impact on real estate and other commercial interests in the Racine area.

It takes faith (and nerve) to project that Taiwan-based, China-built Foxconn, with its jaded corporate history and its faraway officers and major stakeholders, would soon emerge as the kind of corporate citizen that S. C. Johnson has been, pouring untold millions of economic impact into the Racine economy for over 130 years. When I spoke with Charles Postel at San Francisco State University about the Tea Party, he was surprised I hadn't known of Foxconn before its Wisconsin project. "Really?" he asked. "Foxconn is a word we use around here as synonymous with the most brutal and repressive working conditions imaginable."

FOXCONN'S "FAMILY-SUPPORTING" JOBS

One of the puzzling aspects of the Foxconn project was the number and function of all the promised jobs. In its original RFP, Foxconn ("Flying Eagle") had proposed 2,000 jobs, certainly plenty to get the full attention of state economic development agencies. But over time that number morphed to 6,000, then 8,000, and finally 13,000. When Foxconn executives briefed E&Y for the economic impact study in the summer of 2017, they described three-fourths of the 13,000 workers as hourly blue-collar jobs.

At the time, the best operating model for a Gen 10.5 flat-panel factory was the 10.0 Sharp facility in Sakai, Japan. When it opened in 2009, it operated with 1,000 workers, and another 1,000 workers were employed in colocated factories. But most employees were engineers and technicians working at computer screens. Yet the Wisconsin boosters championed the return of blue-collar labor, constantly spoke of "13,000 family-supporting" jobs, and seemed to be imagining the lost automobile factories, with their thousands of assembly-line workers bolting on panels and seats and fitting windshields. It was a discontinuity that was never directly addressed.

The only possible alternative for most of the 13,000 promised jobs was assembly work—the core of Foxconn's historical business. But paying assembly workers in the US anywhere close to $54,000 a year would be completely impractical, even with the 17 percent

Wisconsin taxpayer subsidy. In 2020 Foxconn assemblers across the Mexican border in Ciudad Juárez were doing this sort of labor for less than $2,000 a year, undercutting even Chinese workers.

But then, early in 2019, Foxconn officials dribbled out information that indicated a turn in plans. Yes, they said, a year and a half earlier Foxconn had promoted the notion that three-fourths of the 13,000 workers would be hourly wageworkers. But the world had changed, and the vision had evolved to three-fourths engineers and "knowledge workers," a number later revised to 90 percent of workers at the site.

On January 30, 2019, Louis Woo, special assistant to Terry Gou, made a stunning pronouncement that even a lesser factory wasn't practical. "In terms of TV, we have no place in the US," he said. "We can't compete." Woo went on to explain that, "rather than a focus on LCD manufacturing, Foxconn wants to create a 'technology hub' in Wisconsin that would largely consist of research facilities along with packaging and assembly operations." Perhaps because he had been overly honest and blunt, by the end of September 2019, Woo was no longer employed by Foxconn.

As 2019 unfolded, taxpayer-funded infrastructure work based on Foxconn's original conception of a Gen 10.5 plant was well under way, but the massive construction project itself was hardly moving. Foxconn had provided E&Y with plans that called for 10,000-plus construction workers on site for years, building out more than 20 million square feet of production space. After putting up a spartan 120,000-square-foot warehouse, Foxconn began work on another space of a little less than 1 million square feet. That's a big building—about nine times larger than a Costco store, but still just 5 percent of the promised facility.

At best a few hundred construction workers had been on the job during that time, most being paid by the state and local government. To maximize the state's subsidies, Foxconn's payroll had to hit 2,080 by the end of 2019; 5,200 by the end of 2020. As 2019 wound down Foxconn was scrambling to round up enough employees, including temp workers and interns, just to hit the minimum number, 520, which could trigger the bottom-tier state payments of $4.8 million in salary rebates plus 10 percent of all capital expenses Foxconn could drum up, with a ceiling of $191 million. It was the capital expense rebates that would be more lucrative for Foxconn. As of early 2020, Foxconn had claimed $522 million in capital investments for its 1.1 million square feet in two warehouse structures and five guardhouses and a smoking shack. (This claim belies the industry average for such construction, which for Chicago would be well less than half of this cost per square foot.) This would mean $52 million of state payments, which despite their characterization as tax rebates, would be transferred as cash, since there were no applicable business taxes to rebate. While Wisconsin wasn't getting the factory or the burgeoning manufacturing complex it had been promised, it was still going to be getting the bills.

In short, even if Foxconn built the $10 billion flat-screen factory, it would do very little for the people who needed the jobs most. That facility might indeed be part of a revival of US manufacturing, but it was never a panacea for the loss of traditional manufacturing jobs. Neither would the full-blown megafactory ever pay back the people of Wisconsin. In August 2019, Upjohn Institute's Timothy Bartik, a leading analyst of economic development projects, published a cost analysis of the deal. Bartik estimated the cost per job at somewhere between $172,000 and $290,000, with the cost ramping up as the project's scope diminished. He pegged the range as six to ten times the norm and concluded they were out of scale "whether compared to typical incentives in the US, Wisconsin past practices, or recent incentive offers to Amazon by New York and Virginia." As the University of Georgia economics professor Jeffrey Dorfman has written, "Realistically, the payback period for a $100,000 per job deal is not 20 years, not 42 years, but somewhere between hundreds of years and never."

Wondering whether all the booster hype has been cynical, delusional, or smart politics was a legitimate exercise. In retrospect, it does appear cynical, delusional, and political—but not particularly smart.

CHAPTER 13

The Problem
with Picking Winners

Large development projects are often proposed, debated, and planned, only to be abandoned. In rare cases they even get to the stage of groundbreaking, but the civic leaders involved often later look upon such cases as regrettable embarrassments.

But when I spoke with the Harvard Business School professor Willy Shih, an East Asia expert with extensive business experience in China, he seemed to light up with my question about the Foxconn groundbreaking ceremony: "In China, this happens all the time! They even have a name for it. I'd translate it as 'state visit project.' They announce a large project, everyone basks in the glory of the event and it remains to the economics to determine if anything gets built."

This sheds quite a different light on Foxconn's June 28, 2018, groundbreaking ceremony in Mount Pleasant, where the shovel of honor belonged to President Trump. Additional tools were in the hands of Scott Walker, Terry Gou, and Paul Ryan. All four were happy to bask in the glory, but only one would have had the Chinese vocabulary to name the publicity stunt or a full understanding of what was likely to emerge on the site.

That the original request for proposal had been relatively modest, that Foxconn had consistently presented two alternative factories, that the job numbers seemed fluid since the announcement—none of these factors seemed to take up any significant space in the minds of Wisconsin's promoters and facilitators. Perhaps they were all too dazzled by Foxconn's sales job.

Trying to understand Foxconn's motivation and intent is a frustrating exercise due to the company's opaqueness and its seemingly shifting objectives. It appears that company officials were initially motivated by concerns over tariffs and the opportunity to create a personal relationship with President Trump—a tactic that had aided their success in China. In early 2017, the economies of the LCD flat-panel industry looked considerably more attractive than they would a year or two later, and perhaps Foxconn did see a honest business opportunity to capture the majority share of a new niche of higher-resolution displays with production in both China and the United States. But the best explanation I heard came from Harvard's Shih. He described how US business leaders are like the vacationer who plots every minute of his or her trip; Chinese business leaders are the vacationers who jump into their car and just head out, open to whatever interesting prospects should emerge. Foxconn's team may have been looking past the specifics of LCD flat-panel production, happy to have the billions of incentives in play along with free land and access to almost unlimited fresh water. This variance in business strategy might have been just one example of Wisconsin's negotiating team having sparse understanding of cultural differences. That team had been led by Scott Walker, who had virtually no private business experience, let alone international or Asian know-how. Behind him had been two key administrators, Mark Hogan of WEDC, whose background was in domestic banking, and Scott Neitzel from the state's Department of Administration, who had spent most of his career in utilities and utility regulation. None of the team had any experience with large

Asian or Chinese corporations or with Chinese business culture in general. Nor did they bring in anyone with such experience during the negotiations.

You don't have to go to Harvard to appreciate this suggestion from the Harvard Law School's Program in Negotiations: "Enlist an advisor from your counterpart's culture." On the other side of the table from the Wisconsin team were seasoned Foxconn executives with extensive international experience and ten years of continual contact with their main US business partner, Apple. Many of the key figures had been educated in the US, and all spoke English.

Walker and his team likely never took the time to even consider cultural issues, such as the fact that contracts in China aren't viewed as holding the binding effect assumed in the US. For instance, in China, when the economic situation underlying a contract changes, terms of the contract are expected to be renegotiated. Deb Weidenhamer, an American businesswoman with extensive experience in Asia, agrees that contracts are just the starting point for negotiations and adds that, for the typical Chinese businessman, "a win-win deal is considered impossible." The Chinese believe "that there can only be one winner and one loser—and that foreigners aren't as clever or as capable. They're perceived as easy targets."

This cultural gap might have worked in both directions. Gou had little experience working with fickle American politics. The fact that Walker and Ryan were there for the groundbreaking in June 2018 and out of politics by January 2019 may have unsettled Gou and his executives, and it was likely a factor in the downsizing of Foxconn's capital commitment. At the same time, Gou clearly prized his relationship with President Trump. His company was directly affected by Trump's tariffs, and the US project was leverage for exemptions on key items like smartphones and for possible domestic assembly to skirt imposed tariffs. Foxconn's increased waffling on its US investment beginning in 2019 may have coincided with a wait-and-see period regarding Trump's reelection.

Industry experts in Asian manufacturing and flat-panel fabrication were skeptical from the first about the viability of the LCD panel manufacturing business in the US. Among the problems they foresaw was lack of the prerequisite supply chain and increased construction costs and prevailing labor wages. They also were quick to warn that Foxconn had a history of overpromising and underdelivering—but the Wisconsin negotiating team didn't bother consulting with anyone who might have had that perspective. Mark Hogan later explained that the team didn't think due diligence on Foxconn's history was necessary. They counted instead on their personal judgment of the character of their Foxconn counterparts—another case of preferring faith over fact.

Neither did Walker and friends seem to have a grasp of the potential pitfalls in the auctioning involved in landing megaprojects. This is particularly problematic when the auctioneer is also the seller, as was the case in the Foxconn competition. Even though the states involved are desperate to know the details of their competition's offers, it is clearly in the participant's interests to protect such information. Instead, it is the seller—Foxconn and E&Y in this case—who have to be relied on to relay such information. Not only are the auction bids a prime example of information asymmetry, so is the critical information about the project. To what extent was Foxconn every serious about building a Gen 10.5 fabrication plant? Was the company's vision really for a Gen 6.0 facility, or less? We'll probably never know, but the bidders in this auction couldn't have known either.

It was at the auction stage that Wisconsin could have benefited from some additional negotiating support, from someone studied in the psychology of auctions. Someone who could have explained how often auctions are awarded to the bidder who most seriously miscalculates the value of the auction's object, leading to a well-validated phenomenon known as the winner's curse. As the Stanford professor Paul Milgrom has written: "Even an estimator working in familiar terrain can lose money if he doesn't understand the subtleties of competitive bidding." Imagine what can happen to novices bidding on what amounts to promises for a manufacturing facility in an industry in which they have at best cursory knowledge.

If Wisconsin's professional staff had been self-educated, well briefed, or supported by experts in Asian business culture, the psychology of auctions, and the competitive realities of flat-panel LCD manufacturing, they would have been prepared when Foxconn began moving the cheese. They weren't.

Underlying the Foxconn project and other high-cost development deals are the problems associated with picking the correct industry and company that will provide long-term benefits to the local and regional community and economy. Instead of hedging their bets like a venture capitalist, state and municipal leaders tend to load up on big economic development bets. Cities pour enormous resources into, for instance, a massive convention center or sports stadium, with the belief it will be not only an economic boon but also a spark to revitalize an urban center gutted by first deindustrialization and then the exodus of white-collar jobs to the suburbs and flourishing "edge cities." When this doesn't quite work, they throw more money at convention hotels that can't be built with private money because private money is too smart to throw good money after bad. A familiar scenario has the local sports franchise owner or owners, typically among the wealthiest denizens of the city, deciding that without a new stadium it will be time to move. While powered by the fear of political backlash, stadium spending is typically justified on economic grounds. A stadium is sold as an essential ingredient in urban revitalization. Even if the city is financially stressed, even if its schools and road and social services are underfunded, somehow it finds the money to back the stadium. Milwaukee looked past its deep social problems and began taxing its citizens in 1996 to support its new baseball park for the Brewers. Through 2020 the region collected $650 million in stadium subsidies through regressive area sales taxes. The entire metro area chipped in, including the most distressed areas of Racine.

Milwaukee's NBA franchise, the Bucks, is valued at more than
$1.5 billion, but it gladly accepted the $250 million in state funds for
a new arena via a bill Scott Walker signed in 2015. Not coincidentally, in 2015 Walker contributed to a wave of distress and faculty
exoduses at the highly acclaimed University of Wisconsin–Madison
when he lopped $250 million off its budget. This was not a singu-
lar move. Republican governors and legislatures made similar cuts
to higher education in North Carolina, Louisiana, Mississippi, and
Iowa. The beneficiary of the state grant, the Bucks, were owned by
a group of hedge-fund managers including Jamie Dinan, whose net
worth is estimated at $2 billion.

While much of the corporate welfare devoted to projects like
Wisconsin's Foxconn is portrayed as investment or "pay as you
go," in reality the projects are massive gambles. Should Foxconn
have met its development goals, Wisconsin taxpayers would have
shipped the Asian corporation hundreds of millions a year in upfront cash incentives on the hope that the state would get its money
back over the course of the next decades through income tax on
Foxconn's thousands of new employees. The fact that the math behind the employment and tax assumptions didn't really work did
not upset the boosters at least partly because it was not just about
Foxconn. It was about Wisconn Valley. It was the dawn of a new age.
It was also a sad cliché. Alec Ross racked up the air miles in his job
as senior advisor for innovation to Secretary of State Hillary Clin-
ton: "If there's a single sentence I've heard in every country I've
been to, it's this one. 'We want to create our own Silicon Valley.'"

Netscape founder and venture capitalist Marc Andreesen has
seen it over and over. City or state officials build a big, beautiful
industrial park with all the infrastructure you could dream of. They
throw in some university connections for research and development
and maybe find an anchor company, the way malls land a major
retailer: "Except this approach to innovation clusters hasn't really
worked. Some have even dismissed these government-driven efforts as 'modern-day snake oil.' Yet policymakers are always search-
ing for the next Silicon Valley because of the critical link between

tech innovation, economic growth, and social opportunity. Previous efforts at such clusters failed for a variety of reasons, but one big reason is that government efforts alone simply don't draw people."

Carnegie Mellon University at Silicon Valley engineering professor Vivek Wadhwa echoes this conclusion: "The formula for creating these clusters is always the same. . . . Most of the top-down cluster-development projects in the United States and around the world have died a slow death in relative obscurity. Politicians who held the press conferences to claim credit for advancing science and technology are long gone. Management consultants have cashed in their big checks. Real estate barons have reaped fortunes, and taxpayers are left holding the bag."

The economists Timothy Bresnahan (Stanford), Alfonso Gambardella (Bocconi University, Milan), and AnnaLee Saxenian (University of California, Berkeley) spent two years studying the origin of technology clusters. "Case studies clearly show the foolishness of directive public-policy efforts to jump-start clusters or to make top-down or directive efforts to organize them. . . . Direct, top-down policies are most likely to fail. Particularly worrisome are policies that would direct at a level of detail such as picking the specific industries or technologies to be sponsored."

In the end, Wisconsin politicians fit the mold of capitulation to corporate demands in the belief that these accommodations were necessary to winning the deal that would transform their states. That meant free land, subsidized electrical infrastructure, access to virtually unlimited Lake Michigan water, and the cutting of all that dastardly red tape, like those time-consuming environmental impact studies so beloved by the tree huggers. The expectations of political gain and the dreams of a commercial boom encourage not only making oversized bets on a particular industry or company but also accepting risks that go far beyond the financial. They power decisions that will have an impact on the very air we breathe and the water we drink.

CHAPTER 14

An Ill Wind Blows

Apple Holler is an 80-acre pick-your-own orchard just off of Interstate 94 in Sturtevant, Wisconsin, a mostly rural municipality that abuts Mount Pleasant. Although it is just a short drive from Racine and Kenosha, most of the fall visitors are day-trippers from the Chicago area. When I visited in the fall of 2017, school buses lined the gravel driveway as long lines of six- and seven-year-olds queued up, clutching plastic bags laden with fresh apples. Mildly scary Halloween scarecrows were propped up on benches in an abandoned old red pickup. White picket fences and rows of pumpkins helped enforce the image of an idealized farm. Paying customers could visit a petting zoo. Next to the entrance of the main building, a reconditioned red barn housing a restaurant and bakery, was a sign that read: "Feel free to breathe deeply. The trees in this orchard are absorbing carbon dioxide laden air and sending out fresh oxygenated air."

From the parking lot I could look directly across the highway to the far west edge of Apple Holler's recently announced new neighbor—"Area 1" of the Foxconn development.

I spoke with an Apple Holler worker from her station behind the counter selling tickets and apple-gathering bags. Gail Knapp had been working at Apple Holler for nine years and lived in the Racine area. Her take on the Foxconn development was one I heard over and over: "We all hate it, the neighbors around here especially. All the local two-lane roads are going to be expanded to four lanes. Taxes are going to go up and there'll be no benefits for us for at least twenty years. And in twenty years the technology could be so different. In twenty years they could be gone."

"This is going to be miserable for Apple Holler," Knapp said. "It's going to do nothing for people like me."

Apple Holler's owner, Dave Flannery, had been running the operation for thirty years, and it was clearly a labor of love. He approached me with one hand for a shake, the other with a glass of freshly squeezed, frothy cider. Like most farmers in Wisconsin, he was old enough to be a grandfather and had the weathered look of having spent a lot of his days outdoors. One of the first things he said to me was that the Foxconn project had been like "watching a locomotive coming down the tracks." I could sense the tension between Flannery's political allegiances and the possible damage that his elected officials wrought. "I'm pro-business," he said. "In the long term this should be good for Wisconsin and Northern Illinois. Of course there will be growing pains with the construction and such. But more people, more jobs, that has to be good for us."

When I asked Flannery if he thought people will still drive in from Chicago for the rustic experience of visiting a farm when that farm is in the shadow of a giant industrial complex, he looked stricken, as if it were the first time he'd been forced to picture such a future.

"That's a good question," he said. "A very good question."

I took a drink of the still-foamy cider. Flannery asked if I liked it, if it wasn't too bitter. It was as sweet as a soft drink, as smooth as a milkshake. I assured him it was delicious, and he broke into a proud smile.

"I've got a neighbor," he said, pointing in the direction of the Foxconn project. "He's going to be forced to sell his land. He's third generation. That's the downside. For him it's so much more than the dollars. For me as well. I'd have no interest in selling this place. I enjoy what I'm doing. I love going out for hikes in my orchard with my dog, in the spring with the blossoms, checking the apples in the summer."

I asked if he was worried about the environmental impact of having an industrial plant so close. "I'm sure the state agencies have done their due diligence," he said.

In 2019 the Environmental Integrity Project, a nonprofit and nonpartisan environmental organization, conducted a ten-year review of every state's pollution control budget. Wisconsin led the nation in cuts, with a 36 percent drop between 2008 and 2018. The steepest declines were in 2017 and 2018, just as Foxconn was breaking ground. This was in line with conservative Republican policy to "cut red tape" and was part of Scott Walker's "open for business" agenda instituted upon his election to his first four-year term in 2010. To compound the effect, under Donald Trump, federal Environmental Protection Agency (EPA) budgets and staffs were also being slashed, with responsibility supposedly being shifted to the states. (Conversely, the Walker administration had eliminated the standard requirement for an environmental impact report for Foxconn, on the justification that the federal government would be keeping an eye on things.) Some states did work on picking up the slack—California, for instance, increased its budget by 74 percent over the same period Wisconsin was cutting its own.

The EPA, under industry-boosting Scott Pruitt, was also ready to step in to the Foxconn project to help cut more "red tape." In this case the subject was air pollution. The EPA issued an exemption to help Foxconn get up and running without the burden of spending millions on smokestack pollution controls. This despite the fact that the area was already suffering from air-quality problems. That Pruitt was overruling the agency's own scientists was hardly an anomaly for the Trump administration. An EPA scientist wrote to colleagues that she could see no "sound technical basis" for the ruling and was at a loss on how to write the justification. "I am still in disbelief," she added. In May 2019, under pressure from environmental groups and action from affected cities the EPA backed off, asking for more time to clarify its ruling. By the end of the year, the EPA had resolved the problem by redefining the air quality in the area as acceptable and therefore confirming that expensive pollution controls for Foxconn were unnecessary.

One of the most controversial aspects of Wisconsin's agreement with Foxconn was arrangement for massive amounts of Lake Michigan water to come via Racine's water authority to the Foxconn complex. The management of Great Lakes water, the largest reservoir of quality fresh water in the world, whose value is steadily increasing as the world degrades its rivers and lakes, is under the authority of the multistate and Canadian provincial Great Lakes Compact. One of the tenets of the compact is to restrict movement of water out of the watershed. The Foxconn property is only partially in that watershed—it straddles the divide between it and the Mississippi River catchment area—so its use of water should be especially regulated, no matter what its use might be.

The Great Lakes Compact has issued withdrawal rates for the communities around the lakes. Racine's allocation had been underutilized over previous decades as its largest industrial customers shrank or left, giving it room to shoot millions of gallons of water a day to Foxconn. Rather cavalierly, Racine requested that the Department of Natural Resources expand its service area to include the Foxconn site, and the DNR rubber-stamped it, noting that Foxconn would be treating the water and returning about half it back to the Lake Michigan watershed. Environmentalists worried that Wisconsin's rash actions would in effect shatter the compact, opening up lake water to aggressive and unregulated expansion.

Even after Foxconn began to waffle on its megafactory, the municipalities continued to construct a multimillion-dollar forty-two-inch water main that could deliver far more water than even Foxconn had ever projected. Because if Foxconn couldn't use it, local thinking must have went, surely Mount Pleasant and Racine County could land other tenants looking for free or cheap land and top-quality fresh water.

Later that day after speaking with Flannery, a half peck of Apple Holler apples in my trunk, I took a call from Ron Doetch, the founder of Solutions in the Land, an agricultural environmental impact consultancy based in Prospect Grove, Illinois. He knew the Racine area well, having worked for years in Wisconsin as head of the nonprofit Michael Fields Agricultural Institute, an organization dedicated to sustainable farming practices. I mentioned my visit to the orchard and the possible impact on Dave Flannery's operation, which included its own on-site irrigation wells.

"It isn't an issue of whether the Foxconn operation will affect Apple Holler; it's a question of when," said Doetch, basing his assessment on what Foxconn was then promising: a significant industrial development. "Once they begin production, they will be releasing heavy metals into the watershed." While Doetch's grim predictions would later be mitigated by Foxconn's steadily diminishing business plans, they remain relevant for two reasons. They first reveal what state and municipal officials were willing to sacrifice in the name of job creation and the associated political gain. Second, the environmental threat remains as long as the expansive area is zoned for industrial development under the umbrella of aggressive environmental waivers.

Early estimates placed Foxconn's water usage at approximately equal to the entire city of Racine's daily pull from Lake Michigan—around 17 million gallons a day. "What a lot of people don't understand is why this project needs so much water," Doetch continued. "It's not so much to wash the glass, but to dilute the heavy metal pollutants down to the currently acceptable parts per million level." This does nothing to mitigate the pollutants' effects. This pollution "solution" requires two components: access to virtually unlimited amounts of quality water and an industrial user cynical enough to employ it to dilute dangerous contaminants.

The heavy metals expert Peter Adriaens from the University of Michigan listed the heavy metals involved in LCD production: copper, mercury, cadmium, and chromium. "Leakage during the manufacturing process is a fairly common occurrence," he told an interviewer in 2017. He indicated that removing them from large amounts of water was particularly challenging. "Once into the environment heavy metals are bioaccumulative—you can't get rid of them." He also characterized the relaxation of environmental regulations for Foxconn as "extreme," giving them far more leeway than is standard for US industrial companies. In 2013 the *Wall Street Journal* reported that Chinese regulators were looking into allegations that Foxconn had been guilty of dumping large amounts of heavy metal pollutants into Chinese waterways. Adriaens has also noted the heavy pollution in rivers adjacent to Foxconn factories in China. While circumstances make it difficult to pinpoint pollution sources, "the correlation is very strong."

"Apple Holler will begin to pump heavy metal onto their land within months of the plant's operation," Doetch continued, sketching a future Wisconsin's Foxconn boosters had readily accepted. "The first thing they will see is plant health issues. The heavy metals discharged by the plant will leach into the groundwater, Apple Holler will pump the water onto their land, and the farm's soil will filter them out. The second stage will be a loss of production as the trees suffer. The third stage will be health issues associated with consuming the apples themselves."

What would become of Apple Holler if Foxconn built a major LCD fabrication facility? Doetch thought it would be a fate similar to other bordering lands: "He'll have to sell the land for low-income housing. It will be the only suitable use for it. The way this works is that Foxconn will attract minimum wage workers, probably a lot of them undocumented, and these workers will eventually pull their families along." These families are not going to be able to afford suburban housing—and demand will bring in the kind of housing they need.

Instead of a booming population of middle-class manufacturing workers, Doetch foresaw a horde of underpaid Foxconn assemblers who would be subsidized by the state by qualifying for government housing and food programs—an additional form of corporate welfare for Foxconn.

"The saddest part of this for me is the inability for state leadership to see the future of Wisconsin agriculture," continued Doetch.

"Wisconsin is widely, and correctly, seen as a source of untainted soil and water. While California is currently the leader in producing organic produce, no one really thinks that the Central Valley and its water sources are unadulterated. Wisconsin is poised to become the national leader in organic production, a hugely profitable and sustainable business, and yet they pick Foxconn as the future of the state. Within a short period of time the Foxconn plant will make at least 5,000 acres of Wisconsin farmland unusable, to say nothing of the damage to the state's reputation. And these aren't just acres of cash crops. This is a part of the state that produces a high volume of high quality produce—broccoli, cauliflower, lettuce—that goes directly and efficiently to Milwaukee and Chicago."

What was Doetch's prediction for Racine County in a decade or so? "People will be asking, 'How did we let this happen?'"

The willingness of the Foxconn promoters and local politicians to sacrifice local farmers and landowners seemed remorseless— likewise their seeming lack of concern over environmental issues that could have dire effects on the entire community. Even as Foxconn's diminishing plans reduced the immediate concerns over environmental impact, the potential for environmental disaster remained because of the way the large industrial site had been zoned.

While one scenario posits that Foxconn might eventually walk away from Wisconsin rather than pay its contracted obligations, other possible legacies exists. Foxconn may remain in the area with a footprint and investment at a fractional level of the one promised. But it will still be liable for paying property taxes on a much larger investment as detailed in its contract with Mount Pleasant and Racine County. Foxconn could mitigate this liability by taking advantage of its prime location of 1,000 deeded acres, replete with fine roads, pristine Lake Michigan water, and more than $100 million in electrical infrastructure by inviting other corporations, likely Asian associates, to its campus. In doing so, they could cut through what Scott Walker denigrated as "excess red tape," such as smokestack emission controls and environmental impact studies that would most likely be required in other areas of the US. Documents that Foxconn filed with the Wisconsin DNR indicated that original plans for the factory would make it one of the largest air polluters in the region, spewing into the air the exact components of smog. The civic leaders of Mount Pleasant and Racine County have retained a vision of a bustling high-tech industrial center in their new 3,900-acre park, neatly cleared of homesteads and ready for development. They may not be ready for what Foxconn brings in the future.

In China, industrial parks and areas are among the worst polluters in the world, with air and water quality in various parts of China at disastrous levels. As summarized by the nonprofit Borgen Project: "Water shortages and water pollution in China are such a problem that the World Bank warns of 'catastrophic consequences for future generations.' Half of China's population lacks safe drinking water." By granting waivers to Foxconn, a company that operates largely in China, Wisconsin officials may have opened the door for Foxconn and its suppliers to own the most inviting locale for polluting industries that would benefit from a North American location. It's possible the landscape in Mount Pleasant will gradually change from farmland to belching factories. This is a vision that only the tight circle of businessmen, contractors, and wealthy professionals who benefit directly from the hundreds of millions of dollars in municipal capital could love.

Down the Road

Charles Heide's grandfather came to southeastern Wisconsin for the same reason that thousands of others did in the 1920s—auto manufacturing. He worked his way up from the assembly line to become supervisor of production at the Nash Motors plant in Kenosha. This success gave him the wherewithal to purchase a small tract of land in the country between Racine and Kenosha; there he built a house and operated what his grandson describes as a "gentleman's farm." Today Heide is well into his second career as steward of the family land. To that end, he's been working on preserving native prairie remnants and establishing a sustainable agricultural model that breaks away from the industrialized conventions of the Midwest.

As the area grew and as the cities sprawled, Charles's mother began to encourage her husband to purchase the surrounding land, in order to control development around the family plot. Eventually the family's holdings grew to include some 380 acres, much along the Pike River—with headwaters in the Foxconn tract flowing to its mouth in Lake Michigan on the north side of Kenosha.

Heide drove the fifteen minutes from his place to the Mount Pleasant village hall for the same public meeting I attended on October 11, 2017. He left deflated. He had hoped to discover Foxconn's production projections, water use, and treatment and development time frame. Instead, he was greeted by the Mueller public relations displays: graphics illustrating the map of the Foxconn acquisition and the broad-stroke explanations of its financing.

"I come from a manufacturing background and am pro-business," added Heide, a reliable Republican donor. "Everyone wants to see good jobs and development, which promotes community stability. We are at a critical stage where we still have the leverage to demand that Foxconn takes absolute responsibility for not polluting our waterways or aquifers, either by intent or neglect. It's well known that LCD manufacturing produces highly dangerous heavy metal by-products, yet I have yet to see the subject even addressed. I'm directly downstream and want assurances that our groundwater and the hundreds of private wells in this area will not be compromised by construction runoff, heavy metal pollution, or other by-products of whatever Foxconn produces."

As part of the Foxconn legislation passed in the fall of 2017, the state gave up its wetlands jurisdiction over the 3,900-acre site. Walker's team promised that they were doing so to avoid redundancy, since the Army Corps of Engineers also oversaw the wetlands. A few months after the legislation had been passed and signed into law, the Army Corps of Engineers issued a statement saying that it had no authority over the project and would not be doing any wetlands impact assessments.

"I just think the whole process has been short-circuited by its massive scale and millions of dollars at stake," said Heide. "If we had directed Foxconn or other industry development onto the land abandoned by the auto or other industries, then I'd be celebrating the deal. Instead it appears that we're giving Foxconn cheap farmland and free water and I'm guessing they couldn't be more delighted."

These environmental policies have been driven not by science but by faith. Scott Walker has said that the faith of his Evangelical Christianity is reflected in all of his decisions. Notably, it is a standard Evangelical tenet that the earth was a gift from God for the use of mankind and that divine oversight precludes humans from doing it any permanent harm. When Walker was campaigning for his first term, he accused the retiring Democratic governor Jim Doyle of losing business development because of his reliance on "discredited scientists" who promoted the idea of global warming. Walker's views on science were further revealed during a 2015 trip to London when he was asked about his belief in evolution. "I'm going to have to punt on that one," was Walker's reply. Walker's faith-based positions on environmental and other science topics proved convenient to him as someone convinced that business expansion was the key to political advancement. Faith, as it turned out, was also a key component behind Mount Pleasant's enthusiasm for the project.

Late in 2018, the Mount Pleasant village president Dave DeGroot was interviewed by Sruthi Pinnamaneni for the popular podcast *Reply All*. After DeGroot ran through his reasons for supporting the Foxconn deal, Pinnamaneni raised the concept of "faith-based development deals," in which the promoters worry less about the numbers than about the general benefits that they believe will multiply in ways that cannot be calculated.

DeGroot hesitated and then agreed with the concept: "I've never seen how pessimism has created one job for anybody anywhere. And, and to a certain extent, yes, it does come down to belief. And that's . . . how you move a village—not only a village, but your greater community—forward. Nothing happens without first believing it can happen."

CHAPTER 15

All Politics Are Local

In the spring of 2017 a new, barebones website launched with an innocuous name: Let's Make a Better Mount Pleasant. The site's creator selected as a background an odd stock photo, one of a bustling street scene from Chicago. The first post was dated May 11, a month after Tea Party–affiliated and Tea Party–sympathetic trustees had taken over governance of Mount Pleasant from more independent, centrist officials. That first post stated the site's purpose was "to provide information to the citizens of the Village of Mount Pleasant that are tired of the constant problems being created by a small group of activists with special interests."

But soon the site's mission and focus narrowed to the "activists" themselves. It seemed to concern itself almost solely with the former majority faction of the village board, and particularly with a resident who maintained a Facebook page called A Better Mt. Pleasant, clearly the inspiration of the new website's name.

That Facebook page posted regular news on Mount Pleasant and happenings at the village board. Its stated purpose was "advancing a fair, accountable and honest Mt. Pleasant local government." It had some 1,700 followers and a couple thousand discrete viewers each month—a significant number in a village where elections are often decided by hundreds of votes. A good sense of the page's tenor comes from a posting from November 2019 in response to an editorial in the *Racine Journal Times* that recommended a referendum on a proposal to spend $23 million on a new swimming pool in Racine. "Are you kidding? Where was the [*Journal Times*'s] editorial board (Mark Lewis, Steve Lovejoy, and Stephanie Jones) when Racine County was meeting in closed door sessions to create a scheme to borrow nearly a billion dollars, move out residents, blight and purchase 3,000 square acres of land to convey to a private foreign corporation—for a deal that was originally brokered on the back of a napkin? Oh, we forgot. Mark Lewis was in the back room too. Funny how they never mentioned the need for a referendum to decide that."

Over its first few months, the new website descended from a focus on the bickering over who would pay for a sewer-line expansion and an ongoing stalemate over an open trustee seat to a dedicated ad hominem attack on the Facebook page's originator, Kelly Gallaher. Gallaher is a self-described progressive Democrat, a painter and former arts educator, a graduate of Bradley University in Peoria, Illinois. The new website described her or her husband variously as a "dimwit," "looser [*sic*]," "dingbat," "potty mouth," and "communist activist."

I first met Kelly Gallaher at the October 11, 2017, village hall meeting where Foxconn was introducing itself to locals. We sat together, and I listened for twenty minutes. She admitted she didn't yet know enough about the Foxconn deal to judge its merit, and while she told me that DeGroot and his allies would assume her opposition, it was the process she was lamenting. DeGroot, who had campaigned for office on a platform of transparency, had agreed to cede 6.2 square miles of his village to a foreign corporation, including multigenerational farm operations and some seventy-five private homes, and he had done it all behind closed doors.

When I spoke with Gary Feest, one of the trustees who was the object of the website's venom, he was surprisingly placid about the entire affair. A lifetime Racine County resident, he dabbled in college before settling into his profession as a woodworker. He originally got involved in local politics when a waste collection center was slated for his neighborhood. In his interactions with the Mount Pleasant Village Board, he reached the conclusion that it had become a sort of "old boys" club controlled by a circle who had similar interests and backgrounds. "I felt like sweetheart deals were commonplace," he told me. The same contractors seemed to be landing the jobs—companies with lower bids were deemed "unqualified" for the work. Feest first joined the board in 2010 and went on to serve for ten years. One of the innovations he championed was prequalifying contractors before bids were received, taking favoritism out of the decision making. But he considers his major achievement the professionalization of the village staff, with the capstone being the hiring of a full-time village administrator. Feest believed that this would create a buffer between whatever private interests or prejudices a trustee might have and the village's actions. Feest was the only trustee to vote against blighting the 3,900 acres allocated to Foxconn, "because it wasn't blighted," he explained to me.

Over the months after its launch, the tone of the website, which showed considerably knowledge of village politics and actions, became even nastier, descending into sexual innuendo and intimidation and harassment, creepily documenting where and what Gallaher ate at restaurants and publishing her home address as the location of a fabricated public meeting. Despite her best efforts, Gallaher was not able to definitively identify the owner of the website.

But the circumstantial evidence pointed in just one direction. On May 20, 2017, one of Mount Pleasant's seven trustees and DeGroot supporter Anna Marie Clausen posted a link on her Facebook account to the new site, recommending that people check it out "to keep up-to-date on what's happening in Mount Pleasant." When asked in a Facebook comment who was responsible for the site,

Clausen responded, "I don't know specifically" but "someone in DeGroot's camp." The site continued to post invective through December 2018. While the author never came forward, revealing clues eventually led Gallaher to take formal action.

After the *Reply All* podcast on Foxconn was released, a tech-savvy listener decided to take a dive into the sharply critical website to see if he could find any footprints. He came up with something, which Gallaher publicized in her formal complaint to the village: "In hundreds of errors logged online, one username is repeated over and over again: 'fchief1951.' South Shore Fire Chief Robert Stedman maintains Yahoo, Flickr and WordPress accounts using 'fchief.' Robert Stedman was born in 1951. I believe Robert Stedman used a familiar username when creating the website thinking no one else would see it except himself." Stedman denied involvement with the website. An independent investigator hired by the village cleared Stedman of wrongdoing in November 2019 on the grounds that he had not violated any statutes in his capacity as fire chief. The website that attacked Gallaher, often crudely, personally, and maliciously, was taken down in 2020.

Where did all of the site's invective come from? In corporations, for example, it is an accepted tenet that culture starts at the top. In the case of little Mount Pleasant, the top-down rule appears to be operative in politics as well. Incessant invective from conservative talk radio and Fox News opened the door to a new level of divisive and personal attacks in the 2016 presidential election. As he worked to manipulate Americans along racial and economic fault lines, Trump's use of degrading nicknames for officials and personal slurs at his rallies and in his tweet storms were more fundamental to his campaign and his governance than were policies.

Mount Pleasant was no different from the rest of the country in its widening political polarization. Although candidates for trustees ran unaffiliated, factions were transparent. There was a sea change in 2013 when power shifted from the old, conservative Republican guard to a more independently minded slate, when the village president Jerry Garski was elected along with three allies, giving them the majority. Back then the issues paled in comparison to those that were to come with Foxconn, but the different styles of government were evident. Garski opposed an ordinance limiting public comment at supervisor meetings and a particularly onerous assessment on certain residents for sewer construction that didn't directly serve them—an assessment high enough that it might force some of them to have to sell their homes.

But that daily drumbeat from the top during the Trump era seemed to crack open underlying tensions in Mount Pleasant. Local Tea Party conservatives, back in control after the 2017 local election, seemed to adopt a more aggressive, Trumpian style. And this tenor wasn't restricted to anonymous websites. On August 28, 2017, as the Foxconn announcement was transitioning to on-the-ground action, the village board meeting drew a larger-than-usual crowd. After a less-than-rousing recitation of the Pledge of Allegiance, the three-minute public comment forum opened. Mount Pleasant resident and community activist Al Gardner took his turn at the microphone in front of the trustees and said: "You know, my whole thing about this whole Foxconn issue is, who is going to benefit? I know in the past that when these jobs come here that people that look like me don't have the opportunity to build on the project and get jobs. I looked at this article today and it says that if we get Foxconn, our taxes are going to go up—property owners. Now, I already paid thousands of dollars in property taxes. If they come here, are my taxes going to go up?"

Meeting protocol and ordinances restrict trustees from interacting or speaking during the public comment section of village meetings. This can seem strained to an outsider, such as when the public asks direct questions of the trustees, or when trustees make no response to a highly emotional presentation, as when residents pleaded with the board to save their homes after learning they were subject to condemnation.

Tensions were evident in this August meeting from the start, particularly with pointed criticism about the hiring of Claude Lois. Speakers noted that there had been no job posting, no job description, no background check. One spoke of Lois's main qualification as having political connections, given that he was a Republican insider, a six-figure state employee under Scott Walker, and a known associate of Wisconsin speaker of the assembly Robin Vos, whose father had served on the Burlington city council alongside Lois. Someone noted that Lois's compensation was considerable higher than even the governor's.

For whatever reason, DeGroot couldn't hold back. "Mr. Gardner," he said in a tone of a teacher reproaching a rude student, "I'd be careful about what you read, and I wouldn't believe everything that you read. . . . I can assure you that everyone in the village will be covered on this regardless of the race."

What followed demonstrated the wisdom of restricting interchanges between the public and trustees during these comment sessions:

GARDNER: OK, can I . . .

DEGROOT: That's enough, sir.

GARDNER: Can I respond to that?

DEGROOT: No, sir.

GARDNER: You responded to me.

DEGROOT: No, sir.

GARDNER: Let me respond back to you.

DEGROOT: Go sit down.

GARDNER: Who you talking to, man?

DEGROOT: You, sir.

GARDNER: What, now you're going to respond to your tax-paying citizens . . .

DEGROOT: Do you want to be called out of order?

GARDNER: But we can't respond back to you.

DEGROOT: No, sir.

GARDNER: That is totally wrong. That is totally wrong.

DEGROOT: Go sit down.

GARDNER: Who you talking to, man?

DEGROOT: You're out of order.

GARDNER: Who you talking to? You not my daddy, man. Who you talking to?

DEGROOT: Chief Zarzecki, um, if this man . . .

GARDNER: You should be ashamed of yourself, man. You should be
ashamed of yourself. You gonna sit up here and talk like this to me . . .

DEGROOT: Remove this person. Remove him now.

GARDNER: I'm gonna remove myself. You a coward, buddy. You a coward, that's what you are. You a damn coward, man, shit.

DEGROOT: Move along.

Kelly Gallaher had been among the most regular of public speakers at village meetings for years, keeping an eye on everything from
the deadline for filing committee minutes to fire department overtime. Perhaps one of the items of her criticism in her Facebook posts
on her A Better Mt. Pleasant page had a particular bite. She noted
that certain trustees had regular breakfast meetings—including the
village president and his close associate, the fire chief Robert Stedman—which Gallaher suggested violated open-meeting laws. It was
this kind of relentless gadflying, as much as political difference, that
kept tempers boiling, especially Dave DeGroot's. It boiled over at
that same August 28 meeting. As Gallaher approached the microphone for her three minutes, DeGroot began talking before she
could utter a word: "Miss Gallaher, before you speak ever again in
these chambers you need to have a way, way better idea of the conduct that is expected of you when you're speaking at a public meeting. By which I mean the last time you spoke here upon leaving the
table and walking away you dropped the f-bomb, not once, but twice
and it was noticed by many, many people in these chambers."

The trustee Jon Hanson, a holdover from the old anti-DeGroot
board, declared a point of order to try to stop DeGroot's rant. He
was almost shouting as he pleaded, "This is public comment, not
public reprimand."

DeGroot ignored the protest and continued: "She is not speaking until some things are taken care of. Anyway, it was seen and
witnessed by our radio station, by police officers."

Feest interrupted with his own point of order, shouting, "This is enough!"

"Miss Gallaher," DeGroot continued. "You're very fortunate I didn't hear your outburst, because I would have thrown you out on your can and either had you cited or arrested for disorderly conduct. You will not be speaking in these chambers again until I hear an oral apology. I will not hear an oral apology under I receive a written one delivered to me at least five days before this board meets so I can check the credibility of it because you have had a long history of having issues with the truth. So go sit back down and maybe we'll hear from you in the future."

The meeting then returned to its normal agenda, beginning with a presentation from the director of the village's sauerkraut festival.

At the subsequent village board meeting, DeGroot opened with a public apology for his lack of the "civility I ask of others," not to Gardner or to Gallaher personally, but to "the citizens of Mount Pleasant." Toward the end of the meeting, Feest introduced a surprise motion to censure DeGroot over his behavior at the previous meeting, a largely symbolic gesture, but one he felt was the best available chastisement. As Feest expected, DeGroot stepped in to vote against the censure, which would have deadlocked the vote, but Feest had arranged to have the village attorney on hand to inform DeGroot he was not allowed to vote on his own censure and the motion passed.

The village trustees serve two-year terms, with the village president up for election in the April of odd years. Finding candidates to oppose the incumbents has been a challenge—the village president is paid $13,263 a year, and trustees just $6,574. Dave DeGroot told the *Racine Journal Times* in 2019: "I can't tell you how many times a resident has come up to me in the past few years and said, 'You're making $12,000 [his salary then] as president of the village of Mount Pleasant? You're crazy. You should be making $100,000 easy.' That's reality. I've heard that time and time and time again. And I'm complimented by that, I appreciate that folks see value in what this board is doing and what I'm doing as president. But I've told them, 'Fat chance that that is ever going to get there.'"

Meanwhile, Claude Lois, DeGroot's working colleague at the village office, was pulling $24,000 a month out of the village's TIF fund while the village's eminent domain law firm continued to draw its more than $1 million annual stipend from the same deep pool.

CHAPTER 16

The Trouble with TIF

A friend connected me with Mick Michel, the city administrator of the small eastern Iowa town of Dyersville, to talk about tax-increment financing. As I described this book, Michel balked. "Books always trash TIF," he said. "Please don't do that. It's the only tool I've got." Consciously or not, Michel was echoing former Chicago mayor Richard M. Daley, who in 2007 declared that TIF "was the only game in town" and the city's "only tool" for economic development. At the time Chicago led the nation with 155 TIF districts. While scale and situations vary enormously from small town to large city, this does show just how attractive, even seductive, direct involvement in economic development via TIF can be to civic leaders across the board.

I grasped Michel's challenge of promoting development in this town of 4,000 people. In high school I'd visited there with a friend. We spent Saturday night cruising the main street between the church and the city's lone drive-in. On Sunday morning I joined my cruising compatriots for mass at the Catholic basilica, the most prominent building in town. A newer attraction that emerged in the years after my visit was the nearby baseball diamond in the cornfield where the movie *A Field of Dreams* had been shot. To my mind, the field wasn't much of a destination. I could see that without being able to offer cheap land and infrastructure at the town's little industrial park, where development includes a warehouse that can store up to 14,700 tons of fertilizer, Dyersville could be a tough sell.

So, yes, let it be said: TIF can offer a municipality advantages. It allows municipalities to borrow money to invest in land and infrastructure that in turn can attract corporate and industrial development. Every state other than Arizona has its own TIF or TIF-like statutes. And in a best-case scenario, the results can seem magical. In the late 1990s, a successful software company in Madison, Wisconsin, was making plans to break ground for its new corporate headquarters. Lucky for the Madison metro area, Epic Systems, which specializes in medical charting and recordkeeping software, wasn't moving far off—just twelve miles from its building on the west side of town to the western edge of Verona, a fast-growing southwestern suburb.

Epic Systems had about seven hundred employees at the time, making it one of the larger firms in the city. It had outgrown its central facility and was leasing additional space in five other buildings. The guarded, privately owned firm was founded in 1979 by Judy Faulkner, who had studied computer science at the University of Wisconsin. Faulkner had despaired at finding within Madison's borders enough space for not only her existing employees but also her vision for a much larger firm housed on an architecturally impressive campus. Perhaps these expansive plans came from her preternatural confidence, or perhaps she sensed the momentum behind the digital medical record boom that was to come.

For Verona, the construction of a 346-acre corporate campus on the edge of town was a sea change. To seal the deal, city officials had offered Epic a relocation package in the form of tax-increment financing of an amount which the press described as "lavish" and large enough to make some Verona officials nervous. The city's upfront costs, largely site improvements and infrastructure, were originally budgeted at $11 million, projected to rise to $14 million after interest payments were stretched out through the life of the TIF district, which extended through 2025. This was a subsidy of $2,000 per job, well within the norm for these kinds of deals. But the total exceeded the city's annual operating budget, making the nervousness understandable. The TIF district was destined to expand over the upcoming years, with costs to the city rising to $31.4 million.

In 2006, the optimistic Verona city administrator Larry Saeger told the area's alternative paper, *The Isthmus*, that the Epic campus could someday be valued at as much as $500 million. The company itself projected significant growth, estimating that employment would rise to 1,500 by 2008, more than doubling the entire workforce.

None of these early estimates was correct. Construction on the campus never stopped: multiple cranes hovering over new campus structures has been the standard view for travelers on nearby Highway 151 since the campus's inception in 2002. By 2017 the showplace campus properties were assessed at more than $1 billion. By 2019 the array of whimsically themed buildings (Jungle, Dungeons and Dragon, Lord of the Rings), was home to some 10,000 employees. The accelerating property taxes allowed for debt on the original TIF investment to be paid off by 2016, nine years ahead of schedule, and the TIF district was closed. The TIF authority's excess revenue on hand resulted in a onetime windfall of some $23 million to area recipients, include more than $11 million to the Verona school district. Once the TIF was closed, tax revenue on the site was allocated instead to the main recipients of Verona property tax, including the school district and community college.

The repercussions of this success story reverberated throughout the Madison metropolitan area. Apartment developments boomed as the young, well-paid workforce settled in, many preferring the more urban and urbane setting of downtown Madison, near the University of Wisconsin. Real estate brokers acknowledged the driving force of Epic in their sales and rentals. Verona itself was transformed, regularly taking the title of fastest-growing city in the state. In 2017 voters approved $182 million for school district spending, the largest school referendum in state history, including a state-of-the-art new high school. Property tax income from Epic, projected to total $140 million over the ensuing twenty years, was a major impetus for school expansions.

When it works, then, TIF appears to be a terrific tool. But that can be something of an illusion, as development that was inevitable is sourced to the TIF alone. For instance, Epic was committed to staying in the Madison area and may well have selected the same site with or without TIF incentives. In fact, the site may have been the only acceptable option. Certainly the city of Madison tried to keep Epic but the necessary land simply wasn't available. While the boosters behind the Foxconn project never mentioned Epic, it was likely on their minds. In fact, everything Foxconn did to promote the project had echoes of Epic, including the model and video of what looked to me like their "Tomorrowland" campus, with its self-driving cars, expansive lakes and fountains, and architecture that rivaled Epic's real buildings and sprawling campus, which over the years had expanded to some 1,000 acres—just about the same size as Foxconn's phase 1 footprint.

But the comparison between the two companies ends there. Epic had grown organically, without significant public funding through its first twenty-six years. In many ways, its location was largely a matter of the intellectual capital available to it at the University of Wisconsin, which had been an early national leader in computer science. The evolution from start-up to national stature spanned the entire working life of its founder. The story of Epic was just the opposite of the almost-instantaneous, top-down conception for the Foxconn industrial complex. In fact, none of the Epic Systems story, beginning with its founder's university connection through its long gradual growth, would be a salutary model to a politician like Scott Walker. His concept for business development involved cutting business and other taxes to the bone, and making commensurate slashes to education in order to balance the budget. But even pro-business tax cuts weren't enough. Walker needed fast results to support his political ambitions, certainly not the kind that came from educational spin-offs and incubation capital, which work slowly and unpredictably and would benefit only his successors decades down the road. Plus he showed an innate antipathy to deeply blue Madison, where most of the state's most successful start-ups had begun, with particular animus toward Madison-based unions as well as universities and professors in general. This aversion fit the general anti-intellectualism of the Tea Party, and was perhaps exacerbated by Walker's apparently unhappy, pregraduation dropping out from Marquette University. His distaste for government and public employees in general was ironic considering that he had spent virtually his entire working life in taxpayer-supported jobs.

For the civic leaders of Verona, their experience with TIF and Epic had the glow of gold. But TIF also comes with risk and the potential for abuse. The fundamental operating principal of TIF is to borrow today against the promise of future earnings. In this way, it's a little like buying stocks on margin—it's great when the investments work out. But taking on debt to buy stocks is not always a good idea; for example, it was a primary factor in the stock market crash of 1929 and the subsequent Great Depression. Another factor limiting the utility of TIF is supply and demand. If only one municipality in the region can offer TIF advantages, then that municipality can win more business development than it might without incentives. But when everyone offers TIF advantages, the likelihood exists that all municipalities get the same commerce they would have gotten without it, with every municipality paying more than they would have otherwise. When everyone is using TIF, then it risks becoming an auction in which the real winners are the businesses and corporations that get the breaks. The losers are the taxpayers.

The shiny object of commercial development often blinds officials to real costs and the likely course of nonintervention. This is one of the rubs of TIF: it's impossible to confidently predict the alternative to TIF development. Would the farmland along I-94 in

Mount Pleasant have been developed gradually, sitting as it does on a major corridor between Milwaukee and Chicago where other major developments, including a massive Amazon warehouse, were located? More than one local resident seemed perfectly aware that Amazon paid more per acre than what Mount Pleasant was offering through its eminent domain threat. In 2013, the land for the Amazon fulfillment center, located five miles south of the Foxconn project, sold for $110,760 per acre. Development without TIF can produce immediate property tax benefits to support schools and community coffers that finance libraries, fire and police departments, and parks. Property tax within a TIF stays within the TIF, typically for decades, to pay off debt or expenditures.

The ways that TIF can backfire or be subject to abuse are many. In Sherrard, Illinois, for example, with the Fyre Lake golf development, the introduction of a TIF district was a charade designed so the developers could wash their interest payments and future earnings through the village, creating a twenty-year stream of tax-free income.

Another interstate battle for an industrial site had taken place twenty years before the Foxconn project, also on the Illinois/ Wisconsin border. Beloit, Wisconsin, just a forty-five minute drive southwest of the Foxconn development in Mount Pleasant, was once a booming industrial center. In 1994 city officials were delighted when they heard Motorola, the leading cell phone manufacturer in the world, was thinking of building a major production factory in the vicinity.

From Beloit it's just a thirty-five minute drive southeast over the Illinois border to Harvard, Illinois, a smaller city also in the Motorola mix. With a population that hit 8,000 in 2000 the city was a dairy center, A large fiberglass Holstein remains the downtown's most prominent landmark. But perhaps the most important part of the city's recent history was an accident of birth. Native sons Paul and Joseph Galvin moved to Chicago as young men and got into the radio business near the tail end of the Roaring Twenties. They came up with a snappy name for their company: Motorola.

Co-founder Paul's grandson Christopher took over the reins of the by-now-global giant in 1993.

In the early 1990s Motorola, based in Schaumburg, Illinois, near O'Hare Airport, decided it would develop a new campus, primarily to manufacture cell phones, an industry they had basically founded. Their 1994 Lazr flip phone would become one of the iconic electronic devices of the decade, only later eclipsed by the introduction of digital "smart phones," most notably the iPhone, the first version of which was released in 2007. It wasn't made in America.

Christopher may have been determined to bring the factory back to his grandparents' hometown, but in a game that looked checkers to three-D chess when compared to Amazon's national auction twenty-five years later, he had no qualms about playing Illinois against Wisconsin, Harvard against Beloit.

Harvard won with the help of about $43 million in state and local incentives, about forty percent of Motorola's $100 million capital cost for building their sprawling, 350-acre campus. By the time the showplace facility had its ribbon-cutting in 1997 it consisted of some 1.5 million square feet of office and manufacturing space, including a 500-seat auditorium, a cafeteria that could seat over 1,000, two heliports and two daycare centers. Little Harvard chipped in with $3 million in tax abatements over ten years, an amount that so exceeded Illinois's previous cap of $1 million that state legislation was required (it passed unanimously).

As the little town braced for the influx of 5,000 workers, hopes ran high. A developer got a head start on the expected population boom by building three new subdivisions with a total of 150 homes, all on spec. The economic impact report had projected that 1,000 new homes would be needed.

Much of the promise came true. By the late 1990s, 5,000 workers were on site and workers from as far away as Beloit were commuting to jobs. But some of the promises proved overly rosy. Only a hundred, two hundred at most, of the employees opted to move to Harvard; the rest continued to commute. The hope held by downtown Harvard businesses proved ephemeral: Motorola employees out on the newly annexed edge of Harvard rarely visited. And the cell phone business along with other Motorola divisions, like many technology-based industries, was constantly in flux. Within five years of opening, Motorola dropped its manufacturing activity in Harvard, moving it to Mexico, while it ramped up production capabilities in China. Half of the employees were let go. But Motorola proved to be less than agile at managing the rapid changes in the business and in 2003 closed down its Harvard operation entirely, selling the now empty campus at a fraction of its cost.

The facility went through a series of owners, each buying for a lesser amount, with a common liability being a reluctance to pay property tax on time, even as the assessed value of the development dwindled. The latest owner of the complex is a Canadian businessman, Xiao Hua Gong, who was indicted for securities fraud in 2018. Courts put a hold on the proposed forced sale of the deteriorating Harvard campus. City leaders continue to hold out hope for a new owner that will revitalize the site. They even made a bid to offer the facility to Amazon in its search for a new headquarters. In the end the Motorola campus has been a detriment to taxpayers, rather than a benefit. In an attempt to soften the loss, civic leaders pushed for state legislation to force Motorola to reimburse the city for its added financial burdens, but the bill never became law.

Racine itself had seen some disappointing results of civic-sponsored TIF development. Racine's Tax Increment District No. 18, known as the Machinery Row development, was established in 2014. As one of the developers described it, "Machinery Row is an exciting, $65 million mixed use redevelopment of a formerly industrial portion of Racine's urban riverfront—a 20-acre site that once housed the original manufacturing operations of J. I. Case Main Works, and Golden Books in more recent decades." The project was fueled by $9 million in tax abatements, but it fizzled over the next few years. The property eventually reverted back to the city when the developer defaulted on a $4.5 million loan from Racine. By 2016 the project was dead. In 2018 the city proposed an additional $3.5 million bond issuance for site cleanup. Years later the Machinery Row site remains an eyesore. The other main consequence was a series of lawsuits against Racine from a half dozen of the parties who had been forced to relocate under threat of eminent domain. It was commonplace for locals to reference Machinery Row when asked about their predictions for the Foxconn project.

Mount Pleasant took on so much debt for its Foxconn TIF district that the only way it could find bond buyers was with the partial moral obligation of the entire state's tax base. Even with this backup, the village issued debt at a level that not only violated ordinary prudence levels but also would have been blocked as excessive by state statute without special exemptive legislation. Mount Pleasant is leaning almost entirely on a contractual agreement that Foxconn will pay property tax at a minimum valuation of $1.4 billion beginning in 2023 through the end of TIF period in 2047, regardless of how much capital the company has invested. Meanwhile, local officials were still under the spell of Foxconn's promise of $10 billion in capital spending, which could create an unprecedented tax revenue windfall—if it were to actually happen. No one involved in promoting the project or authorizing the infrastructure expenses has shown any public consternation over this leverage. Yet at least one sign of concern was revealed in Mount Pleasant's commissioning of a new report on future Foxconn property tax payments which was delivered in late 2019.

By 2019 Foxconn had become the village's largest single payer of property taxes, at $8.4 million, but the village had enough qualms to commission the study to look at future collections. Perhaps this was inspired by a look back at the original report the village's TIF experts, Ehlers, the public financing consultant company, had prepared. According to that study, the TIF district would collect $15.4 million in property tax from Foxconn's booming campus in 2019; it actually collected $1 million. In 2020 that figure was expected to rise to $23,134,017, close to four times the likely amount collected on the basis of assessments of Foxconn's buildings. As always, the TIF consultant provided not a range of possible revenues, but a figure exacting to the dollar, with a seemingly hugely overstated $31,089,411 projected for 2021. Other liabilities were also piling up. The City of Racine invested millions of dollars to expand water service to the giant Foxconn factory, which was projected to use 7 million gallons of water a day. Mount Pleasant agreed to compensate Racine for any shortfalls should Foxconn not pay the massive water bill. Because Foxconn shows no signs yet of using more water than needed to flush a few toilets, this shortage bill to Mount Pleasant was set for $1.3 million in 2020 and can amount to as much as $26.8 million through 2039.

With these kinds of potential gaps between projected income and fees, and also the reality on the ground, it's no wonder that Mount Pleasant's municipal leaders asked for a new study. Based on Foxconn's build-out, the report noted that the revenues collected would not cover the debt payments issued for infrastructure by the village and Racine County. The tax income would certainly not be sufficient to allow for the accumulation of assets needed to pay back borrowers when the bonds mature. This overall shortage would still be the case even with the minimal $1.4 billion valuation, which would likely cover only the interest payments due to bondholders. When I pointed this out to the former village trustee Gary Feest, he was nonplussed. "They'll just issue more bonds and kick the can," he explained. "At least that's the way I've heard it's done." Whether the market will be open to such a bond offering remains to be seen.

When asked for a public statement on the report that included the shortfall scenario, Racine County's Office of Corporate Counsel put out assurances that this report was simply a "what-if scenario" and that the "different variables do not reflect actual prediction of developer's performance and the county cautions against drawing any such conclusions."

Although the Foxconn TIF seems to be emerging as a story of village overreach, TIF tends to be used (and abused) more prolifically by large cities such as Chicago for development than by small towns. Illinois passed TIF legislation in 1977, modeling it on Wisconsin's. Forty-three years later, in 2018, Chicago's then 145 TIF districts collected $841 million in property taxes. One-fourth of Chicago's land falls within a TIF district, and in aggregate these districts claim 35 percent of the city's property tax revenue. This massive influx of money has been widely criticized as a slush fund, because tax collected in one TIF district can be shifted to another. Karen Yarbrough, the Cook County Clerk, in 2019 described Chicago TIF funds as "a piggy bank" which officials "use for any number of things." The longtime TIF critic and alternative newspaper *Chicago Reader* stalwart Ben Joravsky has done much to open the public's eyes to what he calls Chicago's "shadow budget." He and his colleagues have broken considerable ground by digging into TIF records across mayoral administrations, finding a consistent pattern of neglect of truly blighted and disadvantaged neighborhoods while money is shuffled to insiders and "vanity projects" like the glitzy tourist attraction of Navy Pier. For instance, the *Reader* tracked funding to discover that the TIF revitalization of a shopping area just outside the prosperous Loop included $8 million for the French Market, a project headed by a wealthy developer who was a reliable donor to the mayor's election coffers. The politicization of TIF was also evident in the allocation of TIF income by ward. One of the poorest wards in Chicago, the Fifteenth Ward—home to the neighborhoods of West Englewood and Back of the Yards—received 0.002 percent of collected TIF taxes through 2010, a result the *Reader* attributed to longtime (serving from 1991 to 2011) alderman Brian Doherty's opposition to TIF projects.

Cities beyond Chicago have become enamored of handing out TIF benefits to specific companies or commercial projects. For instance, in El Paso, Texas, the city went to great lengths to support the opening of the outdoor superstore Cabela's based on promises that it would bring in more people than one of Texas's great tourist attractions, the Alamo. A parcel of open land was declared blighted and the real estate was purchased and improved by the city through $49 million in bond issuance, which by prior agreement had been bought by Cabela's and the project developer. The bondholder's payback was the long-term redirection of two-thirds of sales tax collected—a significant sacrifice for the city, which relies on sales taxes for 21 percent of its revenues. Existing stores in the outdoor category were so upset by the alleged favoritism that they filed a lawsuit. It proved unsuccessful.

Professor David Merriman, of the University of Illinois at Chicago, has had a catbird's view of Chicago TIFs, one of the reasons he's become one of the nation's top authorities on the subject. While Dyersville's Mick Michel would be relieved that Merriman is not prepared to go so far as to recommend the banning of TIF, he's no fan of the way it's working out across the country, especially in the Midwest. In a study from 2000, Merriman and his colleague Richard Dye looked at 235 municipalities in the greater Chicago region (not including Chicago itself) and found that cities, towns, and villages that used TIF "actually grew more slowly than municipalities that did not use TIF." They concluded that "the results are clear and discouraging." In a 2018 follow-up for the Lincoln Institute of Land Policy, Merriman noted that, in practice, "TIF remains highly vulnerable to exploitation, misuse, and uneven application. Additionally, many recent studies show that TIF does little to generate economic growth." But to be fair, he does also conclude that carefully selected TIF projects can generate economic activity but recommends considerably more evaluative rigor than is today's norm before opening a district as well as expanded transparency in operations once established. The historian Sean Dinces did a deep dive into what he concluded was the troubled financing of Chicago's United Center sports stadium. He wrote that successful use of tax incentives like TIF "would rely on careful research to determine whether the incentives would tip the decision of certain businesses to invest in a specific area rather than simply line the pockets of those already intent on investing there regardless of the subsidies on offer."

Overuse or abuse of TIF has not gone unnoticed. More than twenty states have capped the amount of acreage or the percentage of property that a municipality can so designate. New Hampshire, for instance, limits the amount of acreage for any given TIF to 5 percent of the municipality; Maine, to 2 percent. The Foxconn TIF constitutes 18 percent of Mount Pleasant's footprint. In many states, there are statutory limits on the financial commitment a municipality can make for TIF. In Wisconsin, that limit is set at 12 percent of the total assessed value of property within the municipality. But that limit was waived for Mount Pleasant as part of the Foxconn incentive bill passed in the fall of 2017.

The skyrocketing use of TIF has not proceeded without some attempts to rein it in. An increasingly popular variation in TIF operation is for a developer to fund infrastructure or other improvements within a TIF and then bill the municipality for the costs. In Wisconsin these rebates are designated "cash grants." In 2019 Wisconsin's Governor Evers proposed TIF reforms that would limit cash grants to developers and require additional financial reviews of TIF plans. The reforms never got out of committee in the Republican-controlled statehouse.

In addition to fiscal restraints and requirements for additional transparency, a central TIF issue concerns the use of blighting and eminent domain. If land as pristine and well maintained as the acreage and housing in Mount Pleasant is subject to being declared blighted, then no property or home is safe. Court cases, including one involving the seizure of land in Mount Pleasant, may yet provide more clarity on this issue. In the wake of the Supreme Court's *Kelo* decision many states, including Wisconsin, attempted to tighten their eminent domain requirements. However, as Foxconn's project director Claude Lois told resident Kim Mahoney, "We'll find a way."

Further clarification of state statutes may be one solution. In 2016 additional legislation was proposed in California "to ensure that CRIAs [community revitalization and investment authorities, California's version of TIF] are actually used for the purpose for which they are intended: to alleviate blight in our communities and spur economic development in the parts of our state that need assistance most." Along these same lines is the creative allocation of TIF funds, something most cities haven't yet considered. For instance, in Portland, Oregon, some 40 percent of the city's TIF revenues are allocated to affordable housing. Some years ago, a citizens' group in Chicago promoted commonsense reforms: mandated spending on affordable housing, public hearings before the establishment of a TIF district, and a commitment to allocate a percentage of the increment to carefully vetted job-training programs in low-income areas. These recommended reforms, which would have restricted mayoral leverage over TIF revenues, have not been instituted.

As for Mount Pleasant's massive TIF district, known as TID No. 5, the village leaders believe that if Foxconn doesn't pan out, they'll be able to attract any number of new enterprises given their investment in roads, water, sewer, and electricity. This is where the Wisconsin Policy Forum was going with a June 2020 report, "Village of Mt. Pleasant's Fiscal Condition: A Calculated Risk," on the Mount Pleasant TIF. The Wisconsin Policy Forum is a self-defined nonpartisan think tank that produces reports on Wisconsin issues. Though dense with statistics and comparative analyses, the report seemed hesitant to face the eight-hundred-pound gorilla of the massive Foxconn debt. Instead, it lauds Mount Pleasant for its fiscal responsibility through 2017, before it borrowed ten times its operating budget to fund Foxconn's infrastructure. Deep into the report the authors go so far as stating that the magnitude of the Foxconn debt combined with the complications of the COVID-19 pandemic "make it difficult to view the future without some trepidation," but the report still contains what I believe to be one major flaw. If the risk that the village has taken on is "calculated," then it should be possible to report on the considerations that went into the decision. No such evidence appears in the report or elsewhere. The calculations, though, would be fascinating. For instance, what odds did the village put on the promised Gen 10.5 fabrication facility when all the evidence was lining up against it well before it issued $200 million in debt? What about the odds that agencies in other states, like JobsOhio, miscalculated Foxconn's value when they took a pass as the bidding rose? What was the over-under on the percentage chance that Foxconn would break its international pattern of overpromising on development deals? What about the odds that Foxconn would passively accept twenty-four years of taxes on a $1.4 billion physical plant that it may never build, especially should the company face financial hardships? How about the odds that Mount Pleasant can land $1.4 billion or more worth of investments from other companies to make up the difference should Foxconn bail?

The lawyers writing the state's contract and the local TIF agreement with Foxconn were not unaware of the liabilities. Over the years as states and municipalities have been burned in corporate incentive deals, a sort of insurance has been added to these agreements. These "clawbacks" give the sponsoring body authority to reclaim its upfront money if the corporate entity fails to fulfill its promises—typically measured by capital expenditure and job creation. Clawbacks are an important part of the contract between the WEDC and Foxconn, and dispute resolution is part of the TIF agreement with Mount Pleasant and Racine County.

But clawbacks and dispute resolution clauses may induce a false security. Pro-business officials who are personally invested in a project find it hard to activate clawback provisions even when they are triggered out of fear that it will sour their pro-business reputations and confirm their overoptimism. Another factor can be the leverage that a corporation has once it has accepted and used a large amount of public funds. What would municipal officials do if Foxconn demands a rewrite of its property tax liability after the municipalities have already sunk a half billion dollars into the project? Additional complications can be anticipated from the fact that the TIF agreement and all associated liabilities are not with Foxconn itself, but with three subsidiaries: SIO International Wisconsin Inc., FEWI Development Corporation, and AFE Corporation, all incorporated in Wisconsin but with assets limited to the land and structures in Mount Pleasant. The clawbacks at the state level are partially assigned to Foxconn chairman Terry Gou's personal Cayman Islands-based corporation, and any disputes are designated to Wisconsin courts, The TIF agreement relies on arbitration of any arising disputes subject to the rules of the International Chamber of Commerce, with legal action heading to Wisconsin courts.

A window into the kind of complications possible is a long-standing lawsuit brought by Microsoft against Foxconn over contracted payments for software use. The case started in 2011 and remained unresolved at the beginning of 2020, with Gou pledging to not pay a penny in settlements. Instead, Foxconn has attempted to renegotiate its contract with Microsoft. In a separate case, an Illinois company, JST, sued Foxconn, accusing it of pirating proprietary hardware. A lawyer for JST, frustrated with Foxconn's refusal to submit to court-assessed damages, explained, "They think they can't be sued in Illinois, and it's not clear to me whether they think they can be sued in the United States at all." In July 2020, Foxconn's lawyers argued against the suit on jurisdiction grounds, which were upheld in the US Court of Appeals, Seventh District, which agreed that no "causal relationship" existed for damages in Illinois. Promoting development through TIF shouldn't be a casino game. But there's no evidence that Foxconn boosters and leaders in Racine County and Mount Pleasant tried to quantify the upside against the downside. A central problem is Tea Party Republicans, who prefer faith to facts. They preferred to accept the illusion spun by Terry Gou and his minions: $10 billion in investments and 13,000 well-paid jobs. Years into the diminished project they have continued to hang onto that scenario: the wonder world of a Wisconn Valley technology boom and with it the windfall and glory of a mountain of taxes. This stubbornness is not exactly exceptional. The behavioral economist and Nobel laureate Daniel Kahneman has it as one of his tenets of human behavior. Among his findings is the way "statistical information is routinely discarded when it is incompatible with one's personal impressions." He has tracked the kind of wishful thinking that has enveloped Foxconn boosters in Wisconsin, noting that "overly optimistic forecasts of the outcome of projects are found everywhere." And he observes how once a choice is made, the resistance to change direction or admit error is powerful, even when the stakes are high and new information should logically effect a change of mind.

If they had coldly calculated the odds, with numbers, then perhaps the emergence of this glorious technology cluster would have been one in ten or a hundred or a million. But there is no evidence that Foxconn's boosters ever once took their eyes off the shiny object held up by Foxconn to consider the chances of the alternative mapped out in the Wisconsin's Department of Revenue TIF Manual: "If the TID property value does not increase as expected, the municipality may not receive enough tax increment to pay its expenditures. In this case, when the TID terminates, the municipality is responsible for the unpaid debts."

CHAPTER 17

Following the Money

No matter how much money cities, counties, or states collect, they can never do everything they'd like. The demands are endless: road and bridge construction, education, social services. Even in good times cuts are sometimes required—should tax revenues plummet due to recession or contagion, for example, public services and projects can suffer accordingly. Among favorite budget-balancing moves are putting off infrastructure maintenance and slashing education spending. Under Scott Walker's tax-cutting regime, Wisconsin's roads steadily deteriorated, until *US News and World Report* ranked them forty-ninth out of the fifty states. In 2018 the University of Wisconsin–Stevens Point, under pressure from education cuts, proposed eliminating all thirteen of its liberal arts departments, an extreme solution that was eventually rescinded. Between 2012 and 2019, reflecting the legacy of Scott Walker's eight-year tenure from 2010 to 2018, Republican-led Wisconsin provided $3.5 billion less in aid to public schools than if spending had been held at pre-Walker administration levels.

Well-funded far-right lobbyists and think tanks often beat their drums about the need to reduce government in virtually all its functions, with a few exceptions, such as national defense and policing. Among the results in conservative-controlled states are the rise in school vouchers, the imposition of work requirements for public assistance, and the reduction of environmental oversight. Sometimes there are attempts to make major, rather than incremental, changes to government. On the presidential trail in 2011, Texas governor Rick Perry proposed eliminating three federal cabinet-level departments: the Department of Commerce, the Department of Education, and the other one he couldn't remember during a presidential candidate debate, which turned out to be the Department of Energy, which of course Trump later selected him to lead. As Michael Lewis documented with frightening detail in *The Fifth Risk*, the Trump administration worked steadily and stealthily to gut government departments including State and Energy with no other obvious purpose than fulfilling a Koch brothers– and Steve Bannon–inspired goal of undermining the power and efficacy of the state. We saw some of the results in the federal government's crippled response to COVID-19.

But cutting aid to education institutions or making wild and uniformed promises on the campaign trail or moving a state economic agency from within government to a quasi-government status doesn't typically change the fundamental architecture of how we spend our tax dollars. One civic expense that has rarely seen criticism or cuts is economic development. States that can't find the money to fund their K-12 schools or universities or roads or bridges somehow find a way when it comes to digging up the funds to get into a bidding war for a manufacturing plant or a new corporate headquarters. As we've seen, a mutually beneficial circle of consultants, politicians, economic development professionals, contractors, and political donors instigate and fuel these deals. The embedded cost to taxpayers is substantial in both its operating expenses and its end results.

The Governmental Institutionalization of Economic Development

Economic development authorities work to one major end: bringing businesses and jobs to their states or regions. Although on the surface this may seem like a sensible, positive mission, the results, both regionally and nationally, belie this assumption. From a big-picture angle, the bidding between states is a zero-sum game. These incentives don't create an auto plant or an Amazon headquarters. Rather, they simply transfer money, a lot of money, from taxpayers to corporations.

Another problem is the narrowness of the mission and the one-dimensionality of the incentives. Imagine a baseball game in which baserunning is at the full discretion of the player on base. Now add a novel contract for a player in which all earnings are based solely on successful stolen bases, say, $50,000 each. How long would it take to break the record for attempted steals? And would there be commensurate benefits to the team? The institutionalized incentives for economic development are similarly stilted, as are the results. Economic development authorities are not set up to examine opportunity costs or to think about long-term investments, such as poverty abatement or early childhood education. They are designed to look for the next deal: the bigger, the better.

State and regional economic development add up to large bureaucracies. In 2016 the combined budget for state economic agencies was estimated by the Urban Institute to have reached $4 billion. But that figure doesn't include city, county, and regional economic development authorities. In a state with a decentralized economic development structure, like California, the state agency runs on a $3.8 million budget. The City of San Diego Economic Development department alone has a $15 million budget. Most of these state and regional efforts are taxpayer funded. Other states commit much more. For instance, in 2011, under Governor John Kasich, JobsOhio spun off from a government department, with funding coming, as its website explains, "solely from the profits on sales of spirituous liquor." Every time someone buys a fifth of whiskey in Ohio, part of the purchase finds its way to corporate development. JobsOhio's operating expenses have been running close to $1 billion per year, suggesting the Urban Institute's $4 billion figure for all fifty states is underestimated.

And these billions do not include the legislated billions in tax abatements or grant expenses like those approved in Wisconsin for Foxconn or proposed virtually everywhere for Amazon headquarters. This is just the year in, year out background expense of staffing and running the agencies.

Scott Walker came into office in 2010 with a clear agenda to trim government. One of his innovations was to take the state's economic development efforts out of the Department of Commerce and establish the quasi-governmental Wisconsin Economic Development Corporation with himself as chairman. This would, he promised, free the agency from unnecessary political entanglements and give it a free-enterprise efficiency.

A recent organizational chart for WEDC shows a full-time staff of 135 and a $43 million budget in 2017, when Foxconn was landed, about 90 percent sourced directly from taxpayers and two-thirds of the total budget spent on salary and operating expenses, the remainder largely on grants. While state economic agencies do encourage entrepreneurs and support existing businesses, their primary mission is in fomenting job expansion, primarily through landing new enterprises. In other words, in Wisconsin it cost taxpayers some $30 million to find companies that deserve $10 million in grants. Under the leadership of a governor who had promised a daunting 250,000 new jobs in his first term, WEDC's focus was not only narrow but also frantic.

This institutionalized reward system for landing projects can be a recipe for trouble. In 2011 the newly formed WEDC was eager to show off. A fledgling company called Morgan Aircraft made a proposal for a Wisconsin-based factory that would manufacture a new private aircraft that combined elements of helicopter and airplane. The company was set to invest $105 million and hire 340 people, if WEDC would help it get the project off the ground. WEDC wrote a check for a forgivable loan of $686,000 of taxpayer money and approved another $1 million federal loan administered through the state; Sheboygan County threw in $158,000 worth of infrastructure. In 2015 Morgan Aircraft filed for bankruptcy with little or no assets on hand. Wisconsin's chance of getting its money back or seeing a single new job was virtually nil.

Aviation must have been held in high esteem at WEDC because in 2012 it jumped at the chance to back another aerospace venture, Kestrel Aircraft Company. The deal was trumpeted as the biggest economic development deal since World War II for the city of Superior, bringing with it 665 new jobs. The bidding for Kestrel was aggressive, as the firm already had a presence in Maine and Minnesota, and the incentives were cooked up in a hothouse auction atmosphere. In the end, WEDC set the table with $4 million in loans, Superior's redevelopment authority added $2.6 million, and the county dug deep for another $500,000. When Kestrel went bankrupt in 2018 leaving all of these entities on the hook, an audit showed that WEDC had failed in its due diligence, including looking into the company's similar promises and failures in Brunswick, Maine. The Kestrel fiasco was not without its lessons—Superior's mayor Jim Payne tried to alert state leaders that they were making a similar, but much larger, mistake with Foxconn.

Madison's *Capital Times* summarized the early results of WEDC's wide-open race for landing jobs in 2015: "A 2013 audit found that awards were given to ineligible recipients for ineligible projects and some awards exceeded program limits. The review, conducted by the nonpartisan Legislative Audit Bureau, also found that the agency didn't require financial statements from some companies receiving awards and didn't properly track whether promised jobs had been created. According to the audit, one-third of the agency's 30 economic development programs did not meet their expected goals. That audit also found instances of WEDC employees using state funds to purchase University of Wisconsin football season tickets, alcohol and iTunes gift cards."

It can be argued that state economic development agencies are so solidly entrenched because they are uniquely able to "pay for themselves." Each state agency can present to their governor and legislatures an annual tally of the economic impact of all the jobs the agency has "created." Regional economic development agencies can do the same for city councils and mayors. By these measures they appear indispensable.

But imagine a world in which all these agencies suddenly disappeared. Would the engines of economic expansion collapse? Would a company seeking a site for, say, a new automotive assembly plant just give up? Could a company like Foxconn acquire its initial 350 acres all on its own, without hundreds of millions of taxpayer dollars being spent on grooming the site location consultants and Foxconn executives, buying the company its land, paying for its sewers and water mains and roads? And if the Foxconn business plan was unsustainable without so much taxpayer support, was it really the sort of enterprise that the taxpayers should be subsidizing to begin with?

In 2017, 238 cities submitted bids for Amazon's announced new headquarters. These were typically serious, comprehensive efforts, and Amazon paid not a penny of public servants' time and energy. A good deal of the publicly sponsored economic development billions are expended on lost causes like the Amazon proposals. Millions are also spent on providing companies like Foxconn and its site-selection consultant free relocation services not just in Wisconsin but in all the states the company considered, including Michigan, Ohio, and North Carolina. If you are personally relocating from, say, New Jersey to San Jose, which government agency do you call to review housing options, give you free tours of possible locations, and offer you some sweet deals on an empty lot while arranging for ten or twenty years of property tax abatements? Of course, there are no such agencies.

The headline costs for a project like Foxconn are the billions in state incentives. Less visible but still widely reported are the publicly funded infrastructure costs, which in the Foxconn project will run the local municipalities at least $500 million up front, plus another $300 million for decades of annual interest payments on the loans. Uncounted are the public billions spent by state and local economic development agencies in the successful or unsuccessful pursuit of corporate investment. These services are an untallied handout to corporations, the benefits of which are allocated in the usual ways: rising executive salaries and owner or shareholder profits.

A project as large as Foxconn consumes untold hours, weeks, and years of staff time at all levels: municipality, county, and state. The Racine County Economic Development Corporation, with a full-time slate of seventeen, was so devoted to landing and siting Foxconn that its budget jumped from about $2 million a year to almost $6 million in 2017 when it was doing most of this work. In 2018 things settled back to the $2 million level. Meanwhile, in Racine grassroots community service projects for early childhood intervention, housing and food security, or apprentice training are running on shoestring budgets under leadership that is compensated with a fraction of the salaries devoted to economic development staffers. To its credit, the RCEDC was able to get through the frantic Foxconn landing without hiring additional staff, but it did have an agreement with Mount Pleasant to charge back some of its extra work. Those bills would eventually find their way to Mount Pleasant's Foxconn TIF, TID No. 5.

Mount Pleasant TID No. 5: The Foxconn Slush Fund

In chapter 7 we saw how effortlessly the developers of Fyre Lake Golf Club drained Sherrard's $16 million TIF pool. Perhaps no more illustrative example was Claude Lois's generous "donation" of a $16,000 generator to the village, which he would eventually charge back to the TIF pool, funds borrowed by the village. Following the money in this case study is fairly straightforward. The development team was merciless in its exploitation of the pool of funds but not in ways that were necessarily illegal or even untoward. The probability that this was business as usual is even more concerning than if it had been strictly criminal.

Who else benefited from the Sherrard development? A burst of construction jobs early on provided temporary, low-wage income to a set of workers and was a boon to the contractors, at least those who were paid. Local businesses (two bars) might have benefited from increased traffic as the work was being done and would have anticipated long-term growth if the projected home development occurred. If the project had flourished, maybe residents might have gotten parts of their wish list—a grocery store, perhaps. But the project was designed from the beginning to enrich the rich—and in the end the bills were mostly paid by US taxpayers as we bailed out bankrupt Country Bank.

But what about the really big state and municipal investments? Take the Kansas City convention hotel, underwritten by local taxpayers. With that project, what really is being promoted is a kind of tourist economy. Think of a typical Caribbean island, where hordes of locals are employed by chain hotels and resorts as low-wage maids and food service workers while a few high-paid managers (usually outsiders) run the facility. Driving away from the luxury resorts reveals a society living close to, if not deeply mired in, poverty. Any excess revenues go not to the community or the workers but to even higher-paid executives back at headquarters and the generally affluent shareholders.

Foxconn's thirty-year tax-increment-financing project paints the picture of how the funds flow in a much larger manufacturing development. The tax-increment district (Wisconsinese for TIF) didn't open until the summer of 2018, but charges to it had been piling up since July 2017. So examining expenses through April 2020 reflect close to three years of Foxconn project activity. In that period, more than $107 million was spent via the TID No. 5 fund, approximately five times the village's annual budget. The funds were raised via debt issuance, debt that is backed up to 40 percent by the state.

TABLE 1

Among the largest uses of the initial $107 million
spent from the Foxconn TIF/TID fund

USE	COST
Racine Water and Wastewater	$36,643,000
S. J. Louis Construction (Minnesota)	$10,107,000
Land purchases and relocation expenses*	$8,455,000
Super Excavators (Menomonee Falls, WI)	$8,244,000
Foth Infrastructure (West Allis, WI)	$6,073,000
Oakes A. W. & Son (Racine, WI)	$3,638,000
von Briesen & Roper (Marcuvitz's Milwaukee law firm)	$2,348,000
DK Contractors (Pleasant Prairie, WI)	$2,140,000
Guelig Waste Removal (Eden, WI)	$1,624,000
Landmark Title of Racine	$1,498,000
Kapur & Associates, Consulting Engineers (Milwaukee)	$1,150,000 (including $700,000 in charges by Kapur for Claude Lois at $20,000 and $20,000–$24,000 per month)
Mueller Communications (Milwaukee)	$729,000
Sigma Group (Milwaukee)	$404,000

Note: Most of the land purchases, which ran to some $170 million, were paid by other sources, including a $60 million refundable advance from Foxconn to Mount Pleasant. In December 2017 Racine County issued $80 million in bonds for land purchasing. Foxconn pledged to pay a special property tax assessment over time to repay that debt.

Source: Sean Ryan, "Foxconn Fronts $60 Million to Local Governments; Mount Pleasant Preps to Buy Land," *Milwaukee Business Journal*, Dec. 22, 2017, https://www.bizjournals.com/milwaukee/news/2017/12/22/foxconn-fronts-60-million-to-local-governments.html.

The largest single line item for the municipalities was land purchases and relocation costs, which had reached $170 million by early 2019 with all but a few properties in the 3,900-acre zone acquired. These funds were principally found outside of the TID in money raised by the village and county and via a refundable advance of $60 million from Foxconn. The commitment to pay at least seven or eight times the going rate for agricultural land produced a windfall for some farmers, but many homeowners discovered the village's compensation packages were not sufficient to replace their property and houses, let alone compensate them for the distress and anxiety of losing one's home.

One of the natural results for a small town suddenly having access to a pool of a hundred million dollars is a change in perspective. A few years previous, village meetings would descend into acrimony over the cost difference between a new ambulance and a refurbished one. Once the TID was funded, expenses started flowing without a blink of an eye. A farmer was issued a check for $223,695 to dismantle his barn and move it upstate. A businessman with a mobile power-washing business based in a storage building and three trucks tossed out what he thought was an outrageously high bid for relocating his business. He was issued a check for $300,000. The fire chief, the village president's chief ally in government, ordered a rescue boat, a nice Evinrude motor, and a trailer for the boat and charged it all to the TID. Then he stopped at Menards and picked up $800 worth of water rescue gear and added an online order for a top-of-the-line ice rescue kit. All absorbed by the Foxconn TID, miles from any substantial body of water. Some of the spending seemed excessive in another way. Farmhouses were razed in the 1,000-acre Area 2, for instance, in which neither Foxconn nor Mount Pleasant had any immediate plans, even as the farmland around them was not only untouched but still in production as the village leased the land back to farmers. Why did the village first buy and then destroy all the houses and outbuildings if the village might someday need to raise money by selling the properties and land? It was akin to Hernán Cortés burning his ships in the Veracruz harbor. There was no going back.

The economic impact of all these real estate transactions was really an illustration of the old economic saw that two families cannot support themselves by doing each other's laundry. The act of municipal borrowing to purchase residents' houses and land is not in itself an economic benefit to the city, region, or country. Although a small number of land-rich farmers were turned into either rich farmers or rich retirees, homeowners in the 3,900-acre plot were often forced to downsize, move out of the area, or go further into debt. The real stakes were placed on the future value of the real-located land (which the village had transitioned from farming and residential to industrial development) and, on the other side of the coin, the potential liabilities of massive new debt. In other words, the $170 million in land purchases amounted to a municipal gamble that the ensuing development would repay the debt and then some and create such prosperity that the pain of forcing people off the land, out of their homes, would be well worth it.

The bulk of the rest of the money raised by debt issuance in TID No. 5 was actively spent on infrastructure and professional services. The professional services spending is particularly worth scrutiny because it comes without the statutory requirements for open bidding required for infrastructure construction work. This can be seen in the village's steady payment of some $100,000 a month to its eminent domain counsel; compensation at the same rate in 2020 when one property was awaiting litigation as when over a hundred properties were in transition in late 2017.

The biggest spending from the TID fund, as would be expected, was devoted to site preparation, road construction, and water and other utilities. It turns out that you can bulldoze and cart off the remains of a house for around $20,000. I spoke to the local Habitat for Humanity ReStore manager Thom Bowen, who was initially able to collect some materials from displaced owners, but he was shut out once the village took possession. Instead, the chosen contractor extracted whatever resale value it could before laying it all to waste.

Although some infrastructure spending can result in broad economic benefit, this was not the case in Mount Pleasant. Converting a country road to a six-lane highway to facilitate traffic to a massive Foxconn factory is directly beneficial only to the contractors building the road and the company, and only indirectly to the company's potential workforce. Likewise, the millions spent on water and sewers and electrical infrastructure. The immediate beneficiary is not the general community but the owner of the industrial facility being served.

But what about all those construction jobs? While the laborers involved were happy to have the work, the fact is that the projects were limited in scope and time, and often were seasonal. Government spending on construction is much like the tourism industry: it produces a large number of low-paid or modestly paid jobs and just a handful of higher-paid positions for supervisors and engineers. The bulk of the profits are funneled back to owners. The lasting economic impact comes from the benefits of the construction, not the building costs. If there are no long-term benefits, then the government spending only reinforces the same income inequality that is proving a national disaster. The workers receive their modest paychecks for the short interval of the construction, and the owners get rich. The fact that the owners are often active political donors to both parties is not irrelevant.

Research has supported the notion that not all infrastructure spending serves the common good. Sumedha Bajar from the Indian Institute of Advanced Studies reviewed the research and concluded that, while infrastructure spending has the potential to be a social positive, "it is wrong to assume that economic growth attributable to infrastructure development will consequently lead to a reduction in inequality. Literature has shown that economic growth can be associated with rising inequality and poverty." Among the variables that matter, Bajar cites the nature of the infrastructure, the size of the project, the manner in which it is financed, and the populations affected by the development.

Large private-enterprise-focused economic development projects in the US often share many of the variables that move the needle more toward inequality than toward general welfare. Their contributions to the commonweal are especially limited when designated to promote the development and construction of a specific corporate project, whether a convention hotel in Kansas City, a Motorola facility, or a Foxconn Gen 10.5 LCD factory. This puts them in contrast to broad-based government-funded development projects like the interstate highway system or rural electrification, which can be directly associated with increased productivity and national economic interests. Projects like the one that brought Foxconn to Wisconsin tend to be quite targeted and specific, and many of the economic beneficiaries also tend to be narrow and identifiable.

One of the notable characteristics of the Foxconn spending was its momentum. Like one of those complex, multiple-path domino constructions, once the first block was tipped, the chain reaction went on clicking even when Foxconn began waffling about the size and nature of its factory. Much of this can be attributed to the institutions involved. The state leadership under Walker had made this the centerpiece of his administration's achievements and was in no position to shift ground. The economic development professionals were also all in on the project, from the state's WEDC to the Milwaukee Metro Area Chambers' Milwaukee7 to the regional Racine County Economic Development Corporation.

In 2014 the economist Andrew Warner noted that in many large government-spending projects there were issues with "incentive problems," by which he meant that politicians like Scott Walker may be driven by political ambitions and local leaders like Dave DeGroot may have visions of expanding influence and importance. As if speaking directly to the Foxconn project, he cited a worldwide problem with large publicly funded projects: "a pervasive avoidance of rational analysis."

If the Foxconn project was championed for political gain, it was sustained by a neat circle of mutual benefit. The appearance of cronyism was particularly notable when it came to the contractors Foxconn hired. This was hardly new terrain for Foxconn or its chairman Terry Gou. As Minxin Pei wrote in 2018: "Academic research on corruption in China, including my own, finds that the tunneling of state-owned assets by the elite, their family members, and cronies is the surest way to amass large fortunes fast. The secret lies in the way such assets are transacted between government agencies and well-connected private businessmen."

Foxconn's contractor hires were shielded from any bidding requirements because they were conducted by a private firm. Although Foxconn's capital investments in the first years of the project paled against the promised $10 billion, its projects still amounted to hundreds of millions. The lead contractor chosen by Foxconn was a partnership of M+W Group and Gilbane Inc. As tallied by progressive nonprofit One Wisconsin Now, Gilbane had given at least $359,000 to Walker's campaigns. Then the master planner for the Foxconn campus was announced in May 2018: Hammes Company. The head of the company was Jon Hammes, another Republican megadonor who was Walker's campaign finance chairman for his reelection campaign and had served as finance chairman for his presidential bid in 2016. Walker and his team made the hiring of Wisconsin contractors a bragging point for the project's statewide economic benefit. It was a less-publicized joy to reward his loyal supporters.

In 2007 the economists Phillip Keefer and Stephen Knack produced evidence that public investment is "dramatically higher in governments with low-quality governance and limited political checks and balances." In other words, states like Wisconsin in 2017, with not only a firm one-party majority but also a majority whose defining characteristic is party and leadership loyalty.

Foxconn in Wisconsin is not only a case study of economic development gone wrong; it is a cautionary tale because it encompasses common foibles that are replicated over and over across the country, in projects large and small. It's a story in its full scope that could add up to the misappropriation of billions of taxpayer dollars for political gain and ambition, the valuing of industrial development over environmental protection, the enriching of a small number of insiders while simultaneously proclaiming that state coffers have nothing left for those in need. And without a second thought, it proceeded to steamroll the property and rights of those unfortunate to have been in the way.

CHAPTER 18

Foxconn on the Ground

Although local municipalities piled up hundreds of millions in debt to buy land and build roads and sewers, what else was under way after the summer of 2018 groundbreaking? One thing that did not appear to happen in conjunction with the project was any increase in Scott Walker's popularity as his November 2018 reelection approached. In fact, the Foxconn deal was polling negative, with fewer than 40 percent of the state's residents convinced it was worth the cost. Voters outside of the immediate region in Racine County were showing little enthusiasm for spending billions of their tax dollars on a factory that was as far away from northern and western Wisconsin as were Winnipeg and Omaha, respectively. He and his team found this unnerving.

Walker and his election consultants scrambled for a way to turn things around. I spoke with a concrete contractor in the Racine area who had been passed over around the same time for a Foxconn-area paving contract in favor of a company based in La Crosse, 230 miles to the northwest. He was perplexed; hiring a contractor from so far away made little sense in terms of cost or efficiency. But it made sense politically, as Walker began to build a case for statewide economic benefit.

Foxconn itself pitched in on the political message. Its executives might have been novices in the nuances of US politics, but they were old hands at crony capitalism and knew Walker was their best path to achieving the billions in incentives that Wisconsin had allocated to them. Thus, in the summer of 2017 Foxconn began to make announcements that were puzzling as business plans but perfectly understandable in the political context. In late June, for example, Foxconn announced that it would buy a 75,000-square-foot, six-story building in Green Bay for an "innovation center," which it explained in oblique terms as part of its AI, 8K, 5G ecosystem expansion. Green Bay is in northeastern Wisconsin and is not renowned as a technology hub. The *Milwaukee Business Journal* announced on July 16 a second innovation center: "Foxconn Technology Group will open new offices in downtown Eau Claire in early 2019 with about 150 workers to test and develop technology and applications for its products." Eau Claire is in northwestern Wisconsin, about ninety miles east of Minneapolis. Foxconn announced it would buy not one but two buildings there. Foxconn seemed to find Wisconsin real estate attractive, adding a $14.9 million building in Milwaukee in June 2018 and a $9.5 million building in downtown Madison a year later. In April 2018 Foxconn and the University of Wisconsin–Madison inked a deal headlined as a major $100 million grant. The Foxconn expansions into Wisconsin's far reaches immediately became part of the Walker campaign narrative.

In November Tony Evers edged out Walker in the governor's race. This may have been a reflection of the national "blue wave," which gave Democrats control of the House of Representatives and nine new gubernatorial seats. It may have simply been fatigue with Walker. Some political observers thought that voters welcomed Evers's even-temperedness and rationality after so much partisanship and divisive rhetoric. The sense that Walker had overreached on Foxconn seemed a likely factor as well, as a broad spectrum of regional and national media sharpened their critiques of the project and its excessive costs during the first year of the deal.

By early 2019 the political landscape in Wisconsin had shifted, but the public relations effort continued in limited fashion, with Foxconn hosting a statewide "Smart Cities" contest for college students and faculty, with "up to" $1 million in awards over three years, with $60,000 being distributed to the first-year finalists (a figure suspiciously less than one-third of the total $1 million prize). The $100 million "grant" to the University of Wisconsin, the details of which were never completely disclosed to the public, was revealed to be actually a matching offer with so many intellectual property strings attached that it was unlikely to appeal to donors. When aspects of the arrangement leaked, both faculty and graduate students mounted a formal protest. Two years into the arrangement, Foxconn's total donation was $700,000, less than 1 percent of the hyped number.

As for those innovation centers? Foxconn owns one of the two buildings it sought to buy in Eau Claire but has made virtually no improvements or done any hiring. In February 2019, I spoke with the city administrator of Eau Claire, who had no progress to report. When I checked in with the chancellor's office at University of Wisconsin–Eau Claire, where there had initially been support for the project, it was clear they were distancing themselves as far as possible from Foxconn and its local efforts. Reporters who visited the centers in Eau Claire and Green Bay through 2020 found no evidence of any activity.

But all the same, the infrastructure work being supported by Mount Pleasant and Racine County residents had continued unabated. The water and sewer work designed for a $10 billion Gen 10.5 complex was well under way. No substantive changes were made to this build-out, even after Foxconn announced diminished plans, partly because Foxconn continued to make claims for future expansion and partly because of institutional inertia and, perhaps

TABLE 2

Infrastructure expenses for Foxconn complex in Wisconsin

INFRASTRUCTURE EXPENSE	COST
Electrical infrastructure for Gen 10.5 LCD fab (ATC)	$140,000,000[a]
Mount Pleasant TID No. 5 Bonds	$203,000,000[b]
Racine County GO Bonds	$178,000,000[c]
Debt service on municipal bonds over life of bonds	$300,000,000[d]
State grant to Mount Pleasant/Racine Co. for Foxconn	$15,000,000[e]
Federal highway funds reallocated to Foxconn area	$160,000,000[f]
State roadway construction costs for Foxconn area	$221,000,000[g]
State grant to Gateway Community College for Foxconn training	$5,000,000[h]
Total	$1,218,000,000

Sources:

(a) Assessed to ratepayers across Wisconsin, *Milwaukee BizTimes*, "Foxconn Electricity Needs $140 Million in Upgrades," Dec. 12, 2017

(b) *Racine Journal Times*, "Foxconn TID Came with Calculated Risks," June 25, 2020

(c) *Reuters*, "Racine County to Lock In Long-Term Financing for Foxconn," Oct. 18, 2019; *WGTD Public Radio*, "Racine County Authorizes More Bonds for Foxconn, Land Purchases," Sept. 6, 2020

(d) Estimated debt service at 4 percent per year with an average bond maturity of twenty years

(e) City of Mount Pleasant Fact Sheet, "Racine County Welcomes Foxconn," www.mtpleasantwi.gov

(f) *Milwaukee Journal Sentinel*, "Wisconsin Lands $160 Million for I-94 South Upgrade to Help Smooth Foxconn Project," June 6, 2008

(g) Estimated total, *Racine Journal Times*, "Taxpayers Have Spent More Than $225 Million on Roads around Foxconn," Mar. 10, 2019

(h) *Kenosha News*, "Gateway Plans $5 million Expansion to Help Train Foxconn Workers," Sept. 21, 2017

most important, opportunistic enthusiasm from local politicians and economic development professionals who knew this was a one-time shot at building a massive industrial park.

By late 2018 Foxconn's contribution to the work in Mount Pleasant was the opening of a modest 120,000-square-foot "multipurpose" building—a warehouse-like building the size of a big-box retailer. Construction on a second larger building, just under a million square feet, was under way by the summer of 2019. This was the building that Foxconn called its "fab" facility and that local press repeatedly referred to as a Gen 6.0 LCD panel factory, despite the evidence that it was not suitable for this purpose. The facility had originally been described as 3 million square feet, a more appropriate size for LCD production. Still, the *Racine Journal Times* reported in the fall of 2019 that "the building is to become North America's first and only thin-film-transistor, liquid-crystal-display fabrication plant or 'fab.'" When I asked industry expert Bob O'Brien, of Supply Chain Consultants, whether Foxconn could fabricate flat LCDs screens in that building, his response was "depends on what you mean by manufacture." His assessment: it could be used only for token production and that itself seemed unlikely.

A third building in the same area of Mount Pleasant, notable for its nine-story glass dome design, was designated a data center and was under construction by a Foxconn subsidiary in the summer of 2020. It was unclear what data the center would be processing. A fourth, midsized building designated for assembly operations was also under construction. Even a generous valuation of these four buildings would put them at less than 5 percent of Foxconn's promised $10 billion investment.

Intense road work, paid for by Wisconsin taxpayers and federal funds, was under way by August 2018, with I-94 being widened to eight lanes from six. The county highway KR, one of the major east-west roads through the Foxconn TIF district, was being widened from two lanes to six. It had originally been drawn up for nine lanes, but the scaled-back project still appeared excessive for the reduced development. As with many public projects, momentum overrode sense, and six lanes it was. Braun Road, another east-west road that runs just north of Foxconn's initial building area, was mapped as a four-lane highway subsuming all adjacent housing, but reduced to an improved two in later planning. The nonpartisan Wisconsin Fiscal Bureau estimated that Foxconn-related road work would siphon $134 million from other road projects in the state, with additional spending designated for the area expanded and accelerated.

In December 2017 the *Milwaukee Business Journal* had headlined "Foxconn Already Making TVs in Mount Pleasant." They were referring to the modest assembly operation Foxconn had set up in rented space, putting together midsize TVs from imported parts. But soon after the groundbreaking, the line was shut down. So where were the jobs?

As I tracked the job listings for Foxconn in 2018 through 2020, I found a puzzling array of occupations. These varied from a Mandarin-speaking nurse's position in Milwaukee to engineers with experience in cooling solutions for server farms and medical patent attorneys. At first it seemed as if Foxconn were hatching a business plan so complex that it defied unraveling. But over time, interviews with current and recently departed employees revealed these wildly various job listings as evidence of Foxconn's uncoordinated and mismanaged attempts to gain business traction in Wisconsin. The object of these efforts appeared to not be a grand business scheme but a portion of the $3 billion in state incentives that could be triggered by hitting employment targets.

Some of these hires were housed in the 1960s-vintage office building Foxconn had bought in downtown Milwaukee as its "North American headquarters." The gap between interview promises and work reality was soon apparent. Not only were workers expected to bring their own laptops from home; they needed to bring their own office supplies, down to pens and pencils. The elevators in the building were unreliable, and the roof leaked. The recruited workers were given little to do—many filled their days watching movies and playing computer games.

One senior Foxconn executive was fixated on the idea of transforming its "innovation centers" including the buildings in Eau Claire and Green Bay into WeWork-inspired coworking spaces—a plan that fizzled even as WeWork itself crumbled. The search to find some sort of business traction took on a sort of sitcom absurdity as the company toyed with ideas ranging from carp farms to boat storage to a tree farm to exporting ice cream. One idea was to sponsor an e-sports team and set up a training site at one of the innovation centers. Often plans short-circuited when one division of Foxconn refused to authorize funding for projects promoted by another. One such project was Foxconn's "Smart Cities" initiative in which Racine was chosen as the site for futuristic innovation, such as self-driving cars. A bunch of cheap golf carts arrived in Mount Pleasant to be outfitted with autonomous equipment that never materialized. Bored employees from Milwaukee drove down and raced them around the empty warehouse until their batteries died.

Some of the new hires were assigned a novel task: inventing a business at which Foxconn could make money. A few of the early hires were engineers who had been sent to Taiwan for training in the Foxconn way. One described to *The Verge* reporter Josh Dzieza how he was brought back to come up with a viable business for the company. "The most common misunderstanding with Foxconn is people here thought Foxconn had a strategy and business plan. . . . They did not. They had no plans at all." Some people were promised attractive jobs, leading them to leave current employers, only to be left hanging or having the offer rescinded.

All these efforts were geared toward hitting the employment level needed to trigger the lucrative incentives. The contract with Wisconsin called for a snapshot of employment at the end of December, which was in retrospect clearly a weak spot in the deal, particularly with a partner as eager to game the system as Foxconn was. If Foxconn met its minimum 520-job requirement on the 2019 tally date, it would trigger a 10 percent cash rebate from Wisconsin to Foxconn for its to-date capital expenses—as much as $50 million. From the beginning, the Evers administration was skeptical of both Foxconn's job numbers and the state's obligation, taking the position that the contract was based on Foxconn building a Gen 10.5 fab, which all agreed was no longer in the making. And the minimum job threshold of 520 in 2019 continued to escalate in subsequent years: 1,820 in 2020; 3,640 in 2021; 5,200 in 2022; and rising to a cap of 10,400 beginning in 2027. Project boosters had been quick to defend the massive incentives by citing these job requirements. And based on Foxconn's business trajectory, it appeared that they were right to point out how Wisconsin would never be obligated to pay anywhere near its $3 billion incentive maximum. But even that first slice of $50 million was enticing, particularly if Foxconn could staff up for considerably less.

Towards the end of 2019 Foxconn scrambled to hit the 520 mark, including an aggressive effort to recruit a new set of paid interns. The search for warm bodies who could be hired, counted, and then soon dismissed was belied in the internship ranges advertised: "industrial artificial intelligence, 5G networks, industrial big data, human resources, firmware engineering, financing, accounting, legal matters, business analysis, interior design, construction management, sales and marketing." Interior design? In early 2020 the company claimed it had hit this mark. An audit by the state later reduced the number to 216, well below the number needed. Foxconn's disorganization was once again evident: many of the December hires, including interns, didn't receive a paycheck until January, making them ineligible for the 2019 count. After receiving the official rejection, Terry Gou issued a formal response, showing his disappointment in the lack of political enthusiasm for his Wisconsin project and twice citing Donald Trump as an example of the sort of partner Foxconn sought. With Walker and Paul Ryan out, it appeared that Gou was hinting that, should Trump be eliminated from the picture as well, so would Foxconn's enthusiasm for making something out of the Wisconsin venture.

In what was clearly more of a public relations stunt than a viable business, in early 2020 some seventy temp workers were brought in to the onetime Potemkin TV-assembly factory to assemble face masks in response to the COVID-19 epidemic. Take-home pay was $13.00 an hour, which works out to less than half of the $54,000 a year "family-supporting" jobs that Foxconn and its boosters had promised. Meanwhile, Foxconn showed signs of desperation as it scrambled to rent space in its Mount Pleasant buildings. In September 2020 the company's largest building on its Mount Pleasant campus, the 980,000-square-foot big box that it misleadingly called its "fab," was granted a permit to shift its use from manufacturing to storage. Now all Foxconn needed was someone requiring a massive amount of storage space.

Frustration boiled over as Foxconn executives berated hires and complained about how American workers were both overpaid and unproductive. In a move that puzzled the American hires, Foxconn executives insisted they sit through a showing of the 2020 Oscar winning documentary *American Factory*, which tells of the cultural clash in Dayton, Ohio, between former GM employees and their new Chinese managers who repurposed the old plant to make automotive glass. In the film Chinese managers lament the work ethic of their American hires who balk at twelve-hour days or seven-day workweeks. The captive Foxconn employees watched as American managers were gradually replaced with Asian nationals, a trend that Foxconn employees in Wisconsin were already seeing happen around them. If the Foxconn executives thought the showing would be inspirational, it was only as far as creating a wave of résumé distribution.

While much of the $3 billion in incentives looked out of reach, booster claims like Robin Vos's that "Wisconsin wouldn't be out a dollar" if Foxconn didn't perform were playing fast and loose with the facts. The state had redirected more than $200 million in highway funds to the Foxconn project area and had sent Mount Pleasant $15 million to help with its initial efforts. WEDC had devoted a substantial part of its $70 million annual budget to this project for years. But the real liability was concentrated in the municipal expenditures that were shared by Mount Pleasant and Racine County, land acquisition and infrastructure costs that had escalated into the hundreds of millions of dollars.

Repayment of this massive debt would be dependent almost entirely on Foxconn paying its agreed property tax valuation of $1.4 billion beginning in 2023, as well as any special assessments that Mount Pleasant levied. In 2019 Foxconn paid Mount Pleasant $7.2 million in special assessments plus $1 million in property tax. At an effective 2 percent mill rate of market value, the $1.4 billion valuation would bring in about $28 million a year, close to what the municipalities would be dispersing to the bond holders as annual interest. This contracted minimum $1.4 billion assessment in 2023 would produce a substantial jump in taxation for the municipalities: Foxconn's actual investments on the ground appeared to be headed to a tax liability of about one-third of that $1.4 billion. But even the $1.4 billion assessment would not be sufficient to build the nest egg needed to repay the bondholders the face value of the hundreds of millions of dollars in debt when the bonds matured. Should Foxconn's payments fall short of keeping local governments solvent, the state is obligated, via the Foxconn legislation, to backstop local debt to the tune of 40 percent plus interest, payments that could reach hundreds of millions and would still leave the municipalities with substantial liabilities. The village would also be looking down the road at paying back bondholders at least $121 million when the bonds mature. Perhaps they would be able to issue another round of bonds to kick this can a few decades down the road, or perhaps they would be forced to turn back to the state to negotiate some sort of emergency financing. It had been Scott Walker's state government, after all, that had arranged the deal, championed it, and encouraged Mount Pleasant to offer up its land and once solid credit.

CHAPTER 19

Breaking the Cycle

The acclaimed sociologist William Julius Wilson was onto something in his 1996 book *When Work Disappears*. Because of his focus
on the Black working class, Wilson was early to a trend that has
since enveloped a broad swath of American workers. As in Racine,
across much of the US, the Black workers who had been heavily
recruited during and after World War II were often the first victims
of deindustrialization. In 1996 Zenith was still making cathode-ray
tubes in Melrose Park, Illinois; Kenosha Engine was still making
motors for Chrysler; and Western Publishing was still printing Little
Golden Books in Racine. But all these operations were troubled and
had trimmed their workforces. They would be shuttered within a
decade.

The final section of Wilson's book is a summary of positive steps
that could be taken to alleviate the extensive social degradations of
concentrated poverty in urban neighborhoods. Twenty-five years
later many of his observations and potential remedies remain
fresh and, unfortunately, unfulfilled. He highlights the challenges

of globalization, the growing income disparities between skilled and unskilled workers, and the importance of educational opportunities, family stability, and the opportunity gap for those living in cities compared to their suburbs. His solutions involve education reforms, better access to early childhood education, and social support for stressed families. He laments the minimum wage of $7.00 ($11.70 in 2020 dollars) and the lack of health care associated with lower-wage jobs. In terms of jobs themselves, he suggests a government-sponsored job program to pick up the slack, with work focused on repairing urban infrastructure, including housing. He notes with regret "the dramatic retreat from using public policy as a means to fight social inequality." Although it is outside of the scope of Wilson's work, the willingness to continually expand the untrammeled economic development complex in lieu of social services is an example of one of the results.

As long as the incentives exist and the bidding wars stay open, economic development spending will continue unabated and will likely spiral upward. These incentives start with political ambitions, involve a deeply established institutional infrastructure, and are fueled by what for participants is a benign cycle of political donations and commensurate rewards. The end result is a significant engine behind rising income inequality and a beggaring of investments in education, infrastructure, social services, and health care. So not only does economic development money flow freely to the already affluent; it takes money away from the very programs and services that, at a minimum, are needed to begin to reverse the country's falling social and income mobility.

Political Gain

The academic work done on the political motivation for large economic development projects is unequivocal. Politicians have benefited from not only landing big projects but also standing up and giving it a good college try in their losing bids. Here at last is an issue on which Democrats and Republicans agree: sustaining the unholy marriage of government and business. The backlash against the crazed Amazon headquarters auction that began in 2017 or the widespread recognition that Foxconn project backfired on Scott Walker might indicate a tipping point (say, $3 billion in state spending). It might also indicate the benefit of transparency. Most economic impact work, from TIF tax abatement to the kind of funding that Wisconsin spent on its two failed aircraft ventures, goes largely under the radar. This was not the case in the Amazon or Foxconn cases, which received steady, headline treatment from regional and national media. Still, the fact remains that Walker's approval ratings were terrible going into the 2018 election, and he lost by a slim margin. Because there was no exit polling on the Foxconn effect, it's impossible to know how much the Foxconn deal helped or hurt him with various constituencies. But his political instincts were in line with considerable evidence: landing deals has historically garnered votes.

Timothy Bartik at the W. E. Upjohn Institute has been working on economic development issues since joining the think tank in 1989. He dug in deep on the motivations behind big economic development deals in his 2019 book *Making Sense of Incentives*. Bartik's central conclusion is that political ambition and credit is the most important driving force in the incentive game. Certainly the Foxconn case does nothing to contradict this. Bartik summarizes: "Incentives, while economically inefficient, give politicians the opportunity to pander to voters . . . incentives are the perfect pandering tool." He concludes that "politicians overuse incentives for electoral reasons." It is hard to argue with the evidence for political motivation, both from the Foxconn cautionary tale and from the accumulated research. For instance, Bartik shows that municipalities run by an elected mayor spend more on economic development than those run by professional city managers. He also shows a pattern of increased deal making in election years.

One of the problems of challenging the halo effect of inking big deals is the time frames involved. The mayor celebrating the groundbreaking for a civic-backed convention hotel is unlikely to still be in office should the property go bankrupt down the road, as happened in St. Louis and Houston. The manner in which the biggest deals of the recent past, including Foxconn and Amazon, have been challenged may represent a shift in public awareness. Or it may simply warn politicians to stay away from multibillion-dollar deals and stick to the ones that involve hundreds of millions instead. One thing is sure. The country would be better off if American politicians would take a page from their Chinese counterparts with their "state visit projects" and focus on golden shovels rather than incentives.

Dismantling the Economic Development Machine

The first deadly sin of US economic development that begs for reform is the bidding wars between states and between municipalities. Every serious examination comes to the same conclusion: it's economic development as a zero-sum game with taxpayers as losers. Yet the incentive wars continue to expand. Models exist of another way. The European Union, for example, agreed to caps on the size of incentives. Had something similar existed in the US, it might have been a saving grace for Wisconsin's citizens and kept New York from its embarrassing on-off offer to Amazon. Border bidding between the Kansas and Missouri sides of the Kansas City metropolitan area has been at least temporarily paused by a truce. Although it is theoretically possible that all the governors in the US could make a similar pact, and the prospect of regional compacts is an enticing first step, the real answer has to be a national policy.

Bidding wars over economic incentives are just one piston in the economic inequality engine, but the problem is not a complex, multifaceted one, like racial disparity in educational achievement. Instead, it has an easy fix: it can be corrected with direct action via national will and commensurate legislation. One of the reasons, though, for the lack of progress on this and many other crucial issues is the nexus of power. As the Nobel laureate Joseph Stiglitz wrote, "Politics have shaped the market, and shaped it in ways that advantage the top at the expense of the rest. . . . Our political system

seems to be captured by moneyed interests." This is supported by
research that shows definitively that in our current state, even when
there is broad public consensus on an issue, enacted policy follows
the interests of the high-income minority that donates to political
campaigns.

Another reason to put a stop to the billions of dollars of taxpayer
dollars devoted to economic development bidding is how inept the
public sector has proved itself to be in picking winners. Although
Foxconn has been our primary example, the list could go on. Let's
go down to Louisiana to look at just one more. In 2014 Louisiana,
hardly a state with overflowing coffers, put up $257 million in in-
centives and another $800 million in infrastructure costs to land a
South Africa–based Sasol ethane-cracker refinery with the promise
of 1,250 jobs, on the surface a stunning $800,000 per job. Former
governor Bobby Jindal and his secretary of economic development,
Stephen Moret, couldn't say for sure whether it was the money,
Louisiana's lax environmental protections, or the state's existing
refinery supply chain that brought Sasol. But as Moret put it, "If the
state aid played any role in landing such a big fish, it's money well
spent."

In April 2020, before the complex was fully functional, Sasol's
debt was downgraded to junk status as its share price dipped 82 percent from the beginning of the year. The company's finances were
deeply shaken by cost overruns at its Louisiana facility, the price
of which had ramped up to $13 billion from an original estimate of
about $8 billion. Sasol was looking for a partner to buy into and help
bail it out of its not-yet-completely operational facility.

It seems likely that after years of dedicated work by a host of
publicly funded Wisconsin organizations and executives, after
hundreds of millions in infrastructure investments and the seizure
of thousands of acres of productive agricultural land, along with
the coerced displacement of hundreds of homeowners, Wisconsin
will never see a single large-screen TV panel produced. Instead of
achieving the driving vision of a giant LCD fabrication plant and a
massive technology cluster to pump hundreds of millions of dollars

into the state's economy, the village of Mount Pleasant will have a mostly empty industrial park. At its center, fed by virtually empty six-lane highways, will be a smattering of Foxconn structures where a fraction of the promised workers assemble a grab bag of electronic products for a fraction of promised salaries. While no ensuing development may be the nightmare of local politicians, the prospect of Foxconn subleasing its land to environmentally unfriendly industrial operators should be the nightmare of local residents.

Changing the Incentive Infrastructure

At the heart of incentive spending is the question of whether a development would have happened without incentives. Location decisions are complex. They are often driven by factors including consumer markets, labor supply, natural resources, supply-chain development, and transportation. Proximity to executives' and other decision makers' homes and hobbies can be surprisingly decisive. All these factors compromise economic development professionals' assurances that their incentives were the reason for development. Still, they will continue to believe in their victories and make the case that their city, region, or state would be poorer indeed without their labors. As Upton Sinclair famously said, "It is difficult to get a man to understand something, when his salary depends on his not understanding it."

Of course, all things being equal, a company will be hard pressed to refuse to move a few miles from, say, Overland Park, Kansas, to Kansas City, Missouri, if given enough millions. That said, research shows that two-thirds of incentive dollars end up in the coffers of companies that would have made the same investment without the incentives. And the one-third or so of companies that are swayed are given more in tax and other benefits than their presence will ever recover. The point doesn't even pivot on whether the dollars move some investments. It's how when you broaden your lens to include the entire country these municipal or state "victories" reveal themselves as Pyrrhic.

Even without the political halo or even with a cap on the bidding wars, the deeply entrenched economic development infrastructure would continue to push deals. This is due in part to the institutional inertia of publicly funding thousands of economic development professionals whose rewards are winning development deals away from their colleagues in other locales. Stoking these heated battles are the highly compensated site and incentive consultants in the middle, many of whom are directly rewarded for escalating stakes. Equally culpable are the TIF and economic impact consultants. The TIF consultants map out often fantastical returns for a municipality, like the pie-in-the-sky numbers presented to the unsophisticated board of trustees in Sherrard, Illinois. Their accountant colleagues are guilty of misusing I/O models and blindly accepting overly optimistic client numbers to produce scientific-looking reports that always seem to justify the proposed public spending.

A well-established, well-oiled economic development machine serves the interests of a number of powerful interests. Politicians love the aura of favor that a big deal traditionally generates. Corporations are happy to have the handouts. Vendors, consultants, and contractors, often significant campaign donors, line up at the trough. Vast amounts of taxpayer money are siphoned into this narrow constituency, feeding already-profitable corporations and wealthy contractors. This damage doesn't even begin to count the opportunity costs of all this public spending as it erodes K-12 and state university education, beggars non-project-related infrastructure, and helps explain state and municipal neglect of social services, mental health services, and strained safety nets.

Changing the deeply entrenched economic development complex will not be easy. However, there is the possibility of actually finding some nonpartisan support—or more accurately, support from various segments of the partisan spectrum. Progressives will automatically bristle at corporate welfare. Well-funded libertarian and conservative think tanks have been lobbying for incentive cessation for years on the basis of interference in the free market.

But there would be no agreement on what to do with the commensurate savings. The Koch-inspired formula that powers the right-wing lobbying against economic development is in many ways cynical. Koch Industries is happy to take government largesse in the granting of mineral rights or accepting $500 million in state and local incentives to support their own refineries and businesses. And when it comes to the reallocation of economic development dollars there would be no agreement at all. For the fundamentalist conservatives the use is obvious—cut taxes on the rich, "the makers," while eliminating any sort of social services, subsidized health care, or safety nets. In the vision of Tyler Cowen, director of the Koch-sponsored Mercatus Center at George Mason University, look to the favela slums of Brazil and Mexico to get a sense of the future lifestyle of America's poor and uneducated.

On the progressive side there is a growing recognition that without aggressive intervention twenty-first-century income inequality will simply grow rampantly like an uncontrolled pandemic. Technologically driven job loss—an unstated but primary force behind the enthusiasm for the Foxconn development—will only increase over time, with particularly punishing results for the disadvantaged. Universal basic income, as popularized by Andrew Yang during his presidential campaign, is one of the more prominent options proposed.

One aspect of the problem neither conservatives or progressives have tackled is the institutions that foment incentives. On the surface the concept of a complex architecture of public servants serving private corporations should concern both progressive and conservative ideologues. How can the champions of privatization of schools and social security not back the complete privatization of corporate site selection? If Congress could take the bidding billions and company-specific tax abatements off the table, much of the incentive for spending on state and regional economic development authorities would fade. But they wouldn't just disappear, because site-selection professionals could still shop their corporate clients around, looking for noncash subsidies like free land, subsidized infrastructure, and publicly funded worker training.

State-based and regional economic development agencies have a wide mandate to support their indigenous industries. No one wants to stop the shopping of Midwestern soybeans to Asia or to cut off state-based funding for start-up companies. But the redirection of funds wasted on outbidding other states could make these agencies not only leaner and more efficient but also refocused on *meaningful* development. We have strict rules that govern the way lobbyists can spend their money on influence. We should have similar ones for economic development agencies that are tempted to spend their taxpayers' money entertaining and grooming already well-compensated consultants.

In June 2020, under Democratic governor Tony Evers, WEDC issued a road map for future development that demonstrated a distinct change in direction. Rather than encourage spending on six-lane highways leading to a chosen factory, it recommended building out the state's broadband infrastructure to provide access to all. Rather than bet the bulk of the state's economic incentive dollars on one company and one industry, it recommended providing broad support to a wide range of entrepreneurs. Instead of the frantic designing and redesigning of a specific community college curriculum to meet the shifting needs of one client as was the case in Racine County for Foxconn, it recommended increasing practical trade and retraining programs across the state. All these are admirable and sensible adjustments, but the proposal never left committee in the Republican-controlled state legislature.

The end result of the elimination of the grossest abuses of corporate welfare and the publicly funded institutions that service these handouts would not be a net loss of business development in the US but a net gain in public coffers. Take away the incentives and Tesla would still make its batteries, Amazon would continue to pursue its headquarters needs, and Foxconn would come to the same conclusion about the viability of TV manufacturing in the US. The cessation of these needless expenditures would free billions of dollars to help us attack the greatest issues of our time: income inequality, the slipping of our worldwide educational achievement, student debt, climate change, the devastating cycle of poverty.

Cronyism

In his book *Making Sense of Incentives*, Timothy Bartik discounts cronyism by examining the quid pro quo between the chief politicians and the corporate recipient and sees little in the way of direct donations from the main corporate recipient of economic development incentives to the project's elected boosters. Of course, in the Foxconn case, foreign corporations and individuals are prohibited from donating to US campaigns. To find the cronyism in the Foxconn project, you have to peel the onion a bit more to see favoritism fast at work at the vendor and contractor level.

Although transparency, open bidding, and ethical leadership are all counters to cronyism, the best long-term remedy is to reduce the temptations. Capping the amount of spending allowed in a municipal TIF district is a step some states have already taken. A nationwide cap on corporate development and relocation incentives would be another step in the right direction. Dismantling the publicly funded institutional incentives for this spending would make a huge difference over time.

Income Disparity

Looking deeply into the economic incentive process does not reveal the primary driver of income inequality in the United States. It does illustrate how deeply ingrained and broadly institutionalized just one aspect of this engine is. Thomas Piketty demonstrates in *Capital in the Twenty-First Century* how corporate rent seeking and ballooning executive compensation have been key drivers that take us from the relative equanimity of the 1970s to today's lopsided wage and wealth reality. The Foxconn project to date, with

its lavish municipal spending, has been an unfortunate demonstration of the gap between promise and reality in publicly sponsored
developments. Contractors and insiders are flourishing while the
prime justification of the project—13,000 "family-supporting jobs"
for high school–educated workers—have instead devolved into er-
ratic employment for fewer than one hundred people at a time, most
being paid between $13 and $14 dollars an hour without benefits.

The case of struggling Racine and the false hope that Foxconn
would bring back manufacturing jobs only highlights the reality
of our modern economy. Although political gain was an essential
ingredient to Wisconsin's multibillion-dollar offer to Foxconn, it
was exacerbated by the scarcity of reasonably compensated jobs for
blue-collar and low-education workers. Scarcity drives the willingness to accept the cost of skyrocketing incentives. The illusionary
prospect of reviving old-style manufacturing jobs was a primary
feeder of the auction frenzy.

The loss of good-paying blue-collar jobs has rent the fabric of
society. The first and hardest hit from Rust Belt deindustrialization
were largely African Americans who had migrated from the South
for the very jobs that were the first ones to be displaced. Although
they were subject to pernicious and often open racism, they were

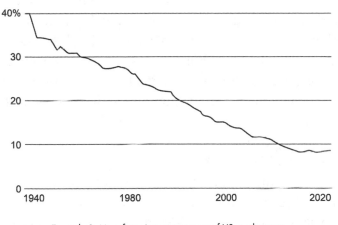

Example 2. Manufacturing as a percent of US employment
Source: Bureau of Labor Statistics

also prized employees who were paid living wages, and this made all the difference. This is what Chester Todd, whose life in Racine began in 1942, meant when he could describe Racine as a paradise for the families from the South even while lamenting that the "racism was thick." Take away the jobs, and what you have in Racine is the American present: the remaining racism with the added disaster of deeply troubled urban populations with little in the way of help, hope, or opportunity to pursue happiness.

There is plenty of good evidence that the job pie is shrinking and will continue to shrink. Careful examinations like the Oxford economist Daniel Susskind's *A World without Work* and the Dartmouth economist David Blanchflower's *Not Working: Where Have All the Good Jobs Gone?*, provide compelling cases that globalization and technological advances make it different this time. A couple of years before promising Wisconsin 13,000 jobs, Foxconn's chairman Terry Gou, a big believer in robotics in manufacturing, declared, "I think in the future young people won't do this kind of work, and won't enter the factories."

The cumulative effect of the loss of jobs and the resulting social disruptions is devastating. As the sociologist Mark Rank and business professor Michael McLaughlin have written, "An essential element of poverty is that it undermines human capabilities and potential." Poverty affects children in profound ways, especially during their critical first five years of development. In America more than 40 percent of children are raised in low-income families, marked by food and housing instability and accompanying stress, along with health-care deficits. Despite well-established research showing the importance of early childhood education, US programs reach a lower of percentage of three-year-olds than do those of twenty-two other nations; for four-year-olds it's less than twenty-seven other nations.

Education is the most commonly cited solution to inequality and the one that receives the most anecdotal support. It may indeed be the best tool we have. But it is no longer the panacea it might have been, for say, GI Bill recipients after World War II. First of all, retraining workers who have been displaced is easy to propose but hard to achieve. Second, jobs for even degreed candidates are dwindling. In today's stressed economy, more college graduates than ever are filling jobs that were once the province of high school graduates. As of 2019, college graduates between the ages of twenty-two and twenty-seven were experiencing serious underemployment. In 1990, 48 percent of these college grads were making more than an inflation-adjusted $45,000 a year; twenty years later, that was down to 38 percent. Even a world-class education can't ensure that the jobs will be there. As David Susskind puts it, "It is hard to escape the conclusion that we are heading toward a world with less work for people to do."

An additional challenge is that the US edge in providing world-class education is disappearing, if it hasn't already. Part of this is the lack of support for education at all levels. Governors like Scott Walker, Sam Brownback, and Bobby Jindal championed education cuts, particularly to land-grant universities. This in turn results in higher tuition and, when combined with cuts in financial aid, narrower access and higher student debt. The sociologists Jacob Hacker, of Yale, and Paul Pierson, of University of California, Berkeley, describe the results: "Older Americans are the most educated in the world. Younger Americans, not even close." By 2017 China was producing eight graduates in science, technology, engineering, or math for every one in the United States.

The response to this educational underachievement is often harsh and political. Wisconsin has become a leader in school vouchers, which siphon money away from public education and allocate it to private schools, many of which have narrow, religious missions and curricula that expand American ignorance of the tenets and methodologies of modern science. Walker famously championed the destruction of public unions in Wisconsin. He cynically campaigned on a self-described "divide and conquer" strategy that convinced struggling members of the working class that teachers and professors were getting more than their fair share in salary and benefits at their expense. Eight years after his union-busting legislation I spoke to teachers in the Racine area who were still looking at paychecks smaller than they'd been receiving prior to his election.

Racine County has been not only the focus of the top-down Foxconn economic development efforts but also the target of state intrusion into public school operation. The state legislature tacked on a provision in their budget bill of 2017 specifically targeting the Racine County schools with a plan that would punish, rather than help, the minority and lower-income children of Racine if the schools didn't meet certain testing benchmarks. Should the legislative mandate lead to the breakup of the county schools into separate urban and suburban district or districts, the result would be resegregation and the beggaring of the schools that serve the children of Racine. The parents of Racine would have no vote or say in this action. This prospect for Racine, to date unexecuted, is a case in point as to how reduced support for education is felt deepest in the communities least able to pay for it themselves, with property tax remaining the main source of school funding in the US.

On top of this, the Foxconn project, if realized in anything close to its original conception, would have likely led to an influx of students into the local school system without a commensurate increase in taxation. Whatever property tax boom it generated from industrial development would be tied up for thirty years to repay TIF debt. If Foxconn's employee track record in Indiana is any indication, these students could be associated with special demands on the local schools, including extensive English-as-a-second-language efforts. Worse, manufacturing employees typically do not make enough to push up demand for single-family houses—they tend to be renters and commuters, and as such, they contribute only marginally to property tax revenue. Dealing with thousands of new students without commensurate revenue was not part of the funding plan for Foxconn.

The Opportunity Cost

The billionaire Warren Buffett has spoken about his fortune—not the zeros after his net worth, but the luck of being born in America to affluence and educational opportunity and not somewhere else in poverty and ignorance. He's spoken of the fortune of having just the right set of native skills to take advantage of investing opportunities that were not available to every past generation and may not be available to future ones. This sense of modesty is not universal—many winners in our economy believe they are home-run hitters, even if they started on third base. The correlations between skills, geography, and birth can be seen in the disparity of success in modern America. Urban centers like San Francisco and New York provide flourishing opportunities to the well educated and well connected and those with the specific skill sets needed in a knowledge economy. The once-prized qualities of high school education combined with work ethic that provided broad financial stability across much of America, particularly the Upper Midwest, have become insufficient. Rural and industrial areas have struggled. Even before the COVID-19 shocks, half of zip codes in the US had fewer jobs than they did in 2007. Automation and artificial intelligence are poised to put additional pressure on working Americans. In 2019 about 3.5 million Americans worked as truck drivers, more than 3 million as cashiers—that's 7 percent of the US workforce in just these two threatened categories.

Upward mobility, once a prized American quality, has become an embarrassing fiction. Seventy-seven percent of children born to the upper quartile of American wealth earn college degrees by age twenty-four, compared to just 9 percent of those in the bottom quartile. Seventy-five years ago the GI Bill propelled an entire generation's social mobility; now, as economist Thomas Piketty summarizes, in the US "parents' income has become an almost perfect predictor of university access." That education has the potential as an economic ladder is no secret: for years for-profit universities and trade schools, including Trump University, have used this awareness to prey on vulnerable students.

Olatoye "Ola" Baiyewu has been running an apprenticeship preparatory program in Racine for more than twenty years. A Nigerian native whose father was a mid-level banker, Baiyewu first came to the US as a young tourist and quickly became fascinated with the country and its consumer-friendly culture. He eventually settled in Milwaukee and later Kenosha and then Racine, where he worked for years for the Urban League. His mainstay was creating a bridge program that could help eighteen- to twenty-four-year-olds of all ethnicities, often with troubled histories, through an intense and comprehensive curriculum to prepare them for a job in such trades as carpentry, plumbing, and pipe fitting. The program focused on soft skills like time and anger management, which Baiyewu found to be major hurdles for landing and retaining jobs.

"I remember one young Black man," he told me, "who came to me with all the baggage—gang banging and drug dealing, high school dropout, a stint in federal prison. He wanted to enroll in my program. I told him he had to go to the library, check out a movie and watch it. If he still wanted to join after doing that, he was in." The movie was *The Shawshank Redemption*, which Baiyewu considered a story on the redemptive power of education and moral rectitude. The young man joined the program and went on to have a steady career, be a homeowner, and get married. Baiyewu also assigns novels such as *Animal Farm* and *The Grapes of Wrath* as part of his program, an aspect of intellectual engagement he believes is essential in the making of good future employees.

Each year Baiyewu has graduated forty to fifty students. He works just as hard on placements as he does on education, and he has a high percentage of success, even though he admits that placing the white students is almost guaranteed while getting the trades to take on Black apprentices is a constant battle. He is called on regularly for projects like helping to build homeless shelters. "They love to use our labor," he says, but the board members of the charities they work for are not always so eager when it comes to promoting the placement of his students, especially in union-run trades that have a history of racial discrimination. He does all of this on an annual budget of $225,000, about $5,000 per student who graduates.

Instead of putting desperate low-income students into mountains of debt under what are often false promises of for-profit trade schools, First Choice Pre-Apprenticeship has been changing lives at no cost to participants while operating on a shoestring budget. For decades Baiyewu has lived on a salary less than his graduates earn today in the trades and has kept the program from collapsing from sheer will, often leaning on the steady support of S. C. Johnson and other supporters, including Dominican nuns.

Instead of being lionized for his efforts, exporting his model to other communities, or ensuring that the program is as well funded as the local economic development authority, Baiyewu has been forced to scramble every few years to find new sponsors and funding. His work started as an Urban League program and has been an independent nonprofit, an arm of a federal jobs training effort, state and city sponsored, a Goodwill Industry program, and most recently an offshoot of the Racine YMCA.

Baiyewu is the first to admit that his program isn't scalable into the thousands—there just aren't enough jobs in the trades. "We touch people one at a time and make a difference in their lives. A key is letting them know that we care about them," he told me.

This isn't to suggest that First Choice is somehow a solution to Racine's deep social problems, but it does illustrate priorities. The struggle of Baiyewu's apprentice program is a perfect example of the choices we make as a society, providing almost unlimited funding to chase chimerical corporate jobs while allowing his proven project to struggle to the point of closure, not once but every few years and over decades. This is one of the opportunity costs of how economic development dollars are allocated today.

Although some argue that the machinery of capitalism invariably creates the sorts of winners and losers we see in the US today, economic analysis suggests otherwise. Such standard actions as raising the minimum wage and supporting unionization are useful and vital steps. Political choices like these make big differences— and our failures to embrace them directly explain why the US has suffered more income inequality than other industrial nations have. Dollars from wage suppression and corporate welfare have made corporate managers, executives, and shareholders the biggest winners. As Piketty concludes, "It is hard to imagine an economy and society that can continue functioning indefinitely with such extreme divergence between social groups."

Nothing better illustrates the ingrained fix favoring the wealthy than the intensely political, highly inefficient shifting of public coffers to handpicked corporate winners via economic development deals like Wisconsin's misadventure with Foxconn. This cautionary tale spotlights a widespread and pernicious trend and a danger. An environment in which cities and states bid against each other for a shrinking number of corporate and industrial jobs simply drives the incentive cost per job into the stratosphere to the benefit of neither the country nor its aggregate workforce. It instead inflates corporate profits at the expense of taxpayers and adds additional fuel to our national trash fire of inequality.

It is nothing but a long con.

The New Contract

On April 20, 2021, the office of Governor Tony Evers announced that a new contract had been inked between Foxconn and the state of Wisconsin. The new agreement, in effect, formalized the diminution of Foxconn's industrial plans. Employment would now top out at 1,454 rather than 13,000 jobs. Instead of up to $3 billion in state support, the project would receive at most $80 million, just 2.7 percent of the original. Foxconn's capital outlay was now projected to be $672 million at best, less than 7 percent of the original project. No TV screens were going to be manufactured.

While the new contract was touted as protecting Wisconsin taxpayers from paying billions in incentives, this explanation was disingenuous. There was already no prospect of Foxconn hitting the employment and capital expenditure targets needed to obtain those incentives, and the Evers administration had made it clear that without the original contract's promise of a massive Gen 10.5 LCD panel factory, no incentives would be forthcoming. So why did the state engineer a new deal that could still pay a generous $55,000 per job? (Reformers who are lobbying for a national cap on incentives have proposed limits between $7,000 and $35,000 per job.) And why was Foxconn willing to formalize its diminished plans?

The answer was Foxconn's sunk costs and Wisconsin's long-term, hidden liabilities. Foxconn's capital investments in Wisconsin were in the hundreds of millions, plus millions more in human capital. They also now owned 1,000 acres of prime land already supplied with state-of-the-art infrastructure and virtually unlimited access to Lake Michigan water. While plans for the site were now modest, this was clearly a long-term corporate asset worth preserving. At the same time, the state, Mount Pleasant, and Racine County had become beholden to Foxconn's promises. For them, the worst-case scenario would be for Foxconn to default on its promised property tax support of Mount Pleasant and Racine County. In the original contract with the municipalities, Foxconn had guaranteed a minimum property valuation of $1.4 billion, taxes on which would be close to $30 million a year. The village and county had borrowed hundreds of millions of dollars to build the infrastructure commensurate with a $10 billion Foxconn site, and they had no alternative way to pay the interest on those loans. In addition, if Foxconn defaulted on its obligation, legislation from 2017 put 40 percent of the liability plus interest back on the state; that could amount to hundreds of millions of dollars as well. If it cost the state $55,000 per job and $80 million to keep Foxconn writing checks to Mount Pleasant and Racine County for the next twenty-five years, it would be worth it. All of which is little consolation to Joy Mueller, who can drive past her old property and see how her house could have coexisted with the new road. Or Jim and Kim Mahoney on their residential island, still waiting for the village to make a good faith offer.

In the end, the new contract only highlights the deep liabilities that can emerge from incentive deals driven by political agendas, cronyism, and ill-placed faith.

Acknowledgments

My work on *Foxconned* began with a series of stories in the online journal *Belt Magazine* under its then editor Jordan Heller. My first piece was carefully honed during a hectic period in which Jordan was relocating from the East Coast to Cleveland. This initial piece and the following two raised fundamental issues about Wisconsin's adventure with Foxconn that set the stage for much of the subsequent reporting. I'm thankful for the opportunity and guidance I received. These three pieces received a collective "Best of 2017" recognition from Longreads.com. I published additional follow-up stories for the *American Prospect* and Madison's *Capital Times* newspaper, the latter under the direction of the experienced hand of editor and publisher Paul Fanlund.

For the transition from long-form journalism to book, I credit my steadfast agent at Trident Media, Alex Slater, and the patient wisdom of my editor at the University of Chicago Press, Tim Mennel. Tim proved a perfect match for this project, quickly recognizing the nuances and import of the story and providing invaluable guidance on specifics, overall organization, and flow. He also arranged for a pair of professional reviews that proved insightful and productive. The resulting manuscript benefited immensely from the line-by-line reading of gimlet-eyed Katherine Faydash. To the rest of the staff at the Press, I thank you all for your design and production work that have made this book possible.

For an early and clearheaded reading of my first draft, I thank my University of Wisconsin economics graduate son, Josh. His suggestions are embedded throughout. My second son, Zach, was here for the early stages of my reporting and was in my heart as I continued working on it after his devastating loss in a car and pedestrian accident in 2018. Both sons and my wife, Diane, put up with my considerable ramblings on the subject as I sorted through the twists and turns of my investigations and the regular surprises in the breaking news.

The telling of this story involved a number of interesting tangents. The Wisconsin Historical Society came through by posting the eight hours of 1974 interviews with Blue Jenkins when I despaired at accessing them in the time of COVID-19. The deep resources of the University of Wisconsin library were invaluable in many ways, particularly in telling the story of Wassily Leontief. Well over a hundred individuals took the time to talk to me at length, and I'm thankful for their time and insights. Of particular note: Bob O'Brien at Supply Chain Consultants; Jenny Thorvaldson, chief economist at IMPLAN; Mark Levine from the University of Wisconsin–Milwaukee; Roy Cordato at the John Locke Institute; Timothy Bartik from the Upjohn Institute; historian Charles Postel at San Francisco State University; and Willy Shih at Harvard Business School.

Despite the continued pressure on the business of daily newspapers, reporters on the ground in Milwaukee and Racine County contributed invaluably in their "first drafts of history." The chronologies of Ricardo Torres at the *Racine Journal Times* and later the *Milwaukee Journal Sentinel*, Sean Ryan at the *Milwaukee Business Journal*, and Rick Romell at the *Milwaukee Journal Sentinel* are reflected repeatedly in this account. Providing the perspective that is often difficult on the daily beat were significant stories from Austin Carr at *Bloomberg*, Corrinne Hess at Wisconsin Public Radio, and particularly Josh Dzieza from *The Verge*. Sruthi Pinnamaneni from Gimlet Media's *Reply All* brought national attention to the local side of the story with her terrific podcast episode "Negative Mount Pleasant." Over the course of reporting on the Foxconn development and writing this book I made numerous attempts to seek responses from Foxconn executives and key figures involved with the project in Racine County. Other than referrals to Foxconn's public relations firm, none of these requests were fulfilled.

For many of the people who helped me tell this story it was far from an academic exercise, as their communities and neighborhoods and even houses were assaulted by the events. I was welcomed with small-town hospitality by my sources in Sherrard, Illinois. In my exploration of Racine history and current reality, I received an education from Gerald Karwowski, Chester Todd, and Al Gardner. In Mount Pleasant I thank Joy Mueller for taking time to tell her story and touring her soon-to-be leveled house and property. Kim and Jim Mahoney, who are the sole residents left in their once-quiet, bucolic suburban development, were consistently open to my inquiries and even presence. I'm also in debt to Kelly Gallaher, who has overcome considerable adversity, including unconscionable personal attacks, in her unyielding efforts to promote transparency and good practice in local government. Her endless curiosity and determination have been both a source of information and an inspiration.

Notes

Introduction

xi. **Diversity was pretty much limited** Encyclopedia of Dubuque, "African Americans," http://www.encyclopediadubuque.org/index.php?title=AFRICAN_AMERICANS; Isabel Wilkerson, "Seeking a Racial Mix, Dubuque Finds Tension," *New York Times*, Nov. 3, 1991.

xvi. **"plutocratic populism"** Hacker and Pierson, *Let Them Eat Tweets*, 5.

Foxconn Timeline

xix. **In response to reports** Mark Sommerhauser, "Foxconn Disputes Report That It's Changing Its Plans for New Wisconsin Campus," *Wisconsin State Journal*, May 24, 2018, https://madison.com/wsj/news/local/govt-and-politics/foxconn-disputes-report-that-its-changing-its-plans-for-new-wisconsin-campus/article_91b6aa35-a543-5ba9-ba98-9d6c2e2aa3ca.html.

xix. **Terry Gou's special assistant** Jessy Macy Wu and Karl Plume, "Exclusive: Foxconn Reconsidering Plans to Make LCD Panels at Wisconsin Plant," *Reuters*, Jan. 30, 2019, https://www.reuters.com/article/us-foxconn-wisconsin-exclusive/exclusive-foxconn-reconsidering-plans-to-make-lcd-panels-at-wisconsin-plant-idUSKCN1PO0FV.

xx. **Racine County** Karen Pierog, "Wisconsin County to Lock In Long-Term Financing for Foxconn Project," *Reuters*, Oct. 18, 2019, https://www.reuters.com/article/us-foxconn-wisconsin-bonds/wisconsin-county-to-lock-in-long-term-financing-for-foxconn-project-idUSKBN1WX2K7.

xx. **Foxconn pledges** Kelly Meyerhofer, "Foxconn Pledged $100 Million to UW-Madison: The School Has So Far Received $700,000," *Wisconsin State Journal*, Sept. 13, 2019, https://madison.com/wsj/news/local/education/university/foxconn-pledged-100-million-to-uw-madison-the-school-has-so-far-received-700-000/article_9f738a83-c280-5f33-9dbf-edad5f454cc6.html.

xx. **Foxconn puts a hold** Lauly Li, Kensaku Ihara, and Gen Nakamura, "Foxconn Terry Gou's Struggling Display Plant Seeks Fresh Capital," *Asia Nikkei*, Sept. 11, 2019, https://asia.nikkei.com/Business/Technology/Foxconn-Terry-Gou-s-struggling-display-plant-seeks-fresh-capital; Yimou Lee, "Exclusive: Foxconn Eyes Sale of $8.8 Billion China Plant amid Trade War Woes," *Reuters*, Aug. 1, 2019.

xxi. **Terry Gou pledges** Debby Wu, "Foxconn's Terry Gou Vows to Fire Up Wisconsin Plant This Year," *Bloomberg*, Jan. 21, 2020, https://www.bloomberg.com/news/articles/2020-01-22/foxconn-s-terry-gou-vows-to-fire-up-wisconsin-plant-this-year.

xxi. **Foxconn begins making** "The Latest: Foxconn Begins Making Masks in Mount Pleasant," *Minneapolis Star Tribune*, Apr. 21, 2020, https://www.startribune.com/the-latest-foxconn-begins-making-masks-in-mount-pleasant/569830272/

Chapter One

3. **"devilishly lethal."** MacLean, *Democracy in Chains*, 220.

3. **His practiced response** Erik Lorenzsonn and Shawn Johnson, "Walker: 'If I Can Take On 100K Protesters, I Can Do the Same' with Islamic Terrorists," *Wisconsin Public Radio*, Feb. 26, 2015, https://www.wpr.org/walker-if-i-can-take-100k-protesters-i-can-do-same-islamic-terrorists.

6. **"This is what eminent** Ricardo Torres, "Properties in Foxconn 'Blighted Area' Await Their Fate," *Racine (WI) Journal Times*, June 17, 2018.

Chapter Two

9. **The *Milwaukee Journal Sentinel*** Tom Daykin, Rick Romell, and Rick Barrett, "With Agreement Signed, Foxconn Era Begins in Wisconsin with

Pomp, Circumstance and a Rush for Land," *Milwaukee Journal Sentinel*, July 27, 2017.

9. **leading trade publication** Ron Starner, "Bagging the Big One, How Wisconsin Landed Foxconn," *Site Selection Magazine*, Sept. 2017.

9. **on April 20, 2016**, "Donald Trump Rally at the Indiana Fairgrounds," *Indianapolis Star*, Apr. 20, 2016, https://www.indystar.com/picture-gallery/news/2016/04/20/donald-trump-rally-at-the-indiana-state-fairgrounds/83278572/.

9. **In it, a manager** Ted Mann, "Viral Video over Plant Closure Gets Attention in GOP Debate," *Wall Street Journal*, Dec. 13, 2016, https://blogs.wsj.com/washwire/2016/02/13/viral-video-over-plant-closure-gets-attention-in-gop-debate.

10. **Trump told his audience** "Trump Speaks to Carrier Employees," *ABC News*, https://www.youtube.com/results?search_query=Trump+Speech+on+Carrier+Jobs.

10. **As a newly laid-off** Amanda Becker, "More Layoffs at Indiana Factory Trump Made Deal to Keep Open," Reuters, Jan. 11, 2018, https://www.reuters.com/article/us-usa-trump-carrier/more-layoffs-at-indiana-factory-trump-made-deal-to-keep-open-idUSKBN1F02TL.

10. **In a later interview** "2016 Person of the Year," *Time Magazine*, https://www.shortlist.com/news/donald-trump-interview-person-of-the-year-2016.

10. **Early in Trump's term** White House, "President Donald J. Trump Announces the White House Office of American Innovation (OAI)" (press release), Mar. 27, 2017, https://www.whitehouse.gov/briefings-statements/president-donald-j-trump-announces-white-house-office-american-innovation-oai/.

10. **Even before the inauguration** "SoftBank's Son Pledges $50 billion, Foxconn Eyes US Expansion as Trump Woos Asian Firms," *Reuters*, Dec. 6, 2016, https://www.reuters.com/article/us-usa-trump-softbank/softbanks-son-pledges-50-billion-foxconn-eyes-u-s-expansion-as-trump-woos-asian-firms-idUSKBN13V2LG.

11. **Over the following few years** Connie Loizos, "SoftBank Says It Has Now Invested $18.5 Billion in WeWork, 'More Than the GDP' of Bolivia, Which Has 11.5 Million People," *TechCrunch*, Oct. 24, 2019, https://techcrunch.com/2019/10/24/softbank-notes-it-has-now-invested-18-5-billion-in-wework-more-than-the-gdp-of-bolivia-which-has-11-5-million-people/.

11. **Two days after the inauguration** Todd Frankel, "How Foxconn's Broken Pledges in Pennsylvania Cast Doubt on Trump's Jobs Plan," *Washington*

Post, Mar. 3, 2017, https://www.washingtonpost.com/business/economy
/how-foxconns-broken-pledges-in-pennsylvania-cast-doubt-on-trumps
-jobs-plan/2017/03/03/0189f3de-ee3a-11e6-9973-c5efb7ccfb0d_story.html.

12.   **In early June** "Rick Rommel, a Blind Proposal, a Summons to Washington and a Jet Trip: Wisconsin's Drive to Win Foxconn," *Milwaukee Journal Sentinel*, July 29, 2017, https://www.jsonline.com/story/money/busi
ness/2017/07/28/blind-proposal-summons-washington-and-jet-trip-wis
consins-drive-win-foxconn/519202001/.

12.   **taxpayer expense: $37,500** Inquiry to WEDC sent and received Feb. 22,
2019. WEDC's statement: "WEDC paid a total of $37,500 for 5 seats,
of which Tricia Braun's [WEDC's chief operating officer] and Governor Walker's seats were paid for by WEDC, in the amount of $15,000.
The remaining $22,500 was reimbursed to WEDC by the Depart-
ment of Administration for Secretary Neitzel's seat ($7,500) and the
Department of Transportation for Governor Walker's security detail
($15,000)." Walker brought along two of his state highway patrol secu-
rity guards.

13.   **In their inscrutable words** "Johnson Controls and Foxconn Industrial
Internet Create Global Strategic Partnership" (joint press release, Johnson Controls and Foxconn), Aug. 28, 2019.

14.   **DeGroot had grown up** Heather Asiyanbi, "Mount Pleasant Trustee
Candidate: David DeGroot," *Patch*, Mar. 25, 2013, https://patch.com
/wisconsin/mountpleasant/mount-pleasant-trustee-candidate-david
-degroot.

14.   **American Majority** "About American Majority," https://app.joinhand
shake.com/employers/american-majority-9169.

14.   **The *Racine Journal Times*** Alison Bauter, "DeGroot Has Right Connections: New Mount Pleasant Board Member Is Top Finisher in Election," *Racine (WI) Journal Times*, Apr. 6, 2013, https://journaltimes.com
/news/local/degroot-has-right-connections-new-mount-pleasant-board
-member-is-top-finisher-in-election/article_abbde008-9f34-11e2-80ef
-0019bb2963f4.html.

15.   **Taj Mahal** Associated Press, "Trump Taj Mahal Casino Sold for 4 Cents
on the Dollar," *Los Angeles Times*, May 9, 2017.

15.   **At a February 2019 conference** Richard Torres, "Foxconn exec:
'We're building the airplane while we're flying,'" *Racine Journal Times*,
Feb. 21, 2019.

15.   **In a November 2020** Jay Lee, "Foxconn Is Making Masks, Ventilators,
Data Servers," *Wisconsin State Journal*, Nov. 13, 2020.

Chapter Three

16. **autonomous vehicle division** Roger Fingas, "Apple Supplier Foxconn So Far Up to 40,000 'Foxbots' in China," *Apple Insider*, May 10, 2016, https://appleinsider.com/articles/16/10/05/apple-supplier-foxconn-so-far-up-to-40000-foxbots-in-china.

17. **Perhaps because bad news** Brian Merchant, "Life and Death in Apple's Forbidden City," *The Guardian*, June 18, 2017.

17. **Workers there are required** "Foxconn in Pardubice, Czech Republic," *Electronics Watch*, Apr. 2017, https://electronicswatch.org/compliance-reports-foxconn-in-pardubice-czech-republic-june-2018_2541758.pdf, https://www.dw.com/en/foxconn-accused-of-exploiting-workers-in-europe/a-17132689.

17. **A 2018 study** Washington Center for Equitable Growth, "Consequences of Routine Work Schedule Instability for Worker Health and Wellbeing," Sept. 26, 2018, https://equitablegrowth.org/working-papers/schedule-instability-and-unpredictability/.

17. **First there was the founder** Jason Dean, "The Forbidden City of Terry Gou," *Wall Street Journal*, Aug. 11, 2007, https://www.wsj.com/articles/SB118677584137994489.

17. **This seemed of a piece** *Asian Market News and Trading Resource*, citing a May 8, 2013, story from Taiwan's *Apple Daily*, https://tw.appledaily.com/new/realtime/20130508/178689/.

17. **Gou is also known** Austin Carr, "Inside Wisconsin's Disastrous $4.5 Billion Deal with Foxconn," *Bloomberg*, Feb. 6, 2019, https://www.bloomberg.com/news/features/2019-02-06/inside-wisconsin-s-disastrous-4-5-billion-deal-with-foxconn.

17. **Foxconn had been sanctioned** Chris Smith and Jenny Chan, "Working for Two Bosses," *Human Relations* 68, no. 2 (2015): 305–26; "Foxconn admits student intern abuse at plant assembling Amazon devices," The Standard, Aug. 9, 2019.

18. **It seemed he swung a deal** Juliette Garside and Yan Thompson, "Apple's Chinese iPhone Plants Employ Forced Interns, Claim Campaigners," *The Guardian*, Apr. 1, 2012, https://www.theguardian.com/technology/2012/apr/01/apple-iphone-china-factories-forced-interns.

18. **The company was also cited** Reuters, "Apple Manufacturer Foxconn Says Underage Workers Used in China," Oct. 16, 2012, https://www.reuters.com/article/us-foxconn-teenagers/apple-manufacturer-foxconn-says-underage-workers-used-in-china-idUSBRE89F1U620121016.

18.   **In December 2016** "How China Built 'iPhone City' with Billions in Perks for Apple's Partner," *New York Times*, Dec. 29, 2016, https://www.nytimes .com/2016/12/29/technology/apple-iphone-china-foxconn.html.

18.   **Take Harrisburg, Pennsylvania** "How Foxconn's Broken Pledges in Pennsylvania Cast Doubt on Trump's Jobs," *Washington Post*, Mar. 3, 2017, https://www.washingtonpost.com/business/economy/how-foxconns -broken-pledges-in-pennsylvania-cast-doubt-on-trumps-jobs-plan/2017 /03/03/0189f3de-ee3a-11e6-9973-c5efb7ccfb0d_story.html.

18.   **But Mark Hogan** Austin Carr, "Inside Wisconsin's Disastrous $4.5 Billion Deal with Foxconn," *Bloomberg*, Feb. 6, 2019, https://www.bloom berg.com/news/features/2019-02-06/inside-wisconsin-s-disastrous -4-5-billion-deal-with-foxconn.

18.   **Alberto Moel covered** Corrinne Hess, "Owners Near Foxconn Say They Were Misled: Now Their Homes Are Gone," *Wisconsin Public Radio*, Sept. 3, 2019, https://www.wpr.org/owners-near-foxconn-say-they-were -misled-now-their-homes-are-gone.

19.   **Although Foxconn promised** "The Impact on the US Economy of Greenfield Projects by US Subsidiaries of Foreign Companies," LocationUSA .com, http://www.locationusa.com/foreignDirectInvestmentUnitedStates /jul08/greenfield-projects-United-States-subsidiaries.shtml.

19.   **An assessment of Foxconn** "Foxconn Culture," Comparably.com, https://www.comparably.com/companies/foxconn/culture.

21.   **"All employees," he told me** All quotes with Williams and Morris come from direct interviews conducted by the author in August and September 2017.

21.   **Using these interviews** Lawrence Tabak, "Wisconsin's Promise of 13,000 jobs," *Belt Magazine*, Sept. 11, 2017, https://beltmag.com/fox conns-wisconsin-promise-13000-quality-jobs-empty-one/.

Chapter Four

22.   **Melrose Park, Illinois** *Encyclopedia of Chicago*, "Melrose Park, Il.," http://www.encyclopedia.chicagohistory.org/pages/809.html.

23.   **As he recalled** WBEZ, rebroadcast as part of "A History of Manufacturing in Five Objects," Oct. 12, 2019, *Americans at Work* series, https:// www.backstoryradio.org/shows/a-history-of-manufacturing-in-5-objects/.

23.   **Zenith might have been** Andrew Zajac and Sallie L. Gaines, "Zenith to Idle Plant in Melrose Park," *Chicago Tribune*, Oct. 6, 1998, https://www .chicagotribune.com/news/ct-xpm-1998-10-06-9810080004-story.html.

23.   **None is manufactured** Katie Reilly, "The Last Major TV Factory in the US Is Shutting Down Because of President Trump's Tariffs," *Time Magazine*, Aug. 8, 2018, https://time.com/5361394/tv-factory-closing-trump-tariffs/.

25.   **Pat Choate, author** Pat Choate, "The Big Squeeze," *Washington Post*, Sept. 20, 1990, https://www.washingtonpost.com/archive/opinions/1990/09/30/japan-and-the-big-squeeze/0fb1617e-8756-4390-a776-f1619d59869a/.

27.   **As the industry insider** Kawamoto, "History," 495.

27.   **As Kawamoto summarized** Kawamoto, 496.

28.   **When Honda constructed** "Honda Breaks Ground on Indiana Plant," ReliablePlant, Mar. 2007, https://www.reliableplant.com/Read/5342/honda-officially-breaks-ground-for-auto-plant-in-indiana.

28.   **In 2016 Japan Display Inc.** "Apple Supplier Japan Display Set to Start Idle LCD Plant," *Nikkei Asia Review*, Dec. 8, 2016.

29.   **The latest Gen 10.5 plant** "BOE 10.5 Generation Line Project Shows Wisdom to Build Black Technology," Shenzhen Enrich Electronics Co., Oct. 15, 2018, http://www.customlcddisplay.com/info/boe-10-5-generation-line-project-shows-wisdom-29840701.html.

29.   **"I think the trip** Daniel Simmons, "What the Residents of Mount Pleasant Really Think about Foxconn Construction," *Milwaukee Magazine*, Aug. 27, 2018.

29.   **Foxconn bought it** Makiko Yamazaki, "Foxconn Agrees to Buy Sharp after Slashing Original Offer," *Reuters*, Mar. 29, 2016, https://www.reuters.com/article/us-sharp-hon-hai/foxconn-agrees-to-buy-sharp-after-slashing-original-offer-idUSKCN0WW03P.

30.   **Japan's losses** "China's Midea Group Buys Toshiba's Home Appliance Business," ChinaDaily.com, Mar. 31, 2016.

30.   **Today Sony** Hiroko Tabuchi, "Sony's Bread and Butter? It's Not Electronics," *New York Times*, May 27, 2013.

30.   **Hitachi sold off** "What Happened to Japan's Consumer Electronics Giants?," *BBC News*, Apr. 2, 2013.

31.   **One of the advantages** "LG Display Open Guangzhou OLED Panel Production Plant," *Korea JoongAng Journal*, Aug. 30, 2019, https://korea joongangdaily.joins.com/news/article/article.aspx?aid=3067421.

31.   **By 2020, OLED TV** Jon Porter, "Samsung Display Is Getting Out of the LCD Business," *The Verge*, Mar. 31, 2020, https://www.theverge.com/2020/3/31/21200859/samsung-display-ending-lcd-panel-production-quantum-dot-oled-south-korea-china-factories.

31.   **The projected cost** "China approves LG Display's Guangzhou OLED

TV fab," *OLED-Info*, July 11, 2018, https://www.oled-info.com/china
-approves-lg-displays-guangzhou-oled-tv-fab.

31.   **However, three major** Michael Herh, "LG Display Puts Off Volume
Production at Guangzhou Plant to Next Year," *Business Korea*, Dec. 24,
2019, http://www.businesskorea.co.kr/news/articleView.html?idxno
=39505.

31.   **In May 2019** Ross Young, "OLEDs Expected to Gain Ground as LCD
Investment Slows," *Information Display*, May 3, 2019.

32.   **Trump's tariffs added** Bob O'Brien, "Tariffs Impact US TV Imports,"
DSCC, Nov. 18. 2019, https://www.displaysupplychain.com/blog/tariffs
-impact-us-tv-imports.

32.   **In early 2019** "Entering a Survival Situation," *TV Veopar Journal*, Feb.
2020, https://www.tvj.co.in/entering-a-survival-situation/.

32.   **Reliable sources reported** "Foxconn Looking to Sell New Gen 10.5
Plant?," *Display Daily*, Aug. 8, 2019, https://www.displaydaily.com/article
/display-daily/foxconn-looking-to-sell-new-gen-10-5-plant.

32.   **The consistently boosterish** Michael Burke, "Foxconn Starts Roof Installation on 'Fab' Plant," *Racine (WI) Journal Times*, Oct. 10, 2019, https://
journaltimes.com/business/local/foxconn-starts-roof-installation-on
-fab-plant/article_0641cd3e-cc12-5f1f-b053-86e1bde91283.html.

Chapter Five

34.   **Joe Janacek** The quotations in this section are my own transcriptions from
the live stream of the meeting.

39.   **As a** *University of Chicago* Briffault, "Most Popular Tool," 67.

41.   **According to eminent** Corinne Hess, "'Blight' Declaration for Foxconn
One of the Largest Ever Seen, Say Experts," *Wisconsin Watch*, Wisconsin
Public Radio, Sept. 3, 2019, https://www.wisconsinwatch.org/2019/09
/blight-declaration-for-foxconn-one-of-the-largest-ever-seen-experts-say/.

41.   **The highway was slated** "Braun Road to Be Widened East of I-94,"
Kenosha (WI) News, July 11, 2018.

Chapter Six

48.   **The Black population** Deon Drane, "Black History in Racine," *Racine (WI)
Journal Times*, Apr. 9, 1995, https://journaltimes.com/news/local/black
-history-in-racine/article_32df8f28-6919-59ba-a31a-9ab77787cf96.html.

48.   **and by 1960** Thompson, *Continuity and Change, 1940–1965*, 338.

48.   **That diversity remains** US Census Bureau, *QuickFacts Racine, WI,* https://
        www.census.gov/quickfacts/fact/table/racinecitywisconsin,racinecounty
        wisconsin/PST045219.

50.   **In 2019 the city** Alana Watson, "Report: Milwaukee, Racine Rank as
        Worst Cities for African Americans to Live," *Wisconsin Public Radio,*
        Nov. 15, 2019, https://www.wpr.org/report-milwaukee-racine-rank-worst
        -cities-african-americans-live.

50.   **In a January 2020 report** Dolores Acevedo-Garcia, Clemens Noelke,
        and Nancy McArdle, "The Geography of Child Opportunity: Why
        Neighborhoods Matter for Equity," Brandeis University, Jan. 2020, 36,
        http://new.diversitydatakids.org/sites/default/files/file/ddk_the-geog
        raphy-of-child-opportunity_2020v2_0.pdf.

52.   **In a sort of indirect reparation** Cary Spivak, "Potawatomi Casino Com-
        plex Laying Off 1,600 Employees as COVID-19 Continues to Hurt Busi-
        ness," *Milwaukee Journal Sentinel,* July 17, 2020.

52.   **producing a pre-COVID $70,000** Cary Spivak, "Gambling Revenue
        Flat as Potawatomi Tribe Wins about $400 Million from Gamblers,"
        Milwaukee Journal Sentinel, Sept. 4, 2017; Cary Spivak, "Potawatomi
        Casino Complex Laying Off 1,600 Employees as COVID-19 Continues
        to Hurt Business," *Milwaukee Journal Sentinel,* July 17, 2020.

52.   **But by 1840** Van Vugt, *British Immigration to the United States,* 91.

54.   **While the Racine area** *Racine: Growth and Change in a Wisconsin County,*
        a compilation written by leading Wisconsin historians (Racine: Racine
        County Board of Supervisors, 1977).

54.   **The modern Case Corporation** "The Company of Jerome Case," 2017,
        http://www.racinehistory.com/jicase.html.

55.   **Labor unions were** "A Case History: Century and a Half of Highlights,"
        Racine (WI) Journal Times, Nov. 8, 1992, https://journaltimes.com/news
        /local/a-case-history-century-and-a-half-of-highlights/article_b3482ec9
        -de8c-5fb3-9064-288a47c7742b.html.

55.   **The robustness** Burckel, *Racine,* 374.

55.   **Case's headquarters** Michael Burke, "Era Ends at Historic Racine
        Factory," *Racine (WI) Journal Times,* July 27, 2002.

55.   **S. C. Johnson is still** Dun & Bradstreet, https://www.dnb.com/business
        -directory/company-profiles.s_c_johnson_son_inc.c009c81e24093adacf
        60e359feb5b62c.html.

55.   **Western Publishing** Jim Higgins, "The Golden Legacy of Racine's
        Western Publishing," *Milwaukee Journal Sentinel,* Feb. 24, 2017, https://
        www.jsonline.com/story/entertainment/books/2017/02/24/golden
        -legacy-racines-western-publishing/98171542/.

56.   **facility closed in 1993** Paul Holley, "230 Jobs Go When Local Plant
        Closes," *Racine (WI) Journal Times*, Jan. 22, 1993, https://journaltimes.com
        /news/local/jobs-go-when-local-plant-closes/article_31ad3758-8a49-5192
        -995b-820c9b5b78b7.html.

56.   **Hamilton Beach now** James Hagerty, "Once Made in China: Jobs Trickle
        Back to US Plants," *Wall Street Journal*, May 21, 2012, https://www.wsj
        .com/articles/SB10001424052702304587704577333482423070376.

56.   **"When the war was over** Oral history interview with William "Blue"
        Jenkins, Civil Rights History Project: Survey of Collections and Repos-
        itories, Wisconsin Historical Society, Library-Archives, https://www
        .loc.gov/folklife/civilrights/survey/view_repository.php?rep_id=712.

56.   **In 1946 a white man** Thompson, *History of Wisconsin*, 331–32.

57.   **Per capita income** Michael B. Sauter and Thomas C. Frohlich, "These
        US Cities Have Gone from Rich to Poor in Less Than Half a Century,"
        USA Today, Dec. 2, 2019, https://www.usatoday.com/story/money/2019
        /12/02/american-cities-that-went-from-rich-to-poor/40662605/.

58.   **The effect of this** US Census Bureau, *Janesville Wis. Quick Facts*, https://
        www.census.gov/quickfacts/janesvillecitywisconsin.

58.   **As a result** Blue Jenkins recorded interview 1974, Wisconsin Historical
        Society.

59.   **In 1944** Burckel, *Racine*, 379.

60.   **It "showed that** Burckel, 422.

60.   **The sad historical** Judt, *Ill Fares the Land*, 77.

60.   **The Black workers** Case and Deaton, "Deaths of Despair," 62.

60.   **"An abundance** Pollin, *Back to Full Employment*, 19.

60.   **By 2012** Stiglitz, *Price of Inequality*, xl–xli.

60.   **Even as the US** Stiglitz, xli.

61.   **At the start of 2020** "Report: Milwaukee, Racine Rank as Worst Cities
        for African Americans to Live," *Wisconsin Public Radio*, Nov. 15, 2019.

61.   **The United States has** Blanchflower, *Not Working*, 5–7.

61.   **The employment crisis** Towncharts.com, "Racine, Wisconsin Education
        Data," data sets based on 2013–2014 information, https://www.town
        charts.com/Wisconsin/Education/Racine-city-WI-Education-data.html.

61.   **As jobs become scarce** Kristof, *Tightrope*, 87.

61.   **by 2000 that number** Case and Deaton, "Deaths of Despair," 51.

61.   **A Brookings Institution** Kristof, *Tightrope*, 35–36.

62.   **When asked whether Foxconn** Sauter and Frohlich, "These US Cities."

62.   **As the Central Racine County** Central Racine County Health Depart-
        ment, *2011–2016 Racine County Fetal, Infant, & Child Death*, 5.

62.   **At the other end** Central Racine County Health Department, "Data and Resources," https://crchd.com/opioid-and-heroin-awareness/data.

62.   **Within the city** "Race and Ethnicity in Racine, Wisconsin," September 2018, https://statisticalatlas.com/place/Wisconsin/Racine/Race-and -Ethnicity.

62.   **Mass incarceration nationwide** Travis, Western, and Redburn, *Growth of Incarceration in the United States.*

63.   **A 2013 study** Cheryl Corley, "Wisconsin Prisons Incarcerate Most Black Men in US," *National Public Radio*, Oct. 3, 2013, https://www.npr.org /sections/codeswitch/2013/10/03/228733846/wisconsin-prisons -incarcerate-most-black-men-in-u-s.

63.   **This growth was not** Pamela Oliver, "The Wisconsin Racial Disparities Project," *Pamela Oliver* (blog), 2015, https://www.ssc.wisc.edu/~oliver /racial-disparities/.

63.   **Across the United States** Blanchflower, *Not Working*, 113.

64.   **Oddly, in the fall** Molly Dill, "At Regional Conference, Woo Works to Clear Up Misconceptions about Foxconn," *Milwaukee BizTimes*, Oct. 30, 2018, https://biztimes.com/at-regional-conference-woo-works-to-clear -up-misconceptions-about-foxconn/.

65.   **I thought about that air base** In the late 1950s work was well under way outside of present-day Kenosha on a major new US Air Force base, R. I. Bong, named after a World War II aviator. More than $168 million (over $1 billion in 2020 dollars) was invested before the Pentagon abandoned the project. For years before being turned into a state recreation area, it was nine square miles of gutted land.

65.   **When asked to explain** Eric Johnson, "Mount Pleasant Officials Pleased with Foxconn Progress," *Racine (WI) Journal Times*, Sept. 27, 2020; Daniel Simmons, "What the Residents of Mount Pleasant Really Think about Foxconn Construction," *Milwaukee Magazine*, Aug. 27, 2018, https://www.milwaukeemag.com/what-mount-pleasant-residents -think-about-foxconn-construction/.

Chapter Seven

72.   **Lois would be** Ben Botkin, "Fyre Lake Developer Uses TIF Funds to Buy Sherrard Generator," *Rock Island Argus*, May 12, 2007.

73.   **They'd been there before** Barb Ickes, "Former Clerk Convicted of Embezzlement Shows Regret, Worries about Future," *Quad-Cities Times*,

June 6, 2010, https://qctimes.com/news/local/former-clerk-convicted
-of-embezzlement-shows-regret-worries-about-future/article_31eef37c
-7109-11df-bf6f-001cc4c002e0.html.

74.   **As the** *Quad City Times* Kay Luna, "Big Plans for Fyre Lake," June 16, 2007.

78.   **In July 2011** Lee Provost, "Bradley: 1 of 2 Local Investors Says Development's Loan Default Was on Purpose," *Kankakee (IL) Daily Journal*, July 27, 2011.

79.   **At the time, Lois** Janine Anderson, "City of Burlington Officials Give Themselves a Pay Hike," *Racine (WI) Journal Times*, Feb. 6, 2005, https://journaltimes.com/news/local/city-of-burlington-s-elected-officials-give
-themselves-pay-hike/article_f8ce2d53-dba3-5ea9-90d0-8df555c1b38f
.html.

80.   **In May 2017 Raufeisen** Megan Noe, "Developer Todd Raufeisen Sentenced to Six Years in Prison," WQAD8 ABC, Sept. 14, 2017, https://wqad
.com/2017/09/14/developer-todd-raufeisen-sentenced-to-prison/.

82.   **Mount Pleasant's village president** Simmons, "What the Residents of Mount Pleasant Really Think."

Chapter Eight

83.   **In their most far-reaching** "Braun Road to Be Widened East of I-94," *Kenosha News*, July 11, 2018, https://www.kenoshanews.com/news/local
/braun-road-to-be-widened-east-of-i/article_c9519c73-fd3b-5a94-8f6c
-7e7f731288c1.html.

84.   **The site-selection business** Cezary Podkul, "Meet the Fixers Pitting States against Each Other to Win Tax Breaks for New Factories," *Wall Street Journal*, May 18, 2019.

85.   **As site selection narrows** Anderson, *Knowledge Is Power*.

85.   **In an industry podcast** "SDG President Mark Williams Reflects on Common Site Selection Mistakes in Recent Podcast Interview," StrategicDev.com, Dec. 5, 2019.

86.   **Peiffer was upbeat** FOIA-obtained WEDC email from Coleman Peiffer, Apr. 28, 2017, titled "MEETING / EVENT BRIEFING" re: "Meeting with Foxconn Chairman Terry Gou," accessed via Public Record Request 32685, obtained January 10, 2020.

88.   **The briefing paper** Coleman Peiffer, "Meeting/Event Briefing" (WEDC briefing paper), May 5, 2017.

89.   **On June 25** Jason Stein, "Michigan Offered Foxconn $3.8 Billion for

Flat-Screen Plant, Still Lost to Wisconsin's $3 Billion Bid," *Milwaukee Journal Sentinel*, Oct. 19, 2017, https://www.jsonline.com/story/news /politics/2017/10/19/michigan-offered-foxconn-3-8-b-flat-screen-plant -still-lost-wisconsins-3-b-bid/772803001/.

89.   **Hogan wrote** Mark Hogan, head of WEDC, to Scott Neitzel, head of the state's Department of Administration, email dated June 26, 2017, FOIA-obtained request.

89.   **His next statement** "Foxconn Factory Could Lead to $1 Billion Corning Plant in Wisconsin," *Milwaukee Business Journal*, July 28, 2017, https://www.tmj4.com/news/local-news/foxconn-possibly-attracting -glass-maker-corning-to-se-wisconsin.

Chapter Nine

91.   **In 1854** "The Birth of the Weather Forecast," *BBC Magazine*, Apr. 30, 2015, https://www.bbc.com/news/magazine-32483678.

91.   **The six-day forecast** Hannah Fry, "Why Weather Forecasting Keeps Getting Better," *New Yorker*, June 24, 2019.

92.   **Wassily Leontief was born** Dietzenbacher and Lahr, *Wassily Leontief*, 136.

92.   **After the Russian Revolution** Leontief, *Genia & Wassily*.

92.   **He was attracted** "Wassily Leontief, 1906–1999," Library of Economics and Liberty, https://www.econlib.org/library/Enc/bios/Leontief.html.

92.   **He was of the mind** Dietzenbacher and Lahr, *Wassily Leontief*, 11.

93.   **Leontief later characterized** Bjerkholt, "Wassily Leontief," 24.

94.   **As he wrote in 1937** Bjerkholt, 5.

95.   **His first impression** Dietzenbacher and Lahr, *Wassily Leontief*, 13–14.

95.   **In 1955, for example** Conference on Research in Income and Wealth, *Input-Output Analysis*, 9.

96.   **In an even stranger irony** Walker and Thiessen, *Unintimidated*, 53.

97.   **They were unable** Dietzenbacher and Lahr, *Wassily Leontief*, 41–43.

97.   **Another pertinent critique** Dietzenbacher and Lahr, 44.

Chapter Ten

117.   **After another moment's pause** Author interview, Apr. 30, 2020.

120.   **This might help explain** Noah Williams, "An Evaluation of the Economic Impact of the Foxconn Proposal," Center for Research on the

Wisconsin Economy, Aug. 21, 2017, https://crowe.wisc.edu/an-evalua
tion-of-the-economic-impact-of-the-foxconn-proposal/.

123.   **In a declassified 1963 report** Abraham B. Beoker, "Memorandum Rm-
3532-Pr March 1963 Input-Output and Soviet Planning: A Survey of Recent Developments," https://apps.dtic.mil/dtic/tr/fulltext/u2/401490
.pdf.

123.   **"The average life expectancy** Author interview, Aug. 2017.

123.   **"The missing ingredient** Author interview, Aug. 2017.

124.   **Their concluding view** Mitchell et al., *Economics of a Targeted Economic
Development Subsidy*, 6.

Chapter Eleven

125.   **While pinning an ideology** Donald Trump repeatedly criticized wind
power. On December 18, 2019, he told a group of conservative investors
in West Palm Beach, "You know, I know windmills very much. They're
noisy. They kill the birds. You want to see a bird graveyard? Go under
a windmill some day." Emily Stewart, "Donald Trump's Issue with
Windmills Might Not Be about Birds," *Vox.com*, Oct. 23, 2020. See also
Gervais and Morris, *Reactionary Republicans*.

127.   **The first act** "Full Historic Timeline," Export-Import Bank of the United
States, https://www.exim.gov/about/history-exim/historical-timeline
/full-historical-timeline.

127.   **According to one extreme** James Conca, "Congressional Tea Party
Vows to Destroy America's Export-Import Bank," *Forbes*, June 22, 2016,
https://www.forbes.com/sites/jamesconca/2015/06/23/congressional
-tea-party-vows-to-destroy-americas-export-import-bank/?sh=1b9309
156e22.

127.   **One of the Koch brothers–supported** Mercatus, "Ex-Im Still 'Boeing's
Bank,'" Aug. 31, 2018, https://www.mercatus.org/publications/govern
ment-spending/ex-im-still-boeings-bank.

128.   **On July 24, 2015** "Sen. Cruz: Corrupt Ex-Im Deal Proves We Have
Government of, by, and for the Lobbyists" (press release, July 14, 2015),
https://www.cruz.senate.gov/?p=press_release&id=2403.

128.   **This tirade** Amber Phillips, "Why Did Ted Cruz Savage Mitch Mc-
Connell on the Senate Floor? The Export-Import Bank," *Washington Post*,
July 24, 2015, https://www.washingtonpost.com/news/the-fix/wp/2015
/06/30/the-expiration-of-the-export-import-bank-explained-for-those
-who-dont-know-what-that-is/.

128.   **Cruz ended** Russell Burman, "Ted Cruz's Cry for Attention," *Atlantic Monthly*, July 24, 2015, https://www.theatlantic.com/politics/archive/2015/07/ted-cruz-mitch-mcconnell-donald-trump-liar-senate/399590/.

128.   **Many Democratic senators** Paul Kane, "Pity the Export-Import Bank, Caught between Warring Republican Factions," *Washington Post*, May 8, 2019, https://www.washingtonpost.com/powerpost/pity-the-export-import-bank-caught-between-warring-republican-factions/2019/05/07/4fcb2140-70ff-11e9-8be0-ca575670e91c_story.html.

128.   **But the core conservatives** Melissa Quinn, "Rubio Takes on Export-Import Bank: 'Government Should Not Be Picking Winners and Losers,'" *Daily Signal*, Apr. 23, 2015, https://www.dailysignal.com/2015/04/23/rubio-takes-on-export-import-bank-government-should-not-be-picking-winners-and-losers/.

129.   **In what has become known** "CNBC's Rick Santelli's Chicago Tea Party," YouTube video, 4:36, posted by Heritage Foundation https://www.youtube.com/watch?v=zp-Jw-5Kx8k.

130.   **The Wisconsin statehouse** "Wisconsin State Senate Elections," Ballotpedia, 2010, https://ballotpedia.org/Wisconsin_State_Assembly_elections,_2010.

130.   **The state senate** "Wisconsin State Senate Elections."

130.   **An exception was** Rosenthal and Trost, *Steep*, 34.

132.   **A study conducted** Jensen and Malesky, *Incentives to Pander*, Kindle loc. 594.

133.   **Politicians who join** Bartik, *Making Sense of Incentives*.

134.   **From his initial election** Wall, *Unethical*, 84.

134.   **As Wall served** Wall, 126–27.

134.   **From Wall's perspective** Wall, 163.

134.   **In 2012 he called** Matthew Defour, "Paul Jadin: Scott Walker 'Defamed' Economic Development Agency to Shift Blame for Failed Jobs Pledge," *Wisconsin State Journal*, Oct. 20, 2018, https://madison.com/wsj/news/local/govt-and-politics/paul-jadin-scott-walker-defamed-economic-development-agency-to-shift-blame-for-failed-jobs-pledge/article_f9e916c7-bcf4-5e14-8433-0126a4f2e520.html.

Chapter Twelve

135.   **One of the oddities** In FOIA-obtained email correspondence; for example, WEDC's Coleman Peiffer's Apr. 26, 2017, email to the governor's

office stating, "Foxconn is looking at reshoring $10 billion and 10,000 jobs."

136. **With Europe and Asia shattered** Piketty, *Capital in the Twenty-First Century*, 61.

136. **In several such** Nicholas Kristof and Sheryl WuDunn, "Who Killed the Knapp Family," *New York Times*, Jan. 9, 2020.

137. **As the economist** Case and Deaton, *Deaths of Despair*.

137. **Although some people may think** Susskind, *World without Work*, 103.

137. **The methodology** US Bureau of Labor Statistics, "Labor Force Statistics from the Current Population Survey," as of Oct. 8, 2015, https://www.bls.gov/cps/cps_htgm.htm#employed.

137. **As jobs have shifted** Blanchflower, *Not Working*, 126–27.

137. **Involuntary part-time** Blanchflower, 127.

137. **No single statistic** Ben Steverman, "The Wealth Detective Who Finds the Money of the Super Rich," *Bloomberg News*, May 23, 2019, https://www.bloomberg.com/news/features/2019-05-23/the-wealth-detective-who-finds-the-hidden-money-of-the-super-rich.

138. **In 2005 there were** Steve Hargreaves, "How an Oil Boom Brought Diversity to North Dakota," *CNN Business*, Feb. 2, 2015.

138. **Piketty and others** Piketty, *Capital in the Twenty-First Century*, 265.

139. **In Donald Trump's 2019** "AP Fact Check: Trump Plays on Immigration Myths," *PBS News Hour*, Feb. 8, 2019, https://www.pbs.org/newshour/politics/ap-fact-check-trump-plays-on-immigration-myths.

139. **This wasn't a new theme** "Donald Trump in Phoenix: Mexicans Are 'Taking Our Jobs' and 'Killing Us,'" *Slate*, July 12, 2015, https://slate.com/news-and-politics/2015/07/donald-trump-in-phoenix-mexicans-are-taking-our-jobs-and-killing-us.html.

139. **"They're taking** "Nothing Donald Trump Says on Immigration Holds Up," *Time Magazine*, June 29, 2019, https://time.com/4386240/donald-trump-immigration-arguments/, accessed Mar. 19, 20.

140. **Actually, immigrant labor** Frey, *Technology Trap*, 280.

140. **In 2017 the New York Times** Farah Stockman, "Becoming a Steelworker Liberated Her: Then Her Job Moved to Mexico," *New York Times*, Oct. 13, 2017, https://www.nytimes.com/2017/10/14/us/union-jobs-mexico-rexnord.html.

141. **As the English-American historian** Judt, *Ill Fares the Land*, 176.

141. **In response, Foxconn** Harrison Jacobs, "Inside 'iPhone City,' the Massive Chinese Factory Town Where Half of the World's iPhones Are Produced," *Business Insider*, May 8, 2018, https://www.businessinsider.com.au/apple-iphone-factory-foxconn-china-photos-tour-2018-5.

141.   **We've already seen** Ross, *Industries of the Future*, 37.

141.   **Early in the project** Milwaukee 7 report circulated May 18, 2017, by WEDC chairman Mark Hogan, Public Record Request 32685, obtained January 10, 2020.

142.   **Even with the ensuing** Gwynn Guilford, "The Epic Mistake about Manufacturing That's Cost Americans Millions of Jobs," *Quartz*, May 3, 2018, https://qz.com/1269172/the-epic-mistake-about-manufacturing-thats-cost-americans-millions-of-jobs/.

142.   **The Massachusetts Institute of Technology** Claire Cane Miller, "The Long-Term Jobs Killer Is Not China: It's Automation," *New York Times*, Dec. 21, 2016, https://www.nytimes.com/2016/12/21/upshot/the-long-term-jobs-killer-is-not-china-its-automation.html.

142.   **In July 2017** *Bloomberg* Thomas Biesheuvel, "How Just 14 People Make 500,000 Tons of Steel a Year in Austria," *Bloomberg Businessweek*, June 21, 2017, https://www.bloomberg.com/news/articles/2017-06-21/how-just-14-people-make-500-000-tons-of-steel-a-year-in-austria.

142.   **In the United States** Miller, "Long-Term Jobs Killer."

142.   **The economist James K. Galbraith** Galbraith, *The End of Normal*, 142.

143.   **In 2009 when GM** Goldstein, *Janesville*, 118.

144.   **He had even gone** "Gov. Walker Fails to Denounce Climate Change Gag Order on State Employees," *One Wisconsin Now*, Apr. 17, 2015, https://onewisconsinnow.org/press/gov-walker-fails-to-denounce-climate-change-gag-order-on-state-employees/.

144.   **Robin Vos, the leader** Frederica Freyberg, "Vos, Hintz Weigh In on Foxconn and Other Fall Legislation," *Here and Now*, Nov. 17, 2017.

144.   **When confronted** Emily Badger, "Are Rural Voters the 'Real' Voters? Wisconsin Republicans Seem to Think So," *New York Times*, Dec. 6, 2018, https://www.nytimes.com/2018/12/06/upshot/wisconsin-republicans-rural-urban-voters.html.

145.   **Scott Walker expressed** "Scott Walker Admits It: Former Wisconsin Governor Argues Votes in Metropolitan Areas Shouldn't Count as Much as Votes in Rural Areas," *Media Matters*, July 18, 2019.

145.   **Among other things** James Rowen, "The Foxconn Road to Ruin," *Urban Milwaukee*, Mar. 9, 2020, https://urbanmilwaukee.com/2020/03/09/op-ed-the-foxconn-road-to-ruin.

145.   **Vos, a master of the superior, smug grin** "Local Perspective—Assembly Speaker Ron Vos," YouTube video, 29:51, posted by League of Wisconsin Municipalities, Aug. 26, 2019, https://www.youtube.com/watch?v=AF47aks1EdI&t=74s.

147.   **In 2020 Foxconn assemblers** "On the Border: Foxconn in Mexico,"
        OpenDemocracy, Jan. 16, 2015, https://www.opendemocracy.net/en
        /on-border-foxconn-in-mexico/.

147.   **"In terms of TV** Jess Macy Yu, "Exclusive: Foxconn Reconsidering
        Plans to Make LCD Panels at Wisconsin Plant," *Reuters*, Jan. 30, 2019,
        https://uk.reuters.com/article/us-foxconn-wisconsin-exclusive/exclusive
        -foxconn-reconsidering-plans-to-make-lcd-panels-at-wisconsin-plant
        -idUKKCN1PO0FV.

148.   **As of early 2020** Lauren Zumbak, "Foxconn's Wisconsin Factory Isn't
        What It Initially Promised: Can It Still Turn Mount Pleasant into a High-
        Tech Hub?," *Chicago Tribune*, Feb. 28, 2020, https://www.chicagotribune
        .com/business/ct-biz-foxconn-wisconsin-changing-plans-20200228
        -hn6wzt4fyzenpdeznicyw642qu-story.html.

148.   **This claim belies** Statista, "Average Construction Costs of Industrial
        Warehouses in the United States in 2019, by Select City," https://www
        .statista.com/statistics/830417/construction-costs-of-industrial-ware
        houses-in-us-cities/.

148.   **Bartik estimated** Melanie Conklin, "Will Taxpayers Give Foxconn
        $172,000–$290,000 per Job?," *Wisconsin Examiner*, Aug. 5, 2019, https://
        wisconsinexaminer.com/2019/08/05/will-taxpayers-give-foxconn
        -172000-290000-per-job/; Bartik, "Costs and Benefits of a Revised
        Foxconn Project."

148.   **As the University of Georgia** Jeffrey Dorfman, "Government Incen-
        tives to Attract Jobs Are Terrible Deals for Taxpayers, *Forbes*, Sept. 6,
        2017, https://www.forbes.com/sites/jeffreydorfman/2017/09/06/govern
        ment-incentives-to-attract-jobs-are-terrible-deals-for-taxpayers/#728
        debf66eff.

Chapter Thirteen

151.   **You don't have to go** "Solutions for Avoiding Intercultural Barriers at
        the Negotiation Table," Program on Negotiation Staff, Harvard Law
        School Program on Negotiation, *Daily Blog*, July 23, 2020, https://www
        .pon.harvard.edu/daily/business-negotiations/solutions-for-avoid
        ing-intercultural-barriers/.

151.   **Deb Weidenhamer** John Grossman, "What Does It Take to Do Business
        in China?," *New York Times*, Sept. 4, 2013, https://boss.blogs.nytimes
        .com/2013/09/04/what-does-it-take-to-do-business-in-china/.

152.   **Mark Hogan** Austin Carr, "Inside Wisconsin's Disastrous $4.5 Billion Deal with Foxconn," *Bloomberg*, Feb. 6, 2019.

152.   **As the Stanford professor** Paul Milgrom, "Auctions and Bidding, a Primer," *Journal of Economic Perspectives* (Summer 1989).

153.   **Through 2020 the region** Joe Taschler, "Sales Take Will Go Away on March 31 after 23 Years," *Milwaukee Journal Sentinel*, Mar. 10, 2020, https://www.jsonline.com/story/news/2020/03/10/miller-park-board -end-sales-tax-helped-fund-brewers-stadium/5002966002/.

154.   **Milwaukee's NBA franchise** Nick Williams, "Forbes: Milwaukee Bucks Now Worth $1.58 Billion, Move Up the Ranks," *Milwaukee Business Journal*, Feb. 12, 2020.

154.   **Not coincidentally** Jennifer Bratburd, "Walker's Cuts to UW Were Devastating," *Wisconsin State Journal*, June 23, 2018, https://madison .com/wsj/opinion/letters/scott-walker-s-cuts-to-uw-were-devastating —/article_edd16f5f-4403-5394-a9a7-200a67a36ac8.html; "Wisconsin Governor Signs Bill to Fund New Milwaukee Bucks Arena," Associated Press, Aug. 12, 2015.

154.   **Republican governors** MacLean, *Democracy in Chains*, xvi.

154.   **The beneficiary** "#945 James Dinan," Forbes, January 30, 2021, https:// www.forbes.com/profile/james-dinan/#21918d9736d1.

154.   **"If there's a single** Ross, *Industries of the Future*, 186.

154.   **Netscape founder** Marc Andreessen, "What Will It Take to Create the Next Great Silicon Valleys," Andreessen Horowitz, https://a16z.com /2014/06/20/what-it-will-take-to-create-the-next-great-silicon-valleys -plural/.

155.   **Carnegie Mellon University** Vivek Wadhwa, "Industry Clusters: The Modern-Day Snake Oil," *Washington Post*, July 14, 2011.

155.   **The economists Timothy Bresnahan** Bresnahan, Gambardella, and Saxenian, "Old Economy Inputs for New Economy Outcomes," 835–60.

Chapter Fourteen

158.   **In 2019 the Environmental Integrity Project** "Thin Green Line," Environmental Integrity Project, Dec. 9, 2019, https://environmental integrity.org/wp-content/uploads/2019/12/The-Thin-Green-Line -report-12.5.19.pdf.

158.   **An EPA scientist** "Trump EPA Backs Away from Smog Breaks for Fox-conn, Indiana Steel Mills," *Chicago Tribune*, May 28, 2019.

159.   **By the end of the year** "The EPA's Stunning Gift to Polluters in Chicago and across the Midwest," *Chicago Sun Times*, Nov. 22, 2019, https://chicago.suntimes.com/2019/11/22/20970669/epa-environmental-protection-agency-bga-brett-chase-veolia-sauget-pollution-midwest-scott-pruitt.

160.   **"Once they begin** Foxconn did not respond to requests to discuss the project's potential pollution issues or their environmental record in China. Over the course of reporting this story and writing this book, phone calls to Foxconn were deferred to their public relation agency and emails remained unanswered.

160.   **Early estimates** "Water Conservation," Jan. 30, 2021, City of Racine website, https://www.cityofracine.org/Water/WaterConservation/.

160.   **The heavy metals expert** PBS Wisconsin, *Here & Now* interview, Aug. 11, 2017, https://pbswisconsin.org/watch/here-and-now/foxconn-manufacturing-environment-LCD-heavy-metals/.

161.   **In 2013** Rik Myslewski, "Chinese Apple Suppliers Face Toxic Heavy Metal Water Pollution Charges," *The Register*, Aug. 5, 2013, https://www.theregister.com/2013/08/05/chinese_apple_suppliers_investigated_for_water_pollution.

161.   **Adriaens has also** Ivan Moreno, "What Are the Environmental Concerns Surrounding the Wisconsin Foxconn Plant," *Chicago Tribune*, Aug. 26, 2017, https://www.chicagotribune.com/business/ct-foxconn-wisconsin-plant-environmental-issues-20170826-story.html.

162.   **Documents that Foxconn filed** "Foxconn Plant Would Add to Air Pollution in Wisconsin," *Wisconsin Public Radio*, Mar. 2, 2018, https://www.wpr.org/foxconn-plant-would-add-air-pollution-wisconsin.

163.   **As summarized by** Carolyn Gibson, "Water Pollution in China Is the Country's Worst Environmental Issue," Borgen Project, Mar. 10, 2018, https://borgenproject.org/water-pollution-in-china/.

163.   **By granting waivers** The Foxconn site was designated through the Foxconn legislation of 2017 as an "Electronics and Information Technology Manufacturing Zone." No limiting specifications were added, leaving the door open to a wide variety of industrial applications, such as the plastics manufacturing and molding operations that would be needed to produce consumer TVs. Hence the broad smokestack pollution waivers granted by Trump's EPA.

164.   **a reliable Republican donor** Wisconsin Democracy Campaign, https://www.wisdc.org/index.php?option=com_wdcfinancedatabase&view=searchadvanced&active_search=1&ic_name=heide%2C+charles.

164.   **A few months** Lee Bergquist, "Foxconn Will Not Need a Permit from

Army Corps of Engineers for Impact to Wisconsin Wetlands," *Milwaukee Journal Sentinel*, Jan. 3, 2018.

165. **When Walker was campaigning** "Most GOP Gubernatorial Candidates Are Climate Science Deniers, Like Their House and Senate Counterparts," *ThinkProgress*, Oct. 23, 2010, https://archive.thinkprogress.org/most-gop-gubernatorial-candidates-are-climate-science-deniers-like-their-house-and-senate-counterpar-d618d1532e3/.

165. **Walker's views on science** "Every Politician Should Tell Us What They Think about Evolution and Climate Change," *Washington Post*, Feb. 13, 2015.

165. **Late in 2018** "#132 Negative Mount Pleasant," *Reply All* (Gimlet Media podcast), Dec. 6, 2018, https://gimletmedia.com/shows/reply-all/wbhjwd.

165. **DeGroot hesitated** "#132 Negative Mount Pleasant."

Chapter Fifteen

166. **That Facebook page** The page is available at https://www.facebook.com/abettermtpleasant.

167. **Where was the [*Journal Times*'s] editorial board** An exaggeration, having been actually handwritten on a sheet of the governor's letterhead.

169. **He came up with** Kelly Gallaher's formal complaint to the Village of Mount Pleasant, May 13, 2018, https://www.scribd.com/document/412281708/PFC-Complaint-Cover-Letter-1.

171. **For whatever reason** All quotes from this meeting were transcribed from the Village's audio archive of meetings available at https://www.mtpleasantwi.gov.

171. **What followed** Mount Pleasant audio archives, https://soundcloud.com/mtpleasantwi/vb-august-28-2018.

173. **Dave DeGroot told** Adam Rogan, "Mount Pleasant OKs Small Raises for Village Board, to Take Effect after Next Elections," *Racine (WI) Journal Times*, Aug. 14, 2019, https://journaltimes.com/news/local/mount-pleasant-oks-small-raises-for-village-board-to-take-effect-after-next-elections/article_0b3aecd2-c198-5c34-837b-feb3d7af7b5d.html.

Chapter Sixteen

175. **Richard M. Daley** Briffault, "Most Popular Tool," 55–56.

176. **To seal the deal** Marc Eisen, "Epic Systems: Epic Decision," *Isthmus*,

June 22, 2008, https://isthmus.com/archive/from-the-archives/epic-sys
tems-epic-decision/.

177.   **The TIF district was destined** Logan Wroge, "Verona Approves Epic
Systems TIF Closure; Windfall Awaits," *Wisconsin State Journal*, May 10,
2016, https://madison.com/wsj/news/local/govt-and-politics/verona
-approves-epic-systems-tif-closure-windfall-awaits/article_97f357cc
-e281-533f-b621-e25503be2f2a.html.

177.   **In 2006** Eisen, "Epic Systems."

177.   **By 2017 the showplace** "Epic Systems Pauses HQ Construction after
15 Years of Constant Growth," *Xconomy.com*, July 20, 2018, https://xcon
omy.com/wisconsin/2018/07/20/epic-systems-pauses-hq-construction
-after-15-years-of-constant-growth/.

177.   **Once the TIF was closed** Wroge, "Verona Approves Epic Systems TIF
Closure."

178.   **Property tax income** Barry Adams, "An Explosion of Growth in Verona
and It's Not Just at Epic Systems Corp.," *Wisconsin State Journal*, May 22,
2017, https://madison.com/wsj/news/local/an-explosion-of-growth-in
-verona-and-it-s-not/article_96d4ab82-41b6-53a8-9e5d-ce0bed54a9b5
.html.

179.   **This aversion** For a full accounting, see Dave Umhoefer, "Solving the
'Mystery' of Scott Walker's College Years and Entry into Politics,"
PolitiFact, Dec. 18, 2013.

180.   **In 2013** BizTimes staff, "Land for Amazon.com Distribution Center Sold
for $17.5 Million," *BizTimes*, Nov. 6, 2013, https://biztimes.com/land
-for-amazon-com-distribution-center-sold-for-17-5-million/.

181.   **Harvard won** Alejandro Cancino, "Illinois Is Poised to Dangle Business
Incentives to Big Companies—But Is It Worth It?," *Crain's Chicago Business*, Oct. 6, 2017.

182.   **In 2018 the city** City of Racine Finance and Personnel Committee Meeting Minutes, Oct. 8, 2018.

184.   **Because Foxconn** Mt. Pleasant Water Agreement, Nov. 2018, https://
www.cityofracine.org/uploadedFiles/_MainSiteContent/Departments
/Water/_Documents/Mt.%20Pleasant%20Water%20Agreement%20
November%202018.pdf.

184.   **When asked** Sean Ryan, "Foxconn Current Projects Valued at $522M
by Local Governments," *Milwaukee Business Journal*, Jan. 17, 2020.

184.   **Illinois passed TIF** The Tax Incremental Financing Law, Section 66.46
An Evaluation by the Wisconsin Legislative Audit Bureau, 1981, I-1.

184.   **Forty-three years** Paris Schutz, "In Chicago, TIF Revenues Soaring,"
WTTW News, July 31, 2019, https://news.wttw.com/2019/07/31/chicago
-tif-revenues-soaring.

184. **One-fourth of Chicago's** "How the City of Chicago Uses Tax Increment Financing Surplus," Civic Federation, May 17, 2019, https://
www.civicfed.org/civic-federation/blog/how-city-chicago-uses-tax
-increment-financing-surplus.

185. **these districts claim** Heather Cherone, "TIFs Claim 35% of City's
Property Tax Revenue," *Daily Line*, Aug. 1, 2019, https://thedailyline
.net/chicago/08/01/2019/tifs-claim-35-of-city-property-tax-revenues
-report/.

185. **Karen Yarbrough** Paris Schutz, "In Chicago, TIF Revenues Soaring,"
WTTW News, July 31, 2019.

185. **The longtime TIF critic** Ben Joravsky, "Chicago's TIF Scam Might Be
Even More Crooked Than We Thought," *Chicago Reader*, July 25, 2017,
https://www.chicagoreader.com/chicago/tif-investigation-navy
-pier-audit-crains-bga-david-orr/Content?oid=28317757.

185. **For instance, the** *Reader* "Exposed, Wealthy Recipients of TIF Funds,"
NBC Chicago, Dec. 11, 2009.

185. **One of the poorest wards** Mick Dumke and Ben Joravsky, "The Shadow
Budget: Who Wins in Daley's TIF Game," *Chicago Reader*, May 20, 2010.

185. **For instance, in El Paso** US PIRG, "Tax Increment Financing," US PIRG
Education Fund, October 11, 2011.

185. **A parcel of open land** "Development around Cabela's Gradually Bringing Returns for Gonzales," *El Paso (TX) Advocate*, May 8, 2017.

185. **The bondholder's payback** Adopted budget of El Paso, Texas, 2020,
114, https://www.elpasotexas.gov/~/media/files/coep/office%20of%20
management%20and%20budget/fy20%20budget/fy%202020%20
adopted%20budget%20book%20-%20updated.pdf.

186. **In a study from 2000** Dye and Merriman, "TIF Districts Hinder Growth."

186. **In a 2018 follow-up** Lincoln Institute of Land Policy, "Improving Tax
Increment Financing (TIF) for Economic Development," 2017, https://
taxpayersci.org/wp-content/uploads/TIF_Lincoln-Institute_2018.pdf.

186. **He wrote that successful** Dinces, *Bulls Markets*, 205.

186. **New Hampshire** "Tax Increment Financing," New Hampshire Office of
Energy and Planning, Nov. 2015, https://www.nh.gov/osi/planning/re
sources/documents/tax-increment-financing.pdf.

186. **Maine, to 2 percent** Portland, Maine, "Tax Increment Financing Report,"
Aug. 2018, https://www.portlandmaine.gov/DocumentCenter/View/26069
/FYE2018-Annual-TIF-Report-to-City-Council---Prepared-8-2018.

187. **In 2019 Wisconsin's Governor Evers** Wisconsin Policy Forum, "Ren-
ovating TIF," *Wisconsin Taxpayer* 87, no. 5, May 2019.

187. **In 2016 additional legislation** AB 2492 (Alejo): Cleanup for CRIA Implementation (AB 2) As Introduced in Assembly, Feb. 19, 2016, https://

caled.org/wp-content/uploads/2014/12/AB-2492-CRIA-Cleanup-Fact
-Sheet-Final.pdf.

187.   **For instance, in Portland** Benjamin Schneider, "CityLab University:
        Tax Increment Financing," *Bloomberg CityLab*, Oct. 24, 2019, https://
        www.bloomberg.com/news/articles/2019-10-24/the-lowdown-on-tif
        -the-developer-s-friend.

190.   **The case started** Liang-rong Chen, Elaine Huang "On Microsoft's At-
        tack against Hon Hai (Foxconn)," *Commonwealth Magazine*, Mar. 20,
        2019, https://medium.com/commonwealth-magazine/on-microsofts
        -attack-against-hon-hai-foxconn-880c2a251998.

190.   **A lawyer for JST** Ricardo Torres, "Foxconn's Legal Issues," *Racine (WI)
        Journal Times*, Apr. 21, 2019, https://journaltimes.com/news/local/fox
        conns-legal-issues-two-lawsuits-could-shed-light-on-how-the-business
        -operates/article_f4745f56-4be6-5469-a1b5-7e8b3dbdd8a2.html.

190.   **In July 2020** *JST Corp. v. Foxconn Interconnect Technology, Ltd.*, No. 19-
        2465 (7th Cir. 2020), Justia US Law, https://law.justia.com/cases/federal
        /appellate-courts/ca7/19-2465/19-2465-2020-07-13.html.

190.   **The behavioral economist** Kahneman, *Thinking, Fast and Slow*.

190.   **Among his findings** Kahneman, 149, 250.

Chapter Seventeen

192.   **Under Scott Walker's** "Candidate Evers Calls Wisconsin's Roads 2nd
        Worst in the US: Are They?," *The Observatory* (UW-Madison School of
        Journalism), May 7, 2019, https://observatory.journalism.wisc.edu/2018
        /09/28/candidate-evers-calls-wisconsins-roads-2nd-worst-in-the-u-s
        -are-they/.

192.   **In 2018 the University of Wisconsin–Stevens Point** Karen Herzog,
        "UW–Stevens Point Rolls Out Transformation That Would Cut 6 Liberal
        Arts Degrees, Focus on Careers," *Milwaukee Journal Sentinel*, Nov. 12,
        2018, https://www.jsonline.com/story/news/education/2018/11/12/uw
        -stevens-point-transformation-trims-humanities-focuses-careers/1976
        108002/.

192.   **Between 2012 and 2019** "Years after Historic Cuts, Wisconsin Still Hasn't
        Fully Restored State Aid for Public Schools," Wisconsin Budget Project,
        July 2, 2018, http://www.wisconsinbudgetproject.org/years-after-histo
        ric-cuts-wisconsin-still-hasnt-fully-restored-state-aid-for-public-schools.

193.   **As Michael Lewis** Lewis, *Fifth Risk*.

194.   **In 2016 the combined** Norton Francis, "What Do State Economic Agen-

cies Do?," *Urban Institute*, July 2016, https://www.urban.org/sites/default
/files/publication/83141/2000880-What-Do-State-Economic-Develop
ment-Agencies-Do.pdf.

194.   **In a state** Allgov California, http://www.allgov.com/usa/ca/departments
/office-of-the-governor/office_of_business_and_economic_development?
agencyid=7452.

194.   **The City of San Diego** City of San Diego website, https://www.sandiego
.gov/sites/default/files/fy20ab_v2econdev.pdf.

195.   **For instance, in 2011** "Understanding JobsOhio Funding," JobsOhio
.com, https://www.jobsohio.com/about-jobsohio/about-us/understand
ing-jobsohios-funding/.

196.   **WEDC wrote a check** Matt DeFour, "$700,000 WEDC Loan to Avia-
tion Company Unpaid," *Wisconsin State Journal*, June 7, 2015, https://
madison.com/wsj/news/local/govt-and-politics/wedc-loan-to-aviation
-company-unpaid/article_08cd4cfc-ec3d-58b5-9e71-b0e9f248868d
.html.

196.   **When Kestrel went bankrupt** Beth Brogan and Whit Richardson,
"Brunswick's Kestrel Aircraft Struggling to Pay Workers, Rent," *Bangor
(ME) Daily News*, Sept. 25, 2013, https://bangordailynews.com/2013/09/25
/news/brunswicks-kestrel-aircraft-struggling-to-pay-workers-rent/.

196.   **The Kestrel fiasco** Danielle Kaeding, "Little Hope Remains for Wisconsin Officials Looking to Recover Funds from Failed Aircraft Deal,"
Wisconsin Public Radio, Aug. 5, 2019, https://www.wpr.org/little
-hope-remains-wisconsin-officials-looking-recover-funds-failed-aircraft
-deal.

196.   **"A 2013 audit** Jessie Opien, "Critics Question Proposed WEDC, WHEDA
Merger in Scott Walker's Budget," *Capital Times*, Mar. 3, 2015, https://
madison.com/ct/news/local/govt-and-politics/election-matters/critics
-question-proposed-wedc-wheda-merger-in-scott-walkers-budget/arti
cle_ad437bf3-6bec-51fc-a807-de023b46cc64.html.

197.   **In 2017, 238 cities** Alison Griswold, "A Nearly Complete List of the 238
Places That Bid for Amazon's Headquarters," *Quartz*, Nov. 4, 2017,
https://qz.com/1119945/a-nearly-complete-list-of-the-238-places-that
-bid-for-amazons-next-headquarters.

199.   **Foxconn's thirty-year** Mount Pleasant website, Ehlers Inc. report, "October 4, 2017 Project Plan for the Creation of Tax Incremental District
No. 5," Ehlers, https://www.mtpleasantwi.gov/DocumentCenter/View
/1239/TID-5-Project-Plan-PDF.

201.   **The largest single** Ricardo Torres, "Local Foxconn Project Estimates
Increase by $150 Million," *Racine (WI) Journal Times*, Jan. 20, 2019,

https://journaltimes.com/local-foxconn-project-estimates-increase-by
-150-million/article_35fbbbf0-011f-5c17-9ea8-6e3a041ae6eb.html.

203.   **Literature has shown** Sumedha Bajar, "The Impact of Infrastructure
        Provisioning on Inequality," National Institute of Advanced Studies,
        Indian Institute of Science Campus, Bangalore, India, July 2018, https://
        www.un.org/development/desa/dspd/wp-content/uploads/sites/22
        /2018/07/1-2.pdf.

204.   **As if speaking directly** Andrew Warner, "Public Investment as an En-
        gine of Growth," IMF eLibrary, August 2014, https://www.elibrary.imf
        .org/view/IMF001/21561-9781498378277/21561-9781498378277/21561
        -9781498378277_A001.xml.

205.   **As Minxin Pei** "Can China Save Itself from Crony Capitalism?," Asia-
        Global Online, Aug. 23, 2018, https://www.asiaglobalonline.hku.hk
        /china-crony-capitalism-corruption-inequality.

205.   **Gilbane had given** "Foxconn Deal Proving Lucrative . . . for Donors
        to Gov. Scott Walker's Campaign," One Wisconsin Now, May 7, 2018,
        https://onewisconsinnow.org/press/foxconn-deal-proving-lucrative-for
        -donors-to-gov-scott-walkers-campaign/.

205.   **In 2007 the economists** Keefer and Knack, "Boondoggles," 566–72.

Chapter Eighteen

207.   **In fact, the Foxconn deal** Jason Stein and Bill Glauber, "Marquette Law
        School Poll: Wisconsin Voters Think State Overpaid on Foxconn Deal,"
        Milwaukee Journal Sentinel, Mar. 5, 2018.

208.   **The *Milwaukee Business Journal*** Sean Ryan, "Foxconn Plans Another
        Innovation Center in Wisconsin," *Milwaukee Business Journal*, July 16,
        2018.

209.   **Reporters who visited** Josh Dzieza and Nilay Patel, "Foxconn's Build-
        ings in Wisconsin are Still Empty, One Year Later," *The Verge*, Apr. 12,
        2017; Jonathan Sadowski, "Foxconn's Promise for 'Innovation Sites'
        Going Nowhere," *Up North News*, May 13, 2020.

211.   **Still, the** Michael Burke, "Foxconn Begins Roof Installation on 'Fab'
        Building Plant," *Racine (WI) Journal Times*, Oct. 10, 2019.

211.   **The nonpartisan Wisconsin Fiscal Bureau** Matthew DeFour, "Fiscal
        Bureau: Foxconn Roads Could Draw $134 Million from Other State
        Highway Projects," *Wisconsin State Journal*, Dec. 15, 2017, https://madi
        son.com/wsj/news/local/govt-and-politics/fiscal-bureau-foxconn-roads

-could-draw-134-million-from-other-state-highway-projects/article_f7a8 a608-c245-5dce-acf3-7f83a19e615e.html.

212. **Not only were workers** Josh Dzieza, "The 8th Wonder of the World," *The Verge*, Oct. 19, 2020.

212. **One senior Foxconn** Dzieza.

213. **One described** Dzieza.

214. **The search** "Foxconn Announces Training Program for Students," *Daily Reporter*, Oct. 4, 2019, https://dailyreporter.com/2019/10/04/fox conn-announces-training-program-for-students/.

214. **In September 2020** "Foxconn Announces Training Program for Students."

Chapter Nineteen

218. **He notes with regret** Wilson, *When Work Disappears*, 140.

219. **For instance, Bartik** Bartik, *Making Sense of Incentives*, Kindle locs. 407 and 645.

220. **As the Nobel laureate** Stiglitz, *Price of Inequality*, l, xli.

221. **This is supported** Hacker and Pierson, *Winner-Take-All Politics*, 158.

221. **In April 2020** Andrew Marc Noel, Loni Prinsloo, and Paul Burkhardt, "Sasol Starts Stake Sale in $13 Billion US Chemical Plant," *Bloomberg*, Apr. 21, 2020, https://www.bloomberg.com/news/articles/2020-04-21 /sasol-kicks-off-sale-of-stake-in-13-billion-u-s-chemical-plant.

222. **Proximity to executives'** Garreau, *Edge City*.

222. **That said, research** Bartik, *Making Sense of Incentives*, Kindle loc. 514.

224. **Koch Industries is happy** Good Jobs First, https://subsidytracker.good jobsfirst.org/parent/koch-industries.

224. **In the vision** MacLean, *Democracy in Chains*, 213.

228. **A couple of years** Michael Kan, "Foxconn Expects Robots to Take Over More Factory Work", *PC World*, Feb. 27, 2015, https://www.pcworld.com /article/2890032/foxconn-expects-robots-to-take-over-more-factory -work.html.

228. **As the sociologist Mark Rank** McLaughlin and Rank, "Estimating the Economic Cost of Child Poverty in the United States," 73–83.

228. **Despite well-established** Hacker and Pierson, *American Amnesia*, 35.

229. **As David Susskind** Susskind, *World without Work*, 167.

229. **The sociologists Jacob Hacker** Hacker and Pierson, *American Amnesia*, 33.

229.   **By 2017 China** Niall McCarthy, "The Countries with the Most STEM Graduates," *Forbes*, Feb. 2, 2017, https://www.forbes.com/sites/niall mccarthy/2017/02/02/the-countries-with-the-most-stem-graduates -infographic/#57d79602268a].

230.   **Racine County has** Lawrence Tabak, "The Latest Assault on Public Education by WI Gov. Scott Walker? Attempting to Resegregate Students in Racine County," *Belt Magazine*, Mar. 13, 2018, https://beltmag.com /wisconsin-war-on-education/.

230.   **Worse, manufacturing** Author interview with editor of *Greensburg Daily News*, 2017.

231.   **Even before the COVID-19** Kristof, *Tightrope*, 53.

231.   **In 2019 about** Jennifer Cheeseman Day and Andrew W. Hait, "American Keeps on Trucking," *US Census Bureau*, June 6, 2019, https://www .census.gov/library/stories/2019/06/america-keeps-on-trucking.html. Vickie Elmer, "Most Americans Work One of These Ten Jobs," *Quartz*, Apr. 1, 2014, https://qz.com/194264/sales-and-related-jobs-account-for -11-american-jobs.

231.   **Seventy-seven percent** "College Affordability and Completion: Ensuring a Pathway to Opportunity," US Department of Education, https:// www.ed.gov/college.

231.   **Seventy-five years** Piketty, *Capital in the Twenty-First Century*, 485.

233.   **Dollars from wage suppression** Piketty, 302.

233.   **As Piketty concludes** Piketty, 297.

Bibliography

Anderson, Carol. *One Person, No Vote, How Voter Suppression Is Destroying Our Democracy*. New York: Bloomsbury, 2018.

Anderson, Louise. *Knowledge Is Power: Working Effectively with Site Selectors*. Washington, DC: International Economic Development Council, 2012.

Applebaum, Binyamin. *The Economists' Hour*. New York: Little, Brown and Co., 2019.

Autor, David, David Dorn, and Gordon Hanson. "When Work Disappears: Manufacturing Decline and the Falling Marriage-Market Value of Young Men." *American Economic Review: Insights* 1, no. 2 (2019): 161–78.

Bajar, Sumedha, and Rajeev Meenakshi. "The Impact of Infrastructure Provisioning on Inequality." Working paper, Global Labour University, July 2015.

Bartik, Timothy. *Costs and Benefits of a Revised Foxconn Project*. Kalamazoo, MI: W. E. Upjohn Institute for Employment Research, July 31, 2019.

———. *Making Sense of Incentives: Taming Business Incentives to Promote Prosperity*. Kalamazoo, MI: W. E. Upjohn Institute, 2019.

Bjerkholt, Olav. "Wassily Leontief and the Discovery of the Input-Output Approach." Memorandum No. 18/2016, Department of Economics, Oslo University.

Blanchflower, David G. *Not Working: Where Have All the Good Jobs Gone?* Princeton, NJ: Princeton University Press, 2019.

Blum, Rachel. *How the Tea Party Captured the GOP.* Chicago: University of Chicago Press, 2020.

Boatright, Robert G. *Getting Primaried: The Changing Politics of Congressional Primary Challenges.* Ann Arbor: University of Michigan Press, 2013.

Bresnahan, Timothy, Alfonso Gambardella, and AnnaLee Saxenian. "'Old Economy' Inputs for 'New Economy' Outcomes: Cluster Formation in the New Silicon Valleys." *Industrial and Corporate Change* 10, no. 4 (2001): 835–60.

Briffault, Richard. "The Most Popular Tool: Tax Increment Financing and the Political Economy of Local Government." *University of Chicago Law Review* 77, no. 1 (December 2010).

Bunch, Will. *The Backlash: Right-Wing Radicals, High-Def Hucksters, and Paranoid Politics in the Age of Obama.* New York: HarperCollins, 2010.

Burckel, Nicholas C., ed. *Racine: Growth and Change in a Wisconsin County.* Racine, WI: Racine Board of Supervisors, 1977.

Bureau of Economic Analysis. *RIMS II, An Essential Tool for Regional Developers and Planners.* Washington, DC: US Department of Commerce, 2012.

Carney, Timothy P. *Alienated America: Why Some Places Thrive While Others Collapse.* New York: Harper, 2019.

Case, Anne, and Angus Deaton. *Deaths of Despair and Future of Capitalism.* Princeton, NJ: Princeton University Press, 2020.

Central Racine County Health Department. *Opioid and Heroin Awareness Guide, Racine County 2019.* Racine, WI: Central Racine County Health Department, May 16, 2019.

Choate, Pat. *Agents of Influence: How Japan's Lobbyists in the United States Manipulate America's Political and Economic System.* New York: Knopf, 1990.

Conference on Research in Income and Wealth. *Input-Output Analysis: Studies in Income and Wealth Volume Eighteen.* Princeton, NJ: Princeton University Press, 1955.

Cowie, Jefferson. *The Great Exception: The New Deal and The Limits of American Politics.* Princeton, NJ: Princeton University Press, 2016.

Cramer, Katherine J. *The Politics of Resentment: Rural Consciousness in Wisconsin and the Rise of Scott Walker.* Chicago: University of Chicago Press, 2016.

Dietzenbacher, Erik, and Michael L. Lahr. *Wassily Leontief and Input-Output Economics.* Cambridge: Cambridge University Press, 2004.

Dinces, Sean. *Bulls Markets: Chicago's Basketball Business and the New Inequality.* Chicago: University of Chicago Press, 2018.

Dorfman, Jeffrey, "Government Incentives to Attract Jobs Are Terrible Deals for Taxpayers." *Forbes,* September 6, 2017.

Dye, Richard F., and David F. Merriman. "TIF Districts Hinder Growth." *University of Illinois Institute of Government and Public Affairs* 13 (November 4, 2000).

Environmental Integrity Project. *Thin Green Line, Cuts in State Pollution Control Agencies Threaten Public Health.* Washington, DC: Environmental Integrity Project, December 5, 2019.

Frey, Carl Benedikt. *The Technology Trap: Capital, Labor, and Power in the Age of Automation.* Princeton, NJ: Princeton University Press, 2019.

Galbraith, James K. *The End of Normal.* New York: Simon & Schuster, 2016.

Garreau, Joel. *Edge City.* New York: Doubleday, 1991.

Gervais, Bryan T., and Irwin L. Morris. *Reactionary Republicanism: How the Tea Party in the House Paved the Way for Trump's Victory.* New York: Oxford University Press, 2018.

Giridharadas, Anand. *Winners Take All: The Elite Charade of Changing the World.* New York: Alfred A. Knopf, 2018.

Goldstein, Amy. *Janesville: An American Story.* New York: Simon & Schuster, 2017.

Greenhouse, Steven. *Beaten Down, Worked Up: The Past, Present, and Future of American Labor.* New York: Alfred A. Knopf, 2019.

Hacker, Jacob S., and Paul Pierson. *American Amnesia: How the War on Government Led Us to Forget What Made America Prosper.* New York: Simon & Schuster, 2016.

———. *Let Them Eat Tweets.* New York: Liveright Publishing, 2020.

———. *Winner-Take-All Politics: How Washington Made the Rich Richer—And Turned Its Back on the Middle Class.* New York: Simon & Schuster, 2010.

Hamper, Ben. *Rivethead.* New York: Warner Books, 1992.

Heller School for Social Policy and Management, Brandeis University. *The Geography of Child Opportunity: Why Neighborhoods Matter for Equality.* Waltham, MA: Heller School, January 2020.

Hoene, Christopher, and Michael Pagano. *City Budgets in an Era of Increased Uncertainties.* Washington, DC: Brookings Institute, 2018.

Hofstadter, Richard. *The Paranoid Style in American Politics.* New York: Vintage Books, 1953.

Jensen, Nathan M., and Edmund J. Malesky. *Incentives to Pander.* New York: Oxford University Press, 2018.

Judt, Tony. *Ill Fares the Land.* New York: Penguin Press, 2010.

Kahneman, Daniel. *Thinking, Fast and Slow.* New York: Farrar, Straus & Giroux, 2011.

Kan, Michael. "Foxconn Expects Robots to Take Over More Factory Work." *PC World*, February 27, 2015.

Kavori, John. "Predicting TIF Distress: A Statistical Analysis of Tax Incremental Finance Districts in Wisconsin." *Public Budgeting & Finance*, November 2019.

Kawamoto, Hirohisa. "The History of Liquid-Crystal Displays." *Proceedings of the IEEE* 90, no. 4 (April 2002).

Keefer, Philip, and Stephen Knack. "Boondoggles, Rent-Seeking, and Political Checks and Balances: Public Investment under Unaccountable Governments." *Review of Economics and Statistics* 89, no. 3 (2007): 566–72.

Kristof, Nicholas, and Sheryl WuDunn. *Tightrope*. New York: Alfred A. Knopf, 2020.

Lee, Kai-Fu. *AI Superpowers: China, Silicon Valley, and the New World Order*. Boston: Houghton Mifflin Harcourt, 2018.

Lehman, Nicholas. *Transaction Man: The Rise of the Deal and the Decline of the American Dream*. New York: Farrar, Straus & Giroux, 2019.

Leonard, Christopher. *Kochland: The Secret History of Koch Industries and Corporate Power in America*. New York: Simon & Schuster, 2019.

Leontief, Estelle. *Genia & Wassily, A Russian-American Memoir*. Somerville, MA: Zephyr Press, 1987.

Lepore, Jill. *The Whites of Their Eyes: The Tea Party's Revolution and Battle over American History*. Princeton, NJ: Princeton University Press, 2010.

Lewis, Michael. *The Fifth Risk*. New York: W. W. Norton & Co., 2018.

MacLean, Nancy. *Democracy in Chains: The Deep History of the Radical Right's Stealth Plan for America*. New York: Viking, 2017.

Macy, Beth. *Factory Man: How One Furniture Maker Battled Offshoring, Stayed Local—and Helped Save an American Town*. New York: Little, Brown and Co., 2014.

Mason, Lilliana. *Uncivil Agreement: How Politics Became Our Identity*. Chicago: University of Chicago Press, 2018.

Mason, Susan G., and Kenneth P. Thomas. "Exploring Patterns of Tax Increment Financing Use and Structural Explanations in Missouri's Major Metropolitan Regions." *Cityscape* 20, no. 2 (2018): 203–32.

Mayer, Jane. *Dark Money: The Hidden History of the Billionaires behind the Rise of the Radical Right*. New York: Random House, 2016.

McCarty, Nolan, Keith T. Poole, and Howard Rosenthal. *Polarized America: The Dance of Ideology and Unequal Riches*. Cambridge, MA: MIT Press, 2005.

McChesney, Robert W., and John Nichols. *People Get Ready: The Fight against a Jobless Economy and a Citizenless Democracy*. New York: Nation Books, 2016.

McLaughlin, Michael, and Mark R. Rank. "Estimating the Economic Cost of Child Poverty in the United States." *Social Work Research* 42, no. 2 (2018): 73–83.

Merchant, Brian. *The One Device: The Secret History of the iPhone*. New York: Little, Brown and Co., 2017.

Merriman, David F. *Improving Tax Increment Financing (TIF) for Economic Development*. New York: Columbia University Press, 2018.

———. "Improving Tax Increment Financing (TIF) for Economic Development." Policy Brief, Lincoln Institute of Land Policy, Cambridge, MA, January 2019.

Metzl, Jonathan M. *Dying of Whiteness: How the Politics of Racial Resentment Is Killing America's Heartland*. New York: Basic Books, 2019.

Mitchell, Matthew D., Michael D. Farren, Jeremy Horpedahl, and Olivia Gonzalez. *The Economics of a Targeted Economic Development Subsidy*. Arlington, VA: Mercatus Center, 2019.

Nelson, Robert R., Jan A. DeRoos, and Russell Lloyd. "The Impact of Publicly Subsidized Hotels in the United States on Competing Properties." Working Paper, Cornell University School of Hotel Management, Ithaca, NY, August 6, 2014.

Parker, Christopher S., and Matt A. Barreto. *Change They Can't Believe In: The Tea Party and Reactionary Politics in America*. Princeton, NJ: Princeton University Press, 2013.

Perkins, Suzanne C., Eric D. Finegood, and James E. Swain. "Poverty and Language Development: Roles of Parenting and Stress." *Innovations in Clinical Neuroscience* (April 2013).

Piketty, Thomas. *Capital and Ideology*. Cambridge, MA: Belknap Press of Harvard University Press, 2020.

———. *Capital in the Twenty-First Century*. Cambridge, MA: Belknap Press of Harvard University Press, 2014.

Pei, Minxin. *China's Crony Capitalism*. Cambridge, MA: Harvard University Press, 2016.

Pollin, Robert. *Back to Full Employment*. Cambridge, MA: Boston Review, 2012.

Quart, Alissa. *Squeezed: Why Our Families Can't Afford America*. New York: Ecco, 2018.

Rosenthal, Lawrence, and Christine Trost. *Steep: The Precipitous Rise of the Tea Party*. Berkeley: University of California Press, 2012.

Ross, Alec. *The Industries of the Future*. New York: Simon & Schuster, 2016.

Schlomach, Byron, Stephen Slivinski, and James Hohman. *Multilateral Disarmament: A State Compact to End Corporate Welfare*. Midland, MI: Mackinac Center for Public Policy, 2019.

Schneider, Dan. "The Worst Place in the US to Be Black Is . . . Wisconsin." *Dollars & Sense*, November–December 2015.

Schneider, Daniel, and Kristin Harknett. *Consequences of Routine Work Schedule Instability for Worker Health and Wellbeing*. Washington, DC: Washington Center for Equitable Growth, September 2018.

Shin, Willy. "How Did They Make My Big-Screen TV? A Peek Inside China's Massive BOE Gen 10.5 Factory." *Forbes*, May 15, 2018.

Silva, Jennifer M. *We're Still Here: Pain and Politics in the Heart of America.* New York: Oxford University Press, 2019.

Skocpol, Theda, and Venessa Williamson. *The Tea Party and the Remaking of Republican Conservatism.* Oxford: Oxford University Press, 2012.

Slattery, Cailin, and Owen Zidar. "Evaluating State and Local Business Tax Incentives." Working paper, January 2020.

Smarsh, Sarah. *Heartland.* New York: Scribner's, 2018.

Stiglitz, Joseph E. *The Price of Inequality: How Today's Divided Society Endangers Our Future.* New York: W. W. Norton, 2013.

Susskind, Daniel. *A World without Work.* New York: Metropolitan Books, 2020.

Tabak, Lawrence. "The Con in Foxconn Wisconsin." *American Prospect*, September 21, 2018.

———. "Eminent Domain, Ruined Farmland, Crony Capitalism: Racine County Braces for Foxconn." *Belt Magazine*, October 24, 2017.

———. "How Wisconsin Gov. Walker Got Taken in the Foxconn Deal." *Belt Magazine*, October 5, 2017.

———. "The Latest Assault on Public Education by WI Gov. Scott Walker? Attempting to Resegregate Students in Racine County." *Belt Magazine*, March 13, 2018.

———. "Where to Now with Foxconn." *Capital Times*, March 6, 2019.

———. "Why Foxconn's Promise of 13,000 Quality Jobs Is an Empty One." *Belt Magazine*, September 11, 2017.

———. "Wild about Convention Centers." *Atlantic Monthly*, April 1994.

Thompson, William F. *Continuity and Change, 1940–1965.* Vol. 6 of *History of Wisconsin.* Madison: Wisconsin Historical Society Press, 2013.

Tough, Paul. *The Years That Matter.* New York: Houghton Mifflin Harcourt, 2019.

Travis, Jeremy, Bruce Western, and Steve Redburg, eds. *The Growth of Incarceration in the United States.* Washington, DC: National Academies Press, 2014.

Vance, J. D. *Hillbilly Elegy.* New York: Harper, 2016.

Van Vugt, William E. *British Immigration to the United States, 1776–1914, Volume 2.* New York: Routledge, 2016.

Walker, Scott, and Marc Thiessen. *Unintimidated: A Governor's Story and a Nation's Challenge.* New York: Sentinel, 2014.

Wall, Ed. *Unethical: Life in Scott Walker's Cabinet and the Dirty Side of Politics.* Mineral Point, WI: Little Creek Press, 2018.

Warner, Andrew M. "Public Investment as an Engine of Growth." Working paper, International Monetary Fund, 2014.

Weber, Rachel, and Sara O'Neal-Kohl. "The Historical Roots of Tax Increment Financing; or, How Real Estate Consultants Kept Urban Renewal Alive." *Economic Development Quarterly*, May 8, 2013.

Wilkerson, Isabel. *The Warmth of Other Suns*. New York: Random House, 2010.

William, Noah. "An Evaluation of the Economic Impact of the Foxconn Proposal." University of Wisconsin Center for Research on the Wisconsin Economy, August 21, 2017.

Wilson, William Julius. *When Work Disappears*. New York: Knopf, 1996.

Wisconsin Policy Forum. "Village of Mt. Pleasant's Fiscal Condition: A Calculated Risk." June 2020.

Yang, Andrew. *The War on Normal People*. New York: Hachette, 2018.

Zingales, Luigi. *A Capitalism for the People: Recapturing the Lost Genius of American Prosperity*. New York: Basic Books, 2012.

Index

Page numbers in italics refer to illustrations.